INSIGHT GUIDES
MAURITIUS RÉUNION
& SEYCHELLES

APA PUBLICATIONS
Part of the Langenscheidt Publishing Group

INSIGHT GUIDE
MAURITIUS REUNION & SEYCHELLES

Editorial
Project Editor
Emily Hatchwell
Managing Editor
Cathy Muscat
Editorial Director
Brian Bell

Distribution
North America
Langenscheidt Publishers, Inc.
36–36 33rd Street 4th Floor
Long Island City, NY 11106
orders@langenscheidt.com

UK & Ireland
GeoCenter International Ltd
Meridian House, Churchill Way West
Basingstoke, Hampshire RG21 6YR
sales@geocenter.co.uk

Australia
Universal Publishers
1 Waterloo Road
Macquarie Park, NSW 2113
sales@universalpublishers.com.au

New Zealand
Hema Maps New Zealand Ltd (HNZ)
Unit 2, 10 Cryers Road
East Tamaki, Auckland 2013
sales.hema@clear.net.nz

Worldwide
**Apa Publications GmbH & Co.
Verlag KG (Singapore branch)**
38 Joo Koon Road, Singapore 628990
apasin@signet.com.sg

Printing
Insight Print Services (Pte) Ltd
38 Joo Koon Road, Singapore 628990
Tel: (65) 6865 1600. Fax: (65) 6861 6438

©2010 Apa Publications GmbH & Co.
Verlag KG (Singapore branch)
All Rights Reserved

First Edition 2000
Updated 2009

CONTACTING THE EDITORS
We would appreciate it if readers
would alert us to errors or out-
dated information by writing to:
**Insight Guides, P.O. Box 7910,
London SE1 1WE, England.
insight@apaguide.co.uk**
NO part of this book may be reproduced,
stored in a retrieval system or transmitted
in any form or means electronic, mech-
anical, photocopying, recording or otherwise, without prior written permission of
Apa Publications. Brief text quotations
with use of photographs are exempted
for book review purposes only. Information has been obtained from sources
believed to be reliable, but its accuracy
and completeness, and the opinions
based thereon, are not guaranteed.

www.insightguides.com

ABOUT THIS BOOK

The first Insight Guide pioneered the use of creative full-colour photography in travel guides in 1970. Since then, we have expanded our range to cater for our readers' need not only for reliable information about their chosen destination but also for a real understanding of the culture and workings of that destination. Now, when the internet can supply inexhaustible (but not always reliable) facts, our books marry text and pictures to provide those much more elusive qualities: knowledge and discernment. To achieve this, they rely heavily on the authority of locally based writers and photographers.

This book is carefully structured to convey an understanding of the islands and their culture as well as to guide readers through the principal sights and activities:

◆ The **Features** section, indicated by a yellow bar at the top of each page, covers the history and culture of the islands in a series of informative essays.

◆ The main **Places** section, indicated by a blue bar, is a complete guide to the sights and areas worth visiting. Places of special interest are coordinated by number with the maps.

◆ The **Travel Tips** listings section, with an orange bar, provides a handy point of reference for information on travel.

WAZ

INDIAN OCEAN

Serpent I.
(Île aux Serpents)

Round I.
(Île Ronde)

Flat I.
(Île Plate)
Gabriel I.
(Îlot Gabriel)

page 114

Coin de Mire

Pte l'Hortal
Péreybère
Cap Malheureux
Pointe aux Canonniers
Grand Gaube
Grand Baie
Petit Raffray
The Vale
Fond du Sac
A4
A5
Goodlands
Île d'Ambre
Triolet
Plaine
Morcellement
des Papayes
St-Andre
M1
Poudre d'Or
Piton
Pte Lascars
Baie du Tombeau
Pamplemousses
A6
Pte de Roche Noire
A2
Mt Piton
267
Rivière du Rempart
Grande Rosalie
Pte Radeau

page 142
page 104
Pointe aux Sables
Abercrombie
Baillache
La Nicolière
A2
Bon Acceuil
Poste de Flacq
page 124
PORT LOUIS
Salazie
Pte Petite Rivière
Le Pouce
811
M2
Malenga
Centre de Flacq
Belle Mare
Albion
Moka
Roselyn Cottage
St-Julien
Pte Moyenne
Beau Bassin
Côte d'Or
Quartier
Militaire
Colignard
Bel Air
(Rivière Sèche)
Rose Hill
Providence
Mare Jacot
Bambous
Quatre Bornes
A7
Flic en Flac
Palma
Phoenix
Blanche Mtn
Deux Frères
A3
Vacoas
page 152
Montagne
Blanche
Pte Sud Flic en Flac
Mt du Rempart
545
Kewal Nagar
Tamarin
Curepipe
Pointe
du Diable
Pte du Tamarin
Tamarin
La Marie
Midlands
Pic Grand Fond
521x
Domaine
d'Anse Jonchée
Curepipe Point
686
M2
Pte Bambou
Grand Rivière Noire
Grande R. Noire
Ferney
Providence
Ste-Médeleine
Petite Case Noyale
Mare aux
Vacoas
Nouvelle
France
Riche en Eau
Île aux Béniliers
Black River Gorges
National Park
Grand Bois
Pte de la Colonie
Pte Pecheurs
Piton de la
Petite Rivière Noire
828
La Chaux
New Grove
Mahébourg
Le Morne Brabant
556
Coteau Raffin
Mt Cocotte
Île aux Aigrettes
Pte Sud-Ouest
L'Embrasure
Valriche
Rivière Dragon
Pointe D'Esny
Pte Corps de Garde
Chemin Grenier
A9
L'Escalier
Le Bouchon
Baie du Cap
Rivière des Anguilles
Savannah
Pte Chaour
Bel Ombre
Surinam
Souillac
Le Gris Gris
page 132

INDIAN OCEAN

N

Mauritius

0   5 km
0   5 miles

The chapters *People of the Indian Ocean, The Impact of Tourism* and *Sailors and Explorers – Discoverers of the Mascarenes* were written by historian **Dr Marina Carter**, who has spent much of the past 10 years living in Mauritius, writing about the island's history and its people. Many of the archive photographs are from her own personal collection.

Carl Jones, passionate ornithologist and conservationist, and a key figure in saving the pink pigeon and Mauritius kestrel from extinction, wrote the chapters on flora and fauna: *Bats, Birds and Banyan Trees* and *Volcanic Habitats*.

Jane Anderson, travel editor for *You & Your Wedding* magazine, wrote *Romancing the Isles*, and supplied the corresponding Travel Tips information. Mauritian journalist, **Jacques Lee**, contributed *The Mauritians*, *Sega* and *Lingua Franca* features.

SEYCHELLES

Judith and **Adrian Skerrett** are keen naturalists and active conservationists who spend much of their time in Seychelles. Authors of several guides on Seychelles, they wrote the majority of chapters and travel tips for the Seychelles section, and supplied a number of the photographs.

David Rowat, marine biologist and managing director of Seychelles Underwater Centre, contributed the chapters on *Marine Life* and the Seychelles' *Underwater World*.

Special thanks to **Nigel Tisdall** for his contribution to the Seychelles section, to **Caroline Radula-Scott** for her help editing a number of features and the Travel Tips, to **Lynn Bresler** for proofreading and to **Elizabeth Cook** for compiling the index. **Alexia Georgiou** edited the 2009 update.

The contributors

Insight Guide: Mauritius, Réunion and Seychelles was edited by **Emily Hatchwell**, a London-based editor who also assembled a widespread team of writers and expert contributors, and by **Cathy Muscat**, a managing editor at Insight Guides.

MAURITIUS, RODRIGUES AND RÉUNION

Mauritian-born **Katerina Roberts** and her husband **Eric Roberts** are travel writers and photographers specialising in the Indian Ocean. After years of visiting and writing about the Mascarene Islands, they were perfectly placed to complete the Places and Features sections, and compile the corresponding information for the Travel Tips. They also supplied many of the outstanding photographs.

Map Legend

–·–	International Boundary
– – –	District Boundary
–●–	National Park/Reserve
– – –	Ferry Route
✈ ✈	Airport: International/Regional
🚌	Bus Station
❶	Tourist Information
✝ ✝	Church/Ruins
☪	Mosque
∩	Cave
⚊	Statue/Monument
★	Place of Interest
⚑	Beach
▲	Mountain Peak
■	Single House
⌘	Lighthouse
✳	Viewpoint
✉	Post Office
↷	Crater

The main places of interest in the Places section are coordinated by number with a full-colour map (e.g. ❶), and a symbol at the top of every right-hand page tells you where to find the map.

CONTENTS

Anse Cocos,
La Digue

THE BEST OF MAURITIUS, RÉUNION & SEYCHELLES

Landscapes and an underwater world to enthrall you, beaches with the wow factor, a wealth of flora and fauna, colonial history, and outdoor pursuits to satisfy the fittest... Here, at a glance, are our recommendations for your visit

BREATHTAKING LANDSCAPES

- **The Cirques, Réunion.** Three huge caldera-like valleys, the remains of an extinct volcano, form a landscape of lush gorges, waterfalls and jagged peaks – all the more stunning when seen from a helicopter. *See page 225.*
- **Vallée de Mai, Praslin.** Mistaken for the Garden of Eden by the British general Charles Gordon in 1881, this is the primeval forest that time forgot, and dense with coco de mer palms and their sensuously suggestive fruit. *See page 319.*
- **Le Morne Brabant, Mauritius.** Former hideout of runaway slaves, the forbidding bulk of Le Morne surges up from a hammerhead peninsula fringed with fine sands and luxury resorts. *See page 149.*
- **Anse Lazio, Praslin.** Consistently tops the polls as the best beach in the world for its butter-soft sands and sculptural boulders. *See pages 33, 317.*
- **Le Gris Gris, Mauritius.** Lashed by wild winds and ferocious seas, the most southerly point of Mauritius still carries a whisper of ancient black magic. *See pages 135.*
- **Piton de la Fournaise, Réunion.** One of the most active volcanoes on the planet, producing blood-red fire fountains and rivers of lava. Watch the eruptions from the safety of the Observatoire Volcanologique. *See pages 188–9, 217.*
- **La Digue, Seychelles.** Live life in the slow lane on the fourth largest island of the granitic group, where bicycles still constitute the main form of transport. *See page 331.*
- **Trou aux Cerfs, Mauritius.** A 300-metre (980-ft) diameter volcanic crater now clogged with vegetation, but with magical views to the pastel-hued mountains beyond. *See page 155.*
- **Chamarel, Mauritius.** A rolling landscape of multi-coloured soil, thought to have been caused by the uneven cooling of lava, viewed from timber walkways and platforms. In the vicinity, Chamarel Waterfall is the highest on the island. *See pages 146–7.*
- **The Aldabra Group, Seychelles.** Virtually untouched by the modern world and an Unesco World Heritage Site, the untamed wilderness of this atoll is home to nearly 95 per cent of the world's giant tortoise population. *See pages 350–51.*

ABOVE: The cirque of Mafate seen from Cap Noir.

SPORTING ACTIVITIES

● **Diving.** The coral reefs of the Indian Ocean, notably around Rodrigues and Seychelles, support hundreds of species of fish, which snorkelling and glass-bottom boats will also allow you to glimpse. *See pages 41–5, 93–6, 271–5.*

● **Adventure sports.** The dramatic terrain of Réunion was made for all manner of adrenaline-pumping activities, from white-water rafting and canyoning to horse trekking, paragliding and bungee-jumping. *See page 183–5.*

● **Big game fishing.** Spending a day on the ocean wave doing battle with a marlin is big business in Mauritius: sit back in the fighting chair, strap on your harness, and wait for the bite. *See pages 97, 276–7.*

● **Hiking.** More than 1,000 km (620 miles) of numbered trails, known as the Grandes Randonnées, criss-cross Réunion, a walker's paradise. *See pages 186–7.*

MUSEUMS

● **Blue Penny Museum, Mauritius.** In 1847, Mauritius became the fifth country in the world to issue postage stamps, some very valuable examples of which are on display here along with maps, coins and prints . *See page 105.*

● **History Museum, Mahé.** No fancy displays but a fine introduction to the history of the islands, from the age of pirates and explorers to the present day. *See page 292.*

● **Museum of Photography, Mauritius.** An intriguing display of 19-century photographic equipment, postcards, memorabilia, daguerreotypes and photos of colonial Port Louis. *See page 107.*

● **Maison du Volcan, Réunion.** At this fascinating museum centred on the research of husband and wife volcanologists Maurice and Katia Krafft, volcanoes are brought to life through interactive video screens. *See page 218.*

● **Musée du Peuplement, Réunion.** Learn about the first settlers and the plight of runaway slaves. *See page 229.*

ABOVE LEFT: Canyoning in the height of the Cirques.
ABOVE: Paul et Virginie, a study in marble at the Blue Penny Museum. **BELOW:** The signature smooth granite boulders and tall palms of Anse Source d'Argent.

BEACHES

● **Anse Source d'Argent, La Digue.** Neck and neck in the polls with Anse Lazio. *See pages 333–4.*

● **Beau Vallon, Mahé.** Busiest beach in the Seychelles but still pristine and excellent for bathing. *See pages 299, 301.*

● **Anse Soleil, Mahé.** Small and perfectly formed. *See page 296.*

● **The Outer Islands, Seychelles.** A plethora of remote, footprint-free beaches, each one as stunning as the last. *See page 343.*

● **Grand Baie, Mauritius.** A vast, horseshoe-shaped turquoise bay dubbed the creole Côte d'Azur. *See pages 116–7.*

● **Ile aux Cerfs, Mauritius.** Limpid waters and lovely beaches make it a favourite with day-tripping Mauritians. *See page 125.*

CULTURE AND HERITAGE

- **Vieux Grand Port and Mahébourg, Mauritius.** The Dutch landed at Vieux Grand Port in 1598, where the remains of Fort Frederick Henry and 18th-century cannons can still be seen. At Mahébourg's National History Museum, eclectic exhibits tell the tale of the colonial periods under the Dutch, French and British. *See page 128.*
- **Plantation houses and *cases créoles*.** Before the concrete tide takes over these lovely wooden homes, with their airy verandahs and delicate 'lacework', visit Eureka and St Aubin (Mauritius) or Bois Rouge and Villa Folio (Réunion). *See pages 135, 153, 205, 228.*
- **Musée de Villèle, Réunion.** Once home to notorious coffee and sugar producer Madame Desbassyns, this colonial mansion houses memorabilia and fine French East

India furniture. *See page 214.*
- **L'Aventure du Sucre, Mauritius.** Sugar cultivation and its history, stylishly presented. *See page 121.*
- **Dauban Mausoleum, Silhouette.** Modelled on the Madeleine in Paris, the mausoleum pays hommage to the Dauban family, owners of the island for more than a hundred years. *See page 311.*
- **Grand Bassin, Mauritius.** Dominated by a sculpture of the Hindu god Shri Mangal Mahadev, this volcanic crater, known as the Lake of the Ganges, is a sacred place of pilgrimage. *See pages 80–81, 148–9.*
- **Arts and craft scene, Seychelles.** Small art studios abound in the Seychelles, selling paintings, batiks and ornaments, often with a chance to meet the artist. *See page 263.*

ABOVE: Madagascar Red Fodies, just one of the bird species that you can expect to see in the Seychelles.
BELOW: Pilgrims at Grand Bassin during Mahi Shivaratri, one of the most important festivals for the Mauritian Hindu community .

WILDLIFE WATCHING

- **Ste Anne Marine National Park, Seychelles.** The first such park in the Indian Ocean, with prolific marine life. Day trips by glass-bottom boat or subsea viewer depart from Victoria. *See page 303.*
- **Aride Island Nature Reserve, Seychelles.** Home to more breeding sea birds and more sea bird species than Seychelles' other granitic islands put together, plus jaw-dropping views at the pinnacle of the nature trail. *See page 327–9.*
- **François Leguat Tortoise Reserve, Rodrigues.** Conservation programmes to restore the island's native habitat are complemented by a colony of 500 Aldabra

tortoises and the only museum devoted to Rodrigues' history, fauna and flora. *See pages 160, 161.*
- **Bird Island, Seychelles.** The sooty tern colony is the most famous attraction here, but guests are encouraged to help with the island's hawksbill turtle conservation project. *See pages 339–40.*
- **Ile aux Aigrettes, Mauritius.** Look out for the bands of pink pigeons, immortalised in the book *Golden Bats and Pink Pigeons* by the late naturalist Gerald Durrell. *See page 129.*
- **Casela Nature and Leisure Park, Mauritius.** Aviaries, walks with lions and cheetahs, and more. *See pages 143–4.*

PARKS AND GARDENS

- **Botanical Gardens at Pamplemousses, Mauritius.** A maze of shady palm-lined avenues lead to beautiful sights such as the Lily Pond, concealed under the floating leaves of the giant Amazon water lily. *See pages 120–21.*
- **Jardin du Roi, Mahé.** Originally laid out in 1771 for the cultivation of spice plants smuggled out of the East Indies, the

present garden is a peaceful plantation reminiscent of 18th and 19th-century farms. *See page 295.*

- **Domaine d'Anse Jonchée, Mauritius.** Nature trails running through forests of spice plants afford a chance of spotting wild boar and monkey, and there are daily appearances from the endangered Mauritian kestrel. *See pages 126–7.*
- **Jardin de l'Etat, Réunion.** A botanical collection born from the European trees brought to the island by botanist Nicolas Bréon in 1817. The centrepiece of the gardens is a natural history museum. *See pages 198–9.*
- **Jardin de Mascarin, Réunion.** A magnificent outdoor museum landscaped into themed gardens, including a cacti enclosure. You can also visit the restored 19th-century villa, stables, hunting lodge and old family kitchen. *See page 213.*

BELOW LEFT: The Lily Pond at Pamplemousses, everyone's favourite photo opportunity.
ABOVE: The natural history museum at the heart of St Denis's State Garden (Jardin de l'Etat).

IN TOWN

- **St Denis.** More than an outpost of France in the tropics, St Denis is worth a visit for its splendid creole homes, clutch of stately buildings, such as the Hôtel de la Préfecture, and a stroll along the waterfront promenade, Le Barachois. *See pages 195–9.*
- **Port Mathurin.** A capital short on monuments, but the vibrant Saturday morning market more than makes up for it. *See pages 157–9.*
- **Victoria.** Some elegant colonial-style buildings are not the only worthwhile sights here: Victoria's most impressive building is Capuchin House, still in use as a seminary. *See pages 289–94.*
- **Port Louis.** Catch the bustle and buzz of Central Market and the Caudan Waterfront, and a view of the southern hemisphere's oldest racecourse, set in the shadow of the Moka Mountains. *See pages 103–110.*

MONEY-SAVING TIPS

Factory shops Explore the local area for shopping opportunities before buying from a factory shop where goods tend to be overpriced (and your taxi driver quite often gets commission on each sale).

Taxi drivers Always agree a fare with taxi drivers but remember, bus travel is much cheaper.

Exchange rate Banks and bureaux de change give a better rate of exchange than your hotel.

Mini-bar Avoid the mini-bar if you're on a budget. Bottled water, wine, spirits, cigarettes and food cost a lot less at the local supermarket.

Eating out Not eating and drinking at your hotel will save you money but remember when ordering food that not all menus include the VAT (value added tax) in their prices. Portions tend to be generous though, so unless you're famished it can be difficult getting through a three-course meal.

Bargaining Don't be shy about haggling with beach hawkers or in shops and markets, particularly if you are buying a number of items.

Lobster Don't let waiters push you into ordering lobster at a restaurant. Priced by the weight, it can work out to be very expensive.

INDIAN OCEAN ISLANDS

The main attraction may be the white beaches and crystal waters, but beyond the palm trees there are cultures to explore

Visitors who have already been to both Mauritius and Seychelles always have a firm favourite: "The beaches are better on the Seychelles"; "But the people are so wonderful in Mauritius… and I've never seen such hotels…"; "But what about the diving?".

And what about Réunion? Few mention this corner of France in the Indian Ocean, with its breathtaking volcanic landscapes. Réunion, with Mauritius, forms part of the Mascarenes, along with Rodrigues, an isolated outpost of Mauritius with unspoilt beaches and a particular serenity.

All these Western Indian Ocean islands share the same history to a certain point: all were colonised and cultivated with tea, sugar or vanilla plantations, and their populations are the descendants of explorers and colonists, slaves and indentured labourers. So, Kreol in one form or another is spoken in all of them, and some of their songs and dances share similar roots, as do their cuisines. But there is also great diversity, both culturally and in the experience that the islands give to tourists.

The cultural diversity of these islands, whose roots spread across three continents, is more visible in the Mascarenes than in Seychelles. The culture of Mauritius, from politics to cooking, is heavily influenced by Asian customs and beliefs, while Rodrigues aligns itself more to the people and character of Africa. In Réunion, where culture is rooted firmly in Gallic tradition, boulangeries sell baguettes and croissants alongside creole snacks.

Seychelles, made up of many islands, has cultural diversity as well as chart-topping beaches and birdlife to make birdwatchers weep; the government's commitment to conservation has resulted in almost half the total landmass being given over to nature reserves and national parks.

This guide sets out both to bring out the truth behind the clichés so often attached to these tropical islands, and also to introduce the lesser-known islands and features of the region.   ❑

PRECEDING PAGES: Touessrok's bar manager tests the *rhum arrangé*, Mauritius; kids with kites, Seychelles.
LEFT: a welcoming Rodriguan smile.

PEOPLE OF THE INDIAN OCEAN

All Indian Ocean islanders are descended from immigrants – whether pioneers or pirates, settlers or slaves – and at least three continents are represented among them

The only thing that distinguishes a Mauritian or Seychellois away from home is the lovely French lilt of their English. Otherwise you could be forgiven for believing that you are meeting a person of European, Asian or East African origin. And, leaping across a few generations, you would be right. The diversity, intermingling and surviving distinctions of the ethnic groups, who have arrived over the past 400 years, create the intriguing hotchpotch of cultures and physiognomies that characterise the Western Indian Ocean peoples today.

Polyglot ports

Travellers to the islands of the southwest Indian Ocean often remarked on the ethnic diversity of the inhabitants. Charles Darwin, visiting Mauritius in 1836 on the *Beagle* noted that "the various races of men walking in the streets afford the most interesting spectacle". He would have seen Arab and Persian traders dressed in long, flowing robes, Malagasy with elaborate hair-styles, turban- and langouti-clad Indians and Chinese shopkeepers with long plaits.

It was the piecemeal settlement of the islands that helps to explain the diversity of the inhabitants. In the 17th and 18th centuries, small groups of French prisoners and pioneers, along with a few Malagasy, Indians and Malays, set up bases, initially in the Mascarenes, and later in Seychelles and Rodrigues. With the importation of women from these same regions, the foundations of "white" and "coloured" communities were laid. Free immigrants were offered grants of land and encouraged to produce cash crops such as cotton, coffee or spices for export to Europe, or to cultivate foodstuffs and raise livestock which could be used to provision the ships calling at the islands on their way to or from the Indies.

PRECEDING PAGES: domino players, Seychelles.
LEFT: Indian Ocean life through the eyes of Seychelles artist, Michael Adams.
RIGHT: Malagasy women *c.*1860.

Merchants, adventurers, pirates and refugees from many nations were soon attracted to these new centres of trade and maritime construction, and the demand for skilled labour spiralled. Asians were cheaper to employ than Europeans, and agreements signed with Indian artisans led to the establishment of a wealthy free

ARTISTS' IMPRESSIONS

In the days before photography, artists travelled from place to place, capturing and publishing famous moments – such as the conquest of an island (for example, R. Temple's drawings of the British conquest of Mauritius in 1810), or sketching and labelling "types" of exotic peoples for a curious European audience who knew very little about life in the tropics. L.A. Roussin and A. D'Hastrel published *Albums of Réunion* in 1863 and 1847 respectively, while Alfred Richard illustrated individuals as diverse as the "Persian Groom", the "Indian Labourer" and the "Muslim Barber" for his *Types de l'Île Maurice* published in 1850.

"Malabar" class in the islands by the late 18th century. The crews of sailing ships were also frequently sourced from Asia, and were known as "Lascars". Many were Muslims. To this day the terms "Malabar" and "Lascar" are local slang for Hindus and Muslims respectively, but visitors should avoid using them, as they can also be considered terms of insult.

Slaves and convicts from countries as diverse as Guinea, the Canary Islands, Bengal, Java and Timor were also off-loaded from passing ships to the labour-hungry colonists. From the mid-18th century, however, organised slaving voyages brought large numbers of Mozambicans and Malagasy to the islands, so that they became the dominant ethnic groups, swallowing up the diverse pre-19th-century minorities into a Creole population that increasingly reflected this East African cultural heritage.

Asian immigrants

The conversion of Mauritius and Réunion into plantation societies in the late 18th and early 19th centuries led to the large-scale introduction of estate workers, chiefly from India. Mauritius recruited indentured labour from several states: Biharis and Tamils were the most numerous; Marathis and Telegus arrived in

smaller numbers. Réunion recruited mostly Tamils. Principally Hindus, some Muslim and Christian Indians were also indentured. Smaller numbers of African and Chinese labourers arrived over the same period. In the 1860s and 1870s several thousand "Liberated Africans" were brought to Seychelles and Mauritius. They are thought to have mostly come from Malawi.

Merchants and other service migrants followed these population flows: Gujarati merchants and Chinese traders (chiefly Hakka and Cantonese speaking) established themselves in wholesale and retail, first on Mauritius and then across the region. Chinese women did not immigrate in large numbers until the turn of the 20th

CATHOLIC PRACTICES

Most Creoles on the islands are devout Catholics and spending an hour or two at one of the many small seaside churches in the Indian Ocean islands can be a delightful experience. The Creoles, and fellow Catholics among the Chinese, Indian and white communities, like to dress up for church and the services are usually well-attended, with the crowded congregation in good voice.

If you travel on public transport in any of the islands, you are likely to see passengers making the sign of the cross on passing a Catholic shrine or church. The islands are dotted with small roadside figures and grottoes at which offerings can be made or prayers said.

century, and the earlier relationships established by Chinese men produced a substantial Creole-Chinese population on the islands.

Seychelles and Rodrigues, less well suited by size and terrain to sugar cane cultivation, received fewer Asian immigrants and have remained principally Creole societies.

Old inequalities, new attitudes

The Mascarene and Seychelles island groups are all ex-slave societies in which the three tiers of the population – whites, coloureds and slaves – were clearly demarcated and discouraged from intermarrying. Distinctions, grounded in

Tamils have taken Christian first names, has been relaxed recently leading to a rediscovery of separate Hindu and Creole identities.

The ethnic compartmentalisation of present-day Mauritian society is more apparent. Here, a white settler class has survived and maintains its ethnic exclusiveness by marrying within its ranks and with acceptable outsiders – typically white Europeans and, increasingly, white South Africans, who have a shared experience of enclave status in a multicultural environment. The old three-tier society has been replaced by one of five or more subgroups which each claim specific caste, religious, and regional distinc-

membership of these "colour coded" groups remain, in varying degrees, on all the islands.

Vestiges of this old hierarchical society seem to have little relevance in modern Réunion and Seychelles, where intermarriage is now the norm, with equality of opportunity an official policy. A light-skinned elite nevertheless remains influential in Seychelles politics and society, while in Réunion, a new class of *z'oreilles* (white metropolitan French) is complained of as having favoured status. Integrationist French policy in Réunion, which ensured that generations of

LEFT: tea pickers in Seychelles.
RIGHT: Rodriguan boys and Mauritian girls.

CREOLE OR KREOL

The term "Creole" might seem to be a catch-all to the uninitiated and needs to be explained. In its historical sense, the word meant someone born on an island and was applied to white as well as coloured inhabitants. Thus Napoleon's consort, Josephine de Beauharnais, was a French Creole of Martinique. Nowadays, the term "Creole" has become associated with a specific community usually considered to derive from the fusion of African with other ethnic groups. In these societies a colonial language often became the basis of a new lingua franca or "creole". To avoid confusion, the language is often spelt Kreol, as it is throughout this book.

tions, maintained through intermarriage. Most Mauritian communities view marriage with a foreigner as a preferable option to an alliance with a Mauritian of another ethnic group. Inter-marriage is not unusual, but it is not yet the norm. Politically, ethnic divisions are reinforced by a constitution that provides electoral safeguards for minorities and by a tradition dating from Independence of selecting candidates and even ministers according to their community. Every prime minister apart from Paul Bérenger has come from the Vaish subcaste of the North Indian Hindu community, numerically the most powerful ethnic group in Mauritius.

BLUE BLOOD

Some French Mauritian families are genuine descendants of aristocrats who fled the French Revolution, while more outlandish claims of noble descent from Arab princesses and heroic corsairs can be heard in rum shops across the islands.

Distinctive traditions

Despite a shared history, and collective musical, linguistic and other traditions, each of the Indian Ocean islands has evolved a unique brand of Kreol and a distinctive set of social customs and religious practices. The African cultural heritage is strongest in Seychelles and Rodrigues where the proportion of Afro-Creoles is highest. Réunion is greatly influenced by France and the Francophone world – the zouk rhythms of Martinique are as popular as Paris fashions. In Mauritius, the preponderance of people of Indian origin means that cinemas here are as likely to show Hindi as French films, the sari and the *shalwar kamiz* (trousers and tunic) are common forms of dress, and bhojpuri bands compete with sega and European music for the hearts and minds of the island's youth. The ubiquitous red flags or *jhandi* which can be seen in front of houses throughout the island signify that the occupants are Sanatanist or orthodox Hindus – an eloquent symbol of the cultural dominance of this community in modern Mauritius.

While there are latent tensions between ethnic groups, the Indian Ocean islands are characterised more by syncretism, and participation in each other's celebrations, than by communal conflict. Many non-Tamils make vows to participate in the Cavadee fire-walking ceremonies *(see pages 80–81)* and people of all religions light candles at the Catholic shrines.

Superstition and sorcery cut across ethnic divides: individuals perceived to possess the requisite skills – from traditional practitioners of alternative medicine to specialists in the art of black magic – attract followers from every community, and may be called in to administer remedies, settle quarrels and banish evil spirits.

The food of the islands is the best expression of this shared ethnic heritage: creole cuisine incorporates European, Asian and African influences and offers dishes to suit every palate, from creamy gratins, to Indian-style curries and Chinese-style fried noodles. ❏

BRAIN TEASERS

Kreol *sirandanes* or riddles are a legacy of the African storytelling traditions that are now disappearing in the Indian Ocean islands. When someone had a few riddles to tell they would shout "*Sirandane!*", their audience would reply "*Sampek!*" and the brain teasing session would begin. Here are some typical examples:

Dileau dibout? Canne.   Standing water? A sugar cane.
Dileau pendant? Coco.   Hanging water? A coconut.
Menace dimoun, napas koze? Ledoigt.
  I threaten but I do not speak? A finger.
Ki lalangue ki zames ti menti? Lalangue zanimaux.
  Whose tongue never lies? An animal's.

LEFT: Hindu marriage ceremony.

Lingua Franca

A s a legacy of their shared history of settlement during periods of French rule, the mother tongue of the inhabitants of the Seychelles and Mascarene islands is Kreol. The various forms of Kreol spoken have evolved from adaptations of French to which a sprinkling of words and speech patterns from the other languages of immigrants has been added.

The formative period of Indian Ocean Kreol in the late 17th and 18th centuries has left its mark on the language. The Breton origins of many early French settlers means that traces of their regional language survive into modern Kreol while the influence of Malagasy immigrants is reflected in local words such as *frangourin* or cane sugar juice which derives from the Malagasy term *fangorinana*. South Indians who arrived on the islands in the 18th century as slaves and artisans have left their mark not only in the delicious curries of the region but also in culinary terms. The herb known as *kaloupile* in Réunion, *karipoule* in Mauritius and *karipile* in Seychelles is derived from the Tamil word *kariveppilai* or curry leaf. The creole dish known as *rougaille* is also derived from the Tamil word *urkukay* meaning pickled vegetable.

Over time, different islands have developed particular speech patterns. Seychelles Kreol is said to be more sing-song in style, while Réunion Kreol has been exposed to greater influence from the Francophone world, particularly the French Caribbean. Mauritian Kreol uses many words deriving from its large population of North Indian origin. Expressions such as *nisa* (feeling high), *jalsa* (amusement) and *paise* (money) derive from the bhojpuri dialect spoken widely in rural Indian villages on the island. English league football is a popular spectator sport in Mauritius and Seychelles where terms such as "offside" and "goal kick" are commonly used by Kreol speakers.

The emphasis given to Kreol in the various islands is strongly linked to political factors. Because Réunion is a *département* of France, the French language is given priority, and is used in all official communications and in the written media. In Mauritius and Seychelles, where French rule was succeeded by British government, English is the official language. In Seychelles, however, Kreol also has this status and is given equality of treatment in the media and government institutions. A Kreol Institute has even been established on Mahé to nurture the language. In Mauritius, as in Réunion, Kreol is spoken but rarely written.

For all the islands, these varying political solutions to the language question pose further problems. Middle-class Seychellois complain that the prominence given to Kreol restricts the opportunities for their children to become proficient in French. Réunion suffers from being a Francophone island in an Indian Ocean that is largely Anglophone. Mauritius, with its multiplicity of competing Asian ancestral languages and chiefly French media, is continually struggling with internal dis-

sent and controversy. The island is becoming increasingly Francophone while the education system is slanted towards the use of both English and Oriental languages.

As a rule, English is widely understood in Seychelles and Mauritius, but not in Réunion. French is the preferred language of communication in Mauritius and Réunion, but will not be appreciated by all Seychellois. Switching from English to French and back will not daunt a Mauritian who can usually reply in kind. A few words of basic Kreol acquired in any of the islands, should provide a channel of easy communication in all of them. ❑

● *A quick pronunciation guide and glossary of basic terms and phrases appear on page 377.*

RIGHT: exchanging news and views.

islands on his own luxury yacht, and Tony Blair who has chosen La Digue as a family holiday retreat on more than one occasion. Prince William and Kate Middleton also visited in 2008. The Sultan of Bahrain has a home in Seychelles, and the Miss World competition has been staged here on more than one occasion; its co-ordinators exploited the paradise cliché to the full, billing the event as a unique opportunity to see "the most beautiful girls on earth in the most beautiful place on earth".

STAR RATING

It used to be said that Mauritius is a 3-star destination with 5-star hotels while Seychelles is a 5-star destination with 3-star hotels, but Seychelles facilities are rapidly catching up.

standard of service and world class chefs. Supermodels, footballers, pop stars and film stars regularly appear in glossy magazines, captured languishing in their designer swimwear by the poolside cafés and seaside bars of Mauritius' most fashionable hotels. Old favourites, the Touessrok (photogenic and popular as a Bollywood location) and St Géran (holiday haunt of ex-Spice Girl Gerri Halliwell, as well as actor Ewan McGregor and tennis star Roger Federer who stayed here in 2008), com-

With its larger tourist industry, Mauritius has more five-star hotels than Seychelles. Seychelles had no five-star facilities until the late 1990s, but this has since changed dramatically and new hotels have capitalised on the twin advantages of more private islands and better beaches than Mauritius. Both countries have several hotels in the "leading hotels in the world" category. They cater to every whim of their celebrity guests, providing security, a high

---

LEFT: Prince Edward tries his hand at water-skiing at La Pirogue, during a royal visit to Mauritius.
RIGHT: beach-side breakfast at the Paradise Sun Hotel, Anse Volbert, Praslin.

pete with newer glitzy resorts such as Shanti Ananda or The Grand Mauritian. Novelist J.K. Rowling is a regular at the Royal Palm hotel, also a favourite with visiting heads of state. Lesser mortals cannot expect automatic access to these hotels. If you want to have lunch or dinner it's best to make a reservation first.

A "once-in-a-lifetime" holiday

In principle, these islands are luxury destinations. A two-week holiday at a good hotel on Seychelles or Mauritius can cost several thousand pounds per person. That said, you don't have to be a celebrity or tycoon to enjoy the best that the region has to offer. There are so many small islands in the Seychelles group that anyone can find their own "private" cove complete with swaying palms, fine white sand and turquoise lagoon. Cruising the granitics sounds like an expensive luxury but there are a range of options available for those with a more limited budget. Honeymooners and others looking to splash out on an exceptional holiday can spend their fortnight on islands such as La Digue, where cars are rarely seen, or enjoy the utter isolation of Denis or Frégate where your very own island wedding can be arranged. Cousine is also an exclusive hideaway with four to eight rooms that can be reached by helicopter.

The tourist industry on Mauritius targets the well-heeled lover of luxury and exclusivity – no charter flights are allowed to land here. This is the destination of choice for those who want to exploit the service and amenities of a five-star hotel and the tropical beach on its doorstep to the full. Such luxury comes at a price, but the hotels are exquisite and they've got the service down to a fine art. The key to a successful holiday on Mauritius lies in choosing the right hotel to suit you, both in terms of style and location. It's even worth staying in more than one just to compare experiences.

Natural assets

While both places have been effectively marketed as idyllic beach holiday destinations, their other natural assets have been widely exploited to draw in people looking for more than just a "sun, sea and sand" experience. The Seychelles government is anxious to attract the "discerning and environmentally aware" tourist. Top of its list of highlights are two UNESCO World Heritage Sites – the Vallée de Mai on Praslin and far flung Aldabra Atoll. Other designated bird sanctuaries and tropical forests attract twitchers and trekkers, while live-aboard cruises around the Outer Islands are becoming increasingly popular.

In Mauritius although water sports, including diving and big game fishing – the annual World Marlin Fishing competition is a major event on the fishing calendar – remain big business for those who can afford it, ecotourism ventures inland are being promoted as an alternative activity, with some success.

The flora and fauna of Seychelles and Mascarenes is in many respects unique and, like all

---

THE WORLD'S BEST HOTELS

The hotels of Seychelles and Mauritius are the Indian Ocean's best assets. In 2006, according to readers of the international travel magazine *Travel & Leisure*, Seychelles was voted the best island destination in the Africa and Middle East region. In 2008, Seychelles won the vote of readers of *Condé Nast Traveller* for its Best Island award, ranking fifth out of 20 island destinations and close behind Mauritius and Barbados. Meanwhile Condé Nast also named Frégate island amongst 30 finalists for the 2008 World Saver Award, an accolade rating resorts for their social responsibility; and the Best Overseas Leisure Hotel awards went to North Island and Denis Island. Also in 2008, Mauritius scored 19th place in the top 100 Condé Nast Readers' Travel Awards, with firm favourites such as the Royal Palm, St Géran, Touessrok and Prince Maurice hotels continuing to attract a loyal clientele. Add new kids on the block like The Grand Mauritian and Shanti Ananda and it's no wonder that the idyllic locations and friendly service have become firmly entrenched in the psyche of the tropical traveller. By 2013 more than 35 resort properties are set to open in Seychelles and Mauritius. Five-star hotels in Mauritius include the Intercontinental Balaclava and Four Seasons at Anahita while Seychelles has the entirely upgraded Alphonse Resort, due to open in 2009, and another Four Seasons Resort in the southwest of Mahé.

small island ecologies, endangered. Coral reefs are notoriously fragile and prone to destruction by over zealous exploitation. Seychelles has a long tradition of ecotourism, with several islands declared nature reserves and access to them limited to the daytime. Mauritius is belatedly recognising the advantages of exploiting the few remaining areas on which unique species have survived. Thankfully, it's now following the example set by the Seychelles government in requiring permits for visits to some of its islets and in opening them up to responsible, supervised nature tours. Île aux Aigrettes, off the southeast coast, is home to the only remaining example of coastal savannah, which the dodo and other local birds found a natural habitat, and tours have been set up by the Mauritius Wildlife Foundation *(see page 129)*.

Holidaying on a budget

Backpackers are not encouraged, but there are ways of staying more cheaply on the islands. The resorts of Grand Baie/Pereybère and Flic-en-Flac in Mauritius offer numerous flats and guest houses where a studio can be rented for around £25 (US$37) a day. Once you have paid for your flight, this is the one island in the region where you can live more cheaply than at home, and some seasonal workers from European coastal resorts choose to spend the winter here, staying for the three to six months that is allowed them on a tourist visa. Prices of imported goods are higher than in Europe, but essential foodstuffs are subsidised, and if you bring your own luxury items, you can live very cheaply.

Seychelles also has a number of small guesthouses; though not particularly cheap compared to other countries, they are less expensive than hotels, the service is much more personal and standards are generally high. Self-catering establishments are also good quality, and shopping for yourself brings down costs: shop prices for drinks are half those charged by hotels, while local produce including fish is inexpensive.

Adventure playground

Réunion is the most expensive of the Indian Ocean islands because its economy is artificially boosted with regular injections of French capital. Prices are slightly higher here than in France. It has long been popular with French visitors – as an overseas *département* there are no customs or immigration checks for arrivals from the metropolis (mainland France) – but its lack of coral-fringed beaches and monolingualism have lessened the island's appeal to non-French tourists. The Réunionnais themselves often take their annual holidays on Mauritius where, beyond the big hotels, the cost of living is much lower.

As its coastline doesn't fit the tropical island profile, Réunion has escaped invasion from international tourists. Most of us still need per-

LEFT: appetising display of fresh fish and seafood.
RIGHT: the sega performances staged at hotels are formalised versions of the traditional slave dance.

EXTREME WEATHER

The Western Indian Ocean islands' hot season coincides with the European winter. The climate is tropical – average temperatures in Seychelles are hotter than in the Mascarenes and the humidity is higher, but all the islands experience frequent rain showers, especially from December to January. The Mascarenes are prey to cyclones between November and April. These can cause serious disruption to telephone and power lines and to public transport, but hotels are generally equipped with generators so that tourists will experience minimum discomfort. The cool season (May to September) is pleasant, with temperatures more akin to those of an English summer.

suading that hiking – even to an active volcano – is more fun than lounging by a palm-fringed lagoon, and the island's breathtaking landscape remains a well-kept secret from all but the French and the ardent adventure traveller.

The tourist authorities were quick to recognise and exploit its potential as a paradise for backpackers and thrill seekers, and over the years they have built up an efficient infrastructure. The trail network is well-mapped and maintained, as are the purpose-built mountain lodges or *gîtes*. The

> ### BOLLYWOOD'S BEACHES
> Fans of Hindi cinema have a good chance of glimpsing their screen idols in Mauritius where Bollywood films are almost constantly in production.

adventure sport potential has been developed to the full. Other than trekking, organisations and facilities for mountain biking, climbing, horse riding, canyoning, canoeing, even bungee-jumping can be found all over the island

Réunion has also countered its shortcomings with the marketing of its colonial heritage, which it seems to have preserved far better than its neighbours. Plantations and colonial houses have been faithfully restored and opened to the public. However, despite the opportunities for cultural heritage tourism that the rich history and diverse population of Mauritius offer, museum development and tours of cultural and historic sites remain unsophisticated.

The forgotten island

Rodrigues, granted regional autonomy in 2002, is the minuscule and often forgotten partner in the twin-island Republic of Mauritius. Until not so long ago, the island could be reached only by a cargo vessel which docked at Port Mathurin just once a month and only the most determined travellers reached its rugged shores. Nowadays, the *Mauritius Pride* and the *Mauritius Trochetia* make the crossing two or three times a month, bringing in islanders and tourists on short breaks.

Tour operators are beginning to turn their attentions to Rodrigues, but tourism is still very much in its infancy here and further development seems to be hampered by the difficulties of air access, water shortages and concern about its infrastructure. Light aircraft make regular flights to and from Mauritius and visitors from Réunion have to fly via Mauritius before continuing to Rodrigues.

The Association of Rodrigues Tourism Operators is a body of guesthouse and hotel managers, tour operators, car hire companies and shopkeepers who, in conjunction with the Mauritius Tourism Promotion Authority, are promoting cultural and niche tourism, with some success. Their organised activities include staying in islanders' homes, going to folklore shows, walking, fishing and diving. The gigantic lagoon for which Rodrigues is famous, is an unspoilt haven for divers, and is currently the subject of detailed research by scientists studying the Indian Ocean's unique coral islands.

Rodrigues remains uncrowded and unspoiled. There are no high-rise hotels or malls, and chickens still roam the capital's streets. Interestingly, the island is visited mostly by Mauritians looking for a relaxing weekend break and small numbers of European and South African tourists travelling from Mauritius who are keen to discover another facet of life in the Mascarenes.

An extended airport runway, built in 2002 with European funding, may attract more flights, increasing Rodrigues' popularity as another Indian Ocean destination. Developers will one day home in on its beaches, but hopefully with the sensitivity to the natural environment that is essential to the survival of such a small island. ❑

LEFT: cleaning the pool before the tourists arrive.

century sugar estate in the shadow of Le Pouce mountain. Couples can be brought here by horse and cart and have four restaurants to choose from for their reception, or they can head for the mountains.

Sunset weddings

In Seychelles there are registrars on the main islands of Mahé, Praslin and La Digue. However, resorts on the other islands can also assist with wedding arrangements, including photography if required.

BEAT THE RUSH

Couples wanting to marry in Mauritius and Seychelles send their requests as much as 18 months in advance. November and December are particularly popular months, so book early to avoid disappointment.

Most hotels in Seychelles welcome weddings. As they tend to be smaller than in other destinations, they lend themselves to intimate gatherings. Coco de Mer on Praslin decorates its wooden pier with local flowers and banana leaves to create a wedding venue over the water. A wedding just before sunset allows the photographer to capture some stunning sunset shots. Some of the best-known hotels for weddings on Mahé are the Plantation Club, the Berjaya hotels, Coral Strand and Le Northolme. Over on Praslin

Foreign couples can marry anywhere they want to although strictly speaking they are not supposed to marry on the distinctive white sand beaches. However, hotels such as the Plantation Club have pavilions or gazebos beside the beach. A favourite beach wedding setting is Anse Source d'Argent on La Digue. Anse Lazio on Praslin, proclaimed best beach in the world by style guru Giorgio Armani, is equally idyllic. Foreigners can also marry in church, but for an extra charge.

LEFT: honeymooners at the Coco de Mer Hotel on Praslin.
RIGHT: sunset photo shoot.

favourites include Coco de Mer Hotel and the Black Parrot Suites, La Reserve, L'Archipel, Indian Ocean Lodge and the new Lemuria Resort. On La Digue couples can arrive by ox cart for their wedding at Patatran Village, or Hotel L'Ocean, for example. As there are so many islands to choose from, it's worth considering marrying on one island such as Mahé or Praslin and honeymooning on another, or even island hopping by air or sea.

Those who really want to get away from it all can make arrangements on several of the small outer islands: Denis has its own tiny wedding chapel; Desroches, Alphonse and Frégate Island Private all fit the tropical paradise bill. ❑

There are a vast number of hard coral formations. The real reef builders are known as "massive" corals. They form enormous rounded coral heads which coalesce to form reefs. Other hard corals are highly branched, with delicately ornate structures, giving rise to such evocative names as staghorn, elk-horn and table horn.

While the stony corals secrete a calcium casing, many of the soft coral species grow on even more complex structures. Some – the colourful tree corals, for example – support their bodies

called fire coral. If you brush against one, the potent sting it inflicts on your skin feels like the burn from a stinging nettle.

DANGEROUS BEAUTY

Cone shells with their beautiful intricate designs are among the most attractive shells in the world. But beware! Never pick one up by the thin end, for its poison is deadly.

Sea anemones

Related to the corals are the sea anemones – a bit like giant coral polyps without the external shell. These creatures are generally hidden within cracks and ledges of the reef but a few species are conspicuously stuck to the surface of the rocks. They are mostly host anemones and are almost always associated with

with a latticework of tiny calcium needles. Others produce a horny resilient material called gorgonin and develop into long spiral whip corals or intricate fans. These grow at right angles to the current and act as living sieves, filtering out food particles as the water flows through.

All corals are really predatory animals and their polyps have tentacles that are armed with stinging cells that stun microscopic prey. Most of these stings are harmless to humans, but the one coral to learn to recognise and avoid is the so-

LEFT: a green turtle: clumsy on land, graceful in the water.
RIGHT: giant potato cod, motionless on the sea bed.

the anemone fish, also known as the clown fish. Theirs is a classic symbiotic relationship: the anemone fish gains shelter and protection from the anemone, and in return the anemone gets scraps of food from the resident fish. Although the anemone fish is able to develop a protection to the anemone's stings they are still a powerful deterrent to a would-be predator. The exact mechanism of the anemone fish's immunity is not clearly understood but it is thought that the mucus coating covering the scales of the fish, which it wears like a coat, absorbs small amounts of the anemone's sting; the anemone begins to accept this coated fish as being itself and thus no longer tries to sting it.

Kaleidoscope of colours

For many snorkellers, and even divers, it is the brightly coloured and most visible fish which gather in the shallower waters around and above the reef that leave the strongest impression. Many of these fish are in fact deep water species which come into the shallows to feed. Colourful schools of fusiliers, known locally as mackerel, have the characteristic "fishy" shape of a torpedo-like body with small fins, and feed on phyto-plankton above the reefs. Most of the common species have bright blue body colourings with a mixture of stripes and flashes ranging from yellow through to pink,

which shimmer in a vivid colour display as the school moves.

On the reef itself the two most colourful species are the angelfish and butterfly fish, both of which have bodies which are flattened from side to side when viewed from ahead and are almost circular when viewed in profile. Butterfly fish are generally small, around 8–15 cm (3–6 in) across the disc and are predominantly algal and coral grazers; most have body colours that are yellow, black or white. Angelfish species are larger in size, up to 25 cm (10 in), and display a wide range of markings. They also have different patterns in juvenile forms compared to the final adult phases and so add enormously to the colour of the living reef.

A larger visitor to the coral reef is the hawksbill turtle; this is probably the most commonly found marine turtle species in this region and takes its name from its hooked hawk-like beak which it uses to carve chunks off sponges and soft coral formations. In some areas of Seychelles these turtles may be be found nesting on the beaches in daylight – a very unusual sight.

Just like a rock reef, the coral reef offers shelter and protection to a vast number of species as well as being a food source for some of its residents. Some fish are especially adapted to feeding on coral polyps, such as certain butterfly fish and filefish; others feed on small shrimp and other invertebrates that shelter between the branches, such as the razor or shrimpfish.

Molluscs are frequent residents; the most obvious of these are the brightly coloured nudibranchs, or sea slugs. Despite their small size they are the most apparent because of their bright coloration that warns would-be predators that they do not taste good and might be poisonous. A number of shelled molluscs can be found during the day as well but many have highly camouflaged shells to conceal them so they can be difficult to find.

Other animals actually live within the limestone of the coral colony; these include the tube or "feather-duster" worms that are evident from their coloured fans which extend above the surface of the coral colony to trap particles. Some are spectacularly formed into twin spiral cones, as in the Christmas-tree worm, and these pretty structures are often brightly coloured. All fan worms are sensitive to changes in light and therefore will disappear into their tubes on the sudden appearance of a snorkeller or diver.

CORAL BLEACHING

From 1997–8 the coral reefs of the western Indian Ocean were severely impacted by a rise in sea temperature of up to 7°C (12°F) that has been attributed to global warming. Branching corals were predominantly affected, first losing their symbiotic algae and consequently bleaching to a white colour. Many of them died. In areas of good environmental conditions a natural cycle of colonisation by algae was triggered, resulting in the deposition of a limestone film, allowing a gradual re-colonisation by coral larvae. In Seychelles, the reef life was further protected by the underlying granitic structure that maintained shelter for species displaced from the coral structures.

In the deep

The open ocean is a very different and much more inaccessible environment. The deep waters and their currents support marine life from microscopic plankton to some of the largest creatures on the planet but often the concentration of individuals is very low. Due to the constraints of deep water activities, most people will only get the chance to see these creatures when they come to the surface. Luckily, some places seem to have special properties that encourage deep water species to aggregate at the surface.

> **CHEMICAL WEAPONS**
>
> Many molluscs secrete chemical substances which, without being poisonous, are distasteful enough to put off a would-be predator.

of the air performing aerial twists and acrobatics. In some instances these places are special feeding or breeding areas and although the animals may appear to be easily approachable in organised encounter programmes, there are strict codes of conduct to ensure the safety of visitors and the protection of the animals concerned.

Some deep water species are generally only seen when landed by fishing boats; these big game species such as sailfish, marlin, wahoo and dorado are relatively abundant but are sel-

the surface; in these areas it is possible to find whales and dolphins at specific times of the year.

Dolphins are one group that visitors are likely to come across on boat journeys around the islands, although in-water encounters are unfortunately a rare occurrence. There are a number of species in this area and the larger bottlenose and common dolphins are most often seen. In more remote areas there are local populations of the smaller species, notably spinner dolphins, which are readily recognisable by the habit of the youngsters to leap out

dom seen in their natural environment. Other deep water creatures are sometimes washed ashore by the ocean currents. These include several varieties of medusa or jelly-fish; characteristically these have a clear gelatinous bell-shaped body and like their coral cousins they have a ring of stinging tentacles. While some jellyfish are harmless others can deliver a powerful and possibly lethal sting and so contact should be avoided.

The Indian Ocean offers a huge diversity of life. Whether you choose to scuba dive, snorkel or take a glass-bottom boat trip, a glimpse into this magical underwater world will most certainly be a highlight of your trip. ❑

LEFT: one of many colourful species of butterfly fish.
RIGHT: potato lips grouper.

TROPICAL ISLAND BLOOMS

From delicate orchids and hibiscus to vibrant bougainvillaea and flaming red flamboyants, the richness and variety of plant life are astounding

When the first explorers set eyes on the Indian Ocean islands, it was the luxuriant forests and sweet-smelling colourful plants that led them to believe they had found Eden. In Mauritius, three centuries of human habitation have brought plantations, roads and logging, and destroyed many of the island's plants. In Seychelles, the shorter human history, absence of plantations and mountainous islands have helped preserve the environment. Réunion, too, was more fortunate: its rocky and mountainous landscape is more inaccessible, so large areas of its natural forests have remained untouched.

Although many species are still endangered, the islands' flora remains rich: Mauritius has 685 native species of which 311 are endemic; Réunion has 700 indigenous species of which 161 are endemic; Seychelles, too, has a remarkable flora. Of more than 1,100 species, over 400 are native, with 75 endemic to the granitic islands and a further 43 found only in the Aldabra group.

BOTANICAL GARDENS

All the islands have botanical gardens where visitors can admire and learn about the abundant plant life. Mauritius has the famous Pamplemousses gardens near Port Louis, the Curepipe Botanical Gardens and Le Pétrin Native Garden in the Black River Gorges area; Réunion has the Conservatoire Botanique National in St-Leu and the Jardin de l'Etat near St-Denis; and in Seychelles you can visit the Botanical Gardens and the Jardin du Roi spice gardens, both on Mahé.

△ PASSIFLORA
Luxuriant passion fruit vines grow all over Seychelles. The fruit is used for juices.

▷ QUEEN OF THE TROPICS
The delicate hibiscus flower comes in myriad colours, but the bloom only lasts for one day.

◁ BLOOMING BUSINESS
The growing of anthuriums is big business in Mauritius. The waxy blooms come in a variety of colours and sizes, and last for several weeks.

△ LOTUS BLOSSOM
One of around 500 plant species you can see in Mauritius' famous Pamplemousses Gardens, not far from the capital, Port-Louis.

◁ A BLAZE OF COLOUR
With its dense canopy of bright red flowers, the flamboyant tree in bloom is an impressive sight. It flowers between November and January.

▽ BIRD-OF-PARADISE
The stem of this most distinctive of tropical plants calls to mind the long neck of a bird, while its vibrant blossoms are like the tuft of feathers on the bird's crown – hence the name.

△ MAY FLOWER
The essential oil from geraniums cultivated in Réunion is considered by the perfume industry to be the best in the world.

▷ SWEET AROMA
The exquisite-smelling vanilla orchid opens only for a few hours in the morning.

LA VANILLE BOURBON

Vanilla was introduced to Réunion from Central America in 1819, but attempts at natural pollination failed. Then, in 1841, a 12-year-old slave called Edmund Albius discovered that flowers could be pollinated by grafting. By the end of the 19th century Réunion was churning out 100 tons a year. Annual production has dropped significantly since then, but the island remains one of the world's leading producers. Cultivation is concentrated on the lush eastern side of the island where the warm, wet conditions are ideal. The pods are harvested between June and September, about eight months after pollination. Still green, they are scalded in boiling water then laid out in the sun to dry. Now brown, the pods are then left in airtight containers for eight months during which time they develop their strong aroma.

SAILORS AND EXPLORERS: DISCOVERERS OF THE MASCARENES

From the Arabs and Portuguese, to the Dutch, French and English, the history of the Mascarenes has been determined by traders, explorers, colonisers and corsairs

The Mascarenes were all uninhabited until the arrival of European colonisers in the 16th century. Ever since, these islands have been subjected to the whims of European taste and ambitions which have determined their population, their pursuits and, to a large extent, their politics.

The Mascarenes are oceanic islands – they did not break away from continental land masses but developed independently as a result of volcanic action. Mauritius is the oldest at about 8 million years, Réunion and Rodrigues are around 3 and 2 million years old respectively. The islands are affected by volatile weather conditions; and the vagaries of trade winds and cyclones which blew countless sailing ships off course or onto reefs, meant that it was as likely accident and misfortune as intrepid exploration that provoked the first sightings of these small land masses in the southwestern Indian Ocean.

The earliest recorded proof of the identification and location of the islands is from Arab documents and maps. Writings dating back to the 12th century include descriptions of islands which may be the Mascarenes. In 1498, Vasco da Gama saw maps by Ibn Majid in which three islands southeast of Madagascar are named Dina Moraze, Dina Margabim and Dina Arobi, which roughly translate as "eastern", "western" and "deserted" islands.

It was not until the early 16th century that Portuguese explorers became the first recorded European visitors to the Mascarenes. They named Mauritius "Cirne", probably after one of their ships, Réunion "Santa Apolina" after the date of its discovery and Rodrigues, after the navigator Diogo Rodrigues, the only one of the islands to retain its Portuguese name. The Portuguese only occasionally used the Mascarenes route on their way to the Indies but it was a welcome place of respite for damaged ships and weary crews which found themselves blown towards these archetypal desert islands.

Dodos, tortoises and ebony

Still uninhabited in the early 17th century, the fertility and unspoilt nature of the Mascarene islands were extolled by Dutch, French and English visitors. Samuel Castleton, who first set eyes on Réunion in 1613, described thick forest, cascading waterfalls, fat eels in the rivers and plentiful turtles and birds. In homage to its natural beauty, he named the island "England's Forest". The Dutchman, Mandelslo, wrote that Mauritius teemed with figs, pomegranates, partridges and pigeons. There were no cats, pigs, goats, dogs or even rats – at least not until some escaped from ships wrecked near Mascarene shores.

LEFT: early map of Île de France.

RIGHT: engraving of a scene from the 18th-century novel *Paul et Virginie*, a romantic tale inspired by a shipwreck off Île d'Ambre.

These early visitors brought back drawings of a strange flightless bird, indigenous to Mauritius and Réunion. It was described as fat, clumsy and bigger than a turkey. In 1628, Emmanuel Altham sent a live specimen of this "strange fowle" home to his brother in Essex. This was the dodo *(see page 67)* whose relative, the solitaire, was found on Réunion and Rodrigues.

The ebony forests on Mauritius, and its two natural harbours, made it a colonial prize for European traders and explor-

WHAT'S IN A NAME?

The Mascarene Island group is named after the Portuguese navigator Pedro Mascarenhas. Like Columbus, he has probably been given more credit than his due, as he did not discover any of them.

groups combined with soldiers and sailors who deserted from the garrison and visiting ships' crews to form a counter-settlement in the forested interior. They launched frequent raids and arson attacks on the fort and farmers. The difficult conditions of the earlier settlers were made worse by seasonal cyclones, which ripped through their fragile wooden homesteads, and by the depredations of rats who ate the crops and stores. The ruins of the Dutch fort at Grand Port can be seen to this day, having

ers. Annexed for the Netherlands in 1598, the Dutch felled much of the valuable black wood on the island, until a glut in the European market slowed the destruction.

Colonisation begins

The Dutch occupied Mauritius twice, between 1638 and 1658, and again from 1664 to 1710. Their first settlement was around the southeast harbour (where present-day Mahébourg is now situated). The garrison and commander, along with a small group of free farmers, brought convicts and slaves from Southeast Asia and Madagascar to help them with wood-cutting and crop cultivation. Runaways from these

only been excavated by archaeologists in 1977.

While the Dutch were establishing their settlement on Mauritius, the French had annexed the other Mascarene islands. Both nations supplemented piecemeal colonisation by sending unruly settlers from their bases at the Cape, Batavia and Madagascar into exile on the Mascarenes.

Bourbon, later renamed Réunion, was given its royal name by the French governor at Madagascar after hearing from a group of returned exiles of its beauty, abundance and healthiness. In 1654, the French attempted a permanent settlement of the island with a mixed group of French and Malagasy. They left four years later and Bourbon remained unoccupied until 1663.

The next group of settlers included three women, but disputes over them led to the creation of rival camps of French and Malagasy men. Attempts to send volunteers from France met with mixed results – many died en route.

Two events then proved a turning point for Bourbon: firstly the French were massacred on Madagascar, forcing the abandonment of that base, and secondly war with Holland closed off the Cape to French ships. Bourbon now became an important post for them on the Indies route. A governor was appointed from France, and, in a series of efforts to boost the size of the population, Indian convicts were imported, Indo-Portuguese women were induced to settle, and pirates, tired of a life of plunder, were invited to marry into the growing Bourbon community.

CRUSOE'S ISLAND

The Mascarenes were legendary refuges. Mandelslo's description of a man marooned on Mauritius in 1601 is said to have provided Daniel Defoe with inspiration for his tale of Robinson Crusoe.

Paradise lost

The glowing description of Bourbon made by its first forced inhabitants had also inspired a group of Protestants, persecuted in France, to set up their Eden on the last remaining desert island of the Mascarenes. François Leguat was one of eight males who settled on Rodrigues until the effects of solitude and the lack of women led them to escape in a small boat to Mauritius. Utopia, it seemed, could not be achieved without sex.

The reality of life on a tropical desert island was far removed from the visions of recuperating sailors and persecuted Protestants. The small settlements, peopled with prisoners and pirates, neglected by the trading companies, presided over by frustrated commanders and weakly defended, found survival a struggle. Geographical constraints – isolation and unreliable weather – had been revealed to be major determinants of Mascarenes history.

The impact of these visitors from across the seas was immense. The fragile island ecologies were irreparably damaged by human settlement and the animals they imported that upset the natural balance. The coastal palms and the

---

LEFT: the Dutch settlement at Vieux Grand Port.
RIGHT: Mauritius was named after Maurice of Nassau, son of William of Orange.

ebony forests were depleted. Eventually 30 species of birds, including the dodo and solitaire, and the large tortoises and turtles with whom they cohabited, would become extinct – casualties of the fragility of unique small island populations.

The Mascarene Islands have become the archetypal example of the destruction of ecological systems by outsiders. Once this process began, it took only a few decades for these small island "Edens" to vanish forever.

The French century

Between 1710, when the Dutch left, and 1810 when the British took control, the French had a century of uninterrupted supremacy in the Mascarenes. Over this period the islands served several purposes: as a rest and refuelling point for European ships on the Indies route, where goods could be traded and ships repaired; as cultivating grounds for spices and coffee; and as good vantage points for the study of astronomic phenomena.

Already established on Bourbon, in 1721 the French sent a party of colonists from there to settle on Mauritius, renamed Île de France. A governor and several hundred soldiers and colonists were also sent from France, arriving the following year with 30 Malagasy slaves they had acquired en route. They settled in the southeast of the island, building on top of the Dutch ruins. Administered from Bourbon, both islands struggled to master their environment. One visitor to Île de France at this time sarcastically renamed it "Kingdom of the Rats", describing the discomfort of nights spent trying to ignore them crawling over his body.

SLAVE LABOUR

The French author of *Paul et Virginie*, Bernardin de Saint Pierre, observed: "I do not know whether coffee and sugar are necessary to the happiness of Europe, but they have certainly made much of the world miserable."

A decisive change occurred in the administration of the French Mascarenes in 1735, with the arrival of Mahé de Labourdonnais, and the decision to transfer the seat of government to Île de France. For the rest of the 18th century, Bourbon was relegated to what its colonists believed to be the inferior position of "granary", supplying food for its sister island, and watching as the latter developed into a substantial trading and naval repair post.

Labourdonnais aimed to transform Île de France into a flourishing colony, but his ambitious plans could not be achieved without labour, and from this period, the trickle of West Africans and Asians arriving with visiting ships was regularly supplemented by the organisation of slave trading voyages to East Africa and Madagascar, and the importation of skilled workers from India and France. With serious food shortages threatening the increased population, Labourdonnais introduced manioc to the Mascarenes, which became a staple food of slaves, and began the systematic plunder of tortoises from Rodrigues. This marked the beginning of the irreversible decline of its endemic land and marine fauna, a process accelerated by the periodic presence of naval squadrons.

By 1767 the French East India Company, suffering severe financial losses occasioned by years of warfare, gave up control of the Mascarenes to the French king. Port Louis was able to expand its trading activities which had been limited by the company's monopolistic practices, and developed an air of prosperity and style which led to its designation as the "Paris of the Indian Ocean".

But this facade of culture, elegance and profit concealed an economy based on speculation and a society in which the presence of celebrated intellectuals and naturalists could not prevent the continuing destruction of nature and the differentiation of men by colour and chains.

The French had hoped to use the Mascarenes to further their interest in the spice trade and to cultivate tropical produce. Colonists were encouraged to grow coffee, cotton, indigo, cane, cinnamon, tea and pepper. Cloves and nutmegs were introduced. Many crops failed – eaten by birds, rats and monkeys or destroyed by adverse weather conditions. Coffee and spices grown on Bourbon nevertheless became the principal exports of the Mascarenes, while sugar cane was found to resist the onslaught of the elements best on Île de France. Its cultivation, expanding towards the end of the 18th century, was to become the defining feature of the Mascarenes in the 19th century.

Revolution and rebellion

French rule in the Mascarenes had instituted a kind of social apartheid which subjected slaves to the provisions of the Code Noir – a famous law the French applied to their colonies which prevented the free coloured population from marrying white colonists. After 1789, the revolutionary fervour emanating from France swept away such laws and unleashed a chain of events in the French colonies that culminated in the breakaway of Haiti and provoked a rebellion in the Mascarenes.

News of the French Revolution did not reach the Indian Ocean islands until the following year, but once ships bearing the tricolour arrived, Colonial Assemblies were set up on the islands and the royal name of Bourbon was changed to Réunion. The revolution was not very bloody in the Mascarenes although one notable victim was MacNamara, a royalist naval officer who was hacked to death by a

– they were thrown out within three days. For a while the islands ruled themselves but not without serious disagreements which almost led to Réunion separating from its sister island.

The arrival of Napoleon on the political scene led to the re-establishment of slavery and in 1803 he sent General Decaen to rule, granting him absolute power over the Mascarenes. Réunion was promptly renamed Bonaparte Island but, once again, did not flourish in the shadow of Île de France. The rigid social and fiscal legislation introduced by Decaen was designed for, and discriminated in favour of, the latter.

mob in Port Louis. Restrictions on marriages between white and coloured colonists were lifted and the gulf between social groups was briefly narrowed.

In 1796, however, the Revolutionary government in France took matters too far for the liking of the colonists. Having proclaimed the abolition of slavery, France sent two representatives to the Mascarenes to put this into effect

LEFT: the horrors of slavery. Roughly translated, the French inscription beneath reads "all that serves your pleasure, is soaked with our tears".
RIGHT: engraving of Governor Mahé de Labourdonnais being welcomed by islanders.

MAHÉ DE LABOURDONNAIS

Mahé de Labourdonnais is fêted in Mauritius and his statue stands in the centre of Port Louis, its capital, because in a few short years he transformed this natural harbour into the beginnings of a flourishing port.

Some of the works he undertook are still in evidence today. The renovated mill and granary on the waterfront of Port Louis are vestiges of this formative period. Labourdonnais also built a hospital, established a road network and imported the first primitive sugar processing equipment to be used in Mauritius, which can still be seen in the grounds of Pamplemousses Botanical Gardens, formerly the site of his estates.

Pirates, traitors and spies

For Portuguese and particularly British ships plying the route to the Indies, the French Mascarenes were by now chiefly known for being a "nest of pirates". Between 1793 and 1802 more than a hundred captured ships were brought into Port Louis where the booty on offer attracted neutral peoples like the Danes and Americans. The port was also popular with sailors: the increasing cultivation of sugar cane meant that one of its by-products, rum, was widely available, and it was one of the few places on the Indies route, outside the Cape, where men did not heavily outnumber women,

and where the latter were reputed to be generous in distributing their favours.

These privateering activities led by the king of the corsairs, Robert Surcouf, were the chief reason why the British decided to target the Mascarenes. In 1806 they blockaded Île de France, where the celebrated British explorer and naturalist Matthew Flinders was then imprisoned. Flinders and other British prisoners and reconnaissance agents who had been sent ashore, were offered information and hospitality from colonists who were either royalist sympathisers or pragmatists.

This did not prevent the British from overestimating the strength of French forces. They sent an armada from Bombay and the Cape, which regrouped at Rodrigues and took Bourbon (later Réunion) in July 1810 without much struggle.

Île de France was not so easy a conquest. In August, the British were defeated after a three-day naval battle in Mahébourg bay, known as the battle of Grand Port. In November 1810 they returned to the attack with 70 ships and 10,000 troops, landing on the north coast and marching to the capital. Both sides recognised that the numerical superiority of the British was such as to make unnecessary bloodshed pointless. Decaen therefore negotiated an honourable capitulation.

After the conquest, Île de France and Bourbon were renamed Mauritius and Réunion. The British retained control of Réunion until 1814 when the Treaty of Paris returned the island to French rule. Louis XVIII is supposed to have commented to the British minister who negotiated the deal: "You are leaving us the volcano and you are keeping the port."

Abolitionist movement

The British conquest of Mauritius and Rodrigues, undertaken for strategic motives, did not lead to a large influx of British settlers, and the Francophone character of the Mascarenes has consequently never been lost.

Early British colonial officials not only had to deal with a largely French settler class, but had to implement unpopular slave amelioration laws. The abolitionist movement, which had a massive following in Britain at this time, turned its attention to Mauritius at the worst possible moment for that colony. The island was in the process of converting itself into a plantation

---

FRIENDLY ENEMIES

Despite the relentless conflict between the two nations during the Napoleonic wars, Anglo–French relations remained chivalrous. When the wife of the English officer commanding the squadron blockading the islands between 1803 and 1810 gave birth to a child on board ship, the French Governor, Decaen, sent her a boatload of fresh produce.

After the battle of Grand Port in 1810 – the only Napoleonic victory over the British that is inscribed on the Arc de Triomphe – the wounded leaders of both forces were treated side by side in what is now the Naval Museum of Mahébourg.

society and needed extra labour to clear land and plant canes. When John Jeremie, a known abolitionist, was sent to the island in 1832 to take up an important legal post, the colonists gave him a "welcome" akin to that received by the delegates from France during the Revolution. A general strike was organised which paralysed the capital and the fearful British governor ordered Jeremie to re-embark almost immediately. In response, the British built Fort Adelaide on a

MOUNTAIN REFUGE

In 1811 a slave revolt on Réunion led to the execution of 30 ringleaders. A later uprising in Mauritius was also snuffed out. But for as long as slavery was in force, the Mascarene mountains remained a refuge for runaways.

free labour could produce sugar as cheaply as slaves, by allowing the colony the first opportunity to import Indian workers under the indenture system – which tied immigrants to fixed-wage contracts with penal clauses, so that if a labourer could not or would not work he could be imprisoned. Almost half a million indentured workers were introduced in the 19th century, making Mauritius the largest recipient of Indian labour in the empire and helping the island to achieve the position of

hill overlooking the capital – a striking symbol of colonial power designed to quell its unruly inhabitants. The colonists were appeased by a £2-million compensation package for their slaves (including those that had been illegally introduced) and the day of emancipation passed without incident in 1835.

Immigrant labour

In 1842 the British decided to make Mauritius the site of a "great experiment" to see whether

Britain's premier sugar colony within a decade.

Both Réunion and Mauritius had turned increasingly to sugar production as falling supplies from the British and French West Indies encouraged the newer colonies to fill the gap. Réunion was given the go ahead to import British Indian labour from 1860, and both islands continued to recruit smaller numbers of Chinese, Malagasy, Comorian and Mozambican workers. Africans rescued from slave ships by British naval cruisers were also offloaded at Mauritius and the Seychelles from the mid-19th century and "liberated" into lengthy apprenticeships with local employers.

Réunion adapted to socio-economic change

LEFT: "King of the Corsairs", Robert Surcouf, captures the British vessel, *Kent*, in the Bay of Bengal in 1800.
RIGHT: Indian labourers.

at a more gentle rate than Mauritius. It was slower to abolish slavery (abolition was declared in 1848, 13 years after Mauritius), and slower to develop into a monoculture economy. Both islands, nevertheless, underwent a revolution of sorts, as mechanisation and centralisation of estates transformed them into plantation societies where plantocracies confronted increasing ranks of immigrant labour. Only Rodrigues remained primarily an agricultural colony and did not experience the vast influx of Indian

> ### DEMON DRINK
>
> Mark Twain, who visited Mauritius in 1896, noted a local saying about new settlers: "The first year they gather shells; the second year they gather shells and drink; the third year they do not gather shells."

labour which had transformed the demographic characteristics of its neighbours. Administered from Mauritius, Rodrigues was only rarely visited by British governors.

Indentured labourers were contracted to work at a fixed wage for a varying number of years. Breaches of contract were punishable by imprisonment, and the physical chastisement and limited mobility of Indian workers made their treatment akin to that of slaves. In 1872 and 1877 Commissions of Enquiry were sent to Mauritius and Réunion respectively to compile reports on the conditions of these workers, and they found much evidence of malpractice.

Disease and disaster

When sugar prices began to fall in the last quarter of the 19th century, the distress of the enormously enlarged populations of the islands increased their vulnerability to outbreaks of such deadly diseases as smallpox, cholera and malaria. In 1892, a fierce cyclone hit Mauritius, killing 1,260 people, and making 50,000 homeless, while Réunion experienced periodic eruptions of its active volcano. But the sequence of disasters did not end there – rats once again wreaked devastation on the Mascarenes as bubonic plague struck, and in 1902 a fly-borne parasite necessitated the slaughter of thousands of horses, mules and cattle in Mauritius. The islands were at their lowest ebb and were a far cry from the idyllic Edens encountered barely 200 years before.

With the sugar economy still in a state of depression, the flow of labour immigration had all but ended, but traders, principally Chinese and Gujarati, continued to settle in the Mascarenes, and gradually took over the retail and wholesale sectors. On the other hand, emigration began to take place from Réunion to Madagascar and from Mauritius to South Africa as colonists sought opportunities elsewhere.

Politically, progress was swift in Réunion, which moved from a system of absolute government to one of universal suffrage, and was given the right to be represented in the French Parliament from 1870. Mauritius, by contrast, did not have an elected legislative council until 1885. In both islands, however, a few wealthy planter families continued to wield disproportionate influence.

Post-war Mascarenes

World War I brought an increase in sugar prices and a degree of prosperity was restored to the Mascarenes, but by the 1930s, the disaffection among labourers had transformed into widely orchestrated strikes on both Mauritius and Réunion.

World War II affected the islands much more directly. The British hurriedly set up naval and air bases on Mauritius, while the Vichy regime, installed on Réunion, isolated the island and brought it to the verge of famine. Following the war, both islands were supplied with a regular air service, becoming increasingly accessible to visitors.

Réunion was given the status of a *département* or district of France in 1946 (along with Martinique, Guadeloupe and French Guyana). The flow of capital from France produced a socio-economic power shift from the planter class towards the growing public and commercial sectors of the economy.

Departmentalisation entailed a process of assimilation, which Réunion, little touched by

SUEZ CANAL

The cutting of the Suez Canal robbed the Mascarenes of strategic significance. Ironically, De Lesseps' wife was Mauritian and many of her compatriots worked on the construction of the Canal.

The 1980s was a period of political radicalism in Mauritius also with the rise of the left-wing Mouvement Militant Mauricien, the MMM, which gained a huge following under the banner of "One nation, one people". Both of these movements have ultimately been limited in their effects and the struggle to create a sense of national identity – Réunion against the linguistic and cultural hegemony of France, and Mauritius against the competing claims of ethnic identity – goes on.

the "negritude" movement of the French Caribbean to assert "black power", seemed initially disinclined to resist. However, since 1959 when the Communist Party was set up, there has always been a movement on the island fighting for the recognition of a distinctively Réunionese identity. This was partly achieved in 1981 when the acknowledgement of a "right to difference" produced a kind of cultural revolution to accompany the political departmentalisation revolution.

LEFT: Chinese immigrant women, *c.*1910.
RIGHT: Independence Day celebrations in the Mauritian capital, Port Louis.

Independence

Independence was something of a brokered affair, with Britain willingly divesting itself of the island in 1968 in return for the British Indian Ocean Territory created from a group of smaller, dependent islands. The Americans were promptly leased one of these – Diego Garcia – for use as a military base, which has become of increasing importance to them in Indian Ocean geopolitics.

The growing recognition in Mauritius that independence would lead to rule by the Indian majority led to fears of Hinduisation policies, and the 1968 celebrations were marred by ethnic violence and the emigration of disaffected minorities. Between 1968 and 1982 the ruling Labour Party did indeed become increasingly identified with its Hindu power base, but it was the combination of corruption scandals, over-population and high unemployment, which swept the opposition MMM into office in the early 1980s. The shift to radicalism was short-lived. Since then, Mauritius has been governed by a series of coalitions of four principal parties – Labour, the MMM, the PMSD and the PSM – all of which have a pro-capitalist stance. In 1992, Mauritius became a Republic, and the Queen was replaced as head of state by a locally nom-inated president.

Rodrigues, formerly a dependency of Mauri-tius, is politically integrated with its sister island. In 2002 the island was granted regional autonomy but still sends MPs to the Mauritius Legislative Assembly.

Economically the islands remain fragile, although Mauritius has gone furthest down the road towards diversification with manufactur-ing and textile production. Until 2003 Mauritius earned more money exporting manufactured goods than from sugar exports. But changes to international sugar pricing agreements have hit the sugar industry hard, and textile factory clo-sures caused by cheap competition from India and China have increased unemployment.

Sugar barons are now turning their lands over to tourism and real estate development. Tourism brings around half a million visitors annually, while it is hoped that financial ser-vices and communications technology – the lat-est additions to the economy – will provide new jobs to replace those lost in other sectors.

Some Rodriguans have sought a share in the development of their country's infrastructure by migrating to work on Mauritius, as their own island lags behind in resource-allocation – its economy remains largely agricultural and youth unemployment is high. The economic prosper-ity which has kept ethnic frustrations at bay in this two-island Republic has been indifferently redistributed, with the Afro-Creole populations on both islands feeling increasingly aggrieved. In 1999 widespread rioting on Mauritius con-stituted a clear signal that socio-economic dis-parities are reaching dangerous levels. It remains to be seen whether the Mauritian polit-ical elite will respond effectively.

Réunion inhabits a position midway between the developed and developing nations. Its health and education infrastructure are akin to those of "first world" states, while its economy lags far behind. Unlike Mauritius, Réunion has not been able to develop a significant Export Processing Zone because wages are too high. The island has its own appeal for tourists, but lacks the plentiful beaches that have made the Seychelles and Mauritius internationally known as holiday destinations. The Chaudron riots of February 1991 underscored the problems of social inequalities and high unemployment that persist in Réunion. Ironically, these distur-bances occurred at a time when the French gov-ernment had at last begun to address the demands of the overseas *départements* for social and economic parity. Réunion has also been active in forging a regional identity: tak-ing part in projects of regional cooperation with its Indian Ocean neighbours.

The Mascarenes constitute one of the few regions where Francophony continues to make advances against the worldwide dominance of the English language. The French have clearly returned to their 18th-century bastion in the Indian Ocean, ready to stand their ground in the 21st century, less in military than in politi-cal and cultural terms. ❑

LEFT: Cassam Uteem, first president of Mauritius.

Death of the Dodo

The dodo is Mauritius' most famous export. This giant, flightless bird, which developed from the pigeon family and was killed off in the 17th century, has become a byword for stupidity and a symbol of man's destructiveness, throughout the world.

The dodo was first seen in Asia and Europe in the 17th century when Dutch sailors brought live specimens from Mauritius to the world's attention. Their name for the bird is thought to derive from Dutch words meaning "round arse". The Dutch described the bird as fearless of man, ungainly, so fat that it could not run, and so foolish that it did not recognise danger. In pre-Darwinian days, the dodo was seen as an example of a mistake made by God, and later as an evolutionary failure. In Grant's *History of Mauritius* published in England in 1801 it is described as a "feathered tortoise" which was an easy target for hunters.

For many years, contemporary paintings and written descriptions of the birds were practically all that were known of them – only a disputed claw and other remnants having survived from the birds brought to Europe. Naturalists began to argue that the dodo was a figment of sailors' rum-fuelled imagination. In the mid-19th century, however, dodo bones were dug up at Mare aux Songes (ironically, where the airport now stands) and models of the bird were constructed and placed in museums throughout the world. Lewis Carroll saw one such model at the University Museum in Oxford, which evidently sparked his imagination – the flightless bird was immortalised in *Alice in Wonderland*.

With the reality of the dodo's existence, and its fame now firmly established, naturalists began to turn their attention to the bird itself. Travellers' accounts and cultural artefacts were re-examined along with the skeletal evidence unearthed in the 20th century. Bones excavated in Rodrigues were found to belong to a similar bird with longer legs, named the solitaire. These findings vindicated the account of French Huguenot, François Leguat, two centuries before.

The overweight, ungainly dodo was rehabilitated when it was discovered that the bird ate seasonally and was both fast and trim at other times of the year. The new slimline model of the dodo is now on display in several museums. Nat-uralists also absolved the Dutch from the ignominy of killing the last dodo. While men were the catalyst of its destruction, it was the pigs, rats and monkeys they introduced to Mauritius which ate the eggs and chicks.

Some facts about the dodo remain to be elucidated. Travellers' accounts speak of a grey dodo in Mauritius and a white dodo in Réunion. Others assert that the dodo in Réunion was more like a solitaire. It is clear that a similar large bird to the dodo and solitaire was found on Réunion but no bone discoveries have been made to confirm the various theories. Scientists in the UK are now attempting to use new genetic techniques to re-

create the dodo, so we may one day see the bird back in what remains of its natural habitat. Until then, the dodo remains the world's most famous example of extinction, food for thought when we visit today's examples of rare species in Mauritius.

Île aux Aigrettes, just off the southeast coast of Mauritius, is thought to be the site of the dodo's extinction. Since 1987, the MWF (Mauritius Wildlife Foundation) has been working on restoring the island's original ecosystem. Obviously it's too late for the dodo, but the pink pigeon has been saved from the same fate and can be seen flying free here. Most hotels organise day trips to the island and a percentage of the cost goes towards wildlife conservation. ❑

RIGHT: artist's impression of the dodo, extinct by 1661.

Weddings are another common weekend activity on the island. Hindu nuptials take place over several days, and innumerable sittings are organised in marquees for guests, who are served vegetarian curries on a banana leaf. The bride will wear a traditional red or cream sari, and her groom – probably for the only time in his life – will don an ornate turban, and slippers. Muslim weddings are characterised in Mauritius by the serving of a biryani meal, accompanied by a soft drink, generally Pepsi. The ceremony, or *nikah*, is shorter than that of Hindus, and at some gatherings male and female guests are accommodated in separate

of quirky customs and taboos, ranging from cutting your toenails only at certain times of day to leaving out food to pacify malevolent spirits. Chinese Mauritians are partial to the number 9, as their car number-plates testify.

Local sorcerers, known as *longanistes* or *traiteurs*, have followers from diverse backgrounds, and are called in to settle quarrels, exact revenge, reverse bad luck and administer love potions. When one's spouse or lover loses interest, a rival may well be suspected of having used the services of a sorcerer. Cemeteries are powerful sites for such practitioners of magic, and they can often be seen at mid-

areas. Weddings of Catholics, be they Chinese, Creole or Franco-Mauritian, generally involve a ceremony at the local church, followed by a reception. Sooner or later, at most functions, the sega will be played when guests of all ages will indulge their love of dancing *(see page 79)*.

Folklore and superstition

Diverse beliefs and practices, some originating in the popular customs which African and Asian immigrants brought to the island, have persisted into modern-day Mauritius. There are all kinds

day, sacrificing a small chicken, breaking coconuts, and lighting candles or camphor sticks on the graves, surrounded by a small knot of followers.

The phenomenon of the *loup garou*, or werewolf, is a good example of how a popular belief can become a serious issue in Mauritius given propitious circumstances. In 1994 a serious cyclone, Hollanda, brought down most of the island's electricity pylons, leaving many areas without power for several weeks. During this time, the notion that a *loup garou* was on the loose took hold of the popular imagination. Women claimed to have been raped by the creature, and there were daily sightings. The *loup*

LEFT AND RIGHT: watching the world go by in Port Louis and Curepipe.

garou became front page news for several weeks, and hysteria mounted daily, with women and children barricading themselves indoors. The police issued a communiqué, assuring people that it was tackling the problem, and only when the issue took on a communal dimension, with Muslims asserting that the werewolf was hiding in a Catholic shrine, and inter-religious tensions increasing, did the president intervene, disputing the existence of such a creature.

Community, class and generation

It is one of the peculiarities of Mauritian society that any seemingly insignificant object can

become an ethnic signifier. Here, the company you work for, the kind of car you drive, even the type of soft drink you buy, is often a decision governed by communal factors. The reason may simply be that the importer of a certain make of vehicle or product is a member of your community, influencing your decision. There is a popular saying in Mauritian Kreol, "*sak zako bizin protez so montan*" (each monkey must protect his mountain) which refers to the tendency to put members of one's own ethnic group before others.

That tensions sparked by the prevalence of favouritism and nepotism do not erupt into more serious violence, can be attributed to the pragmatism of most Mauritians and to the elaborate balancing act performed by all governments. In fact, ministerial posts are assigned in cabinet so that members of competing caste and ethnic groups each have at least one representative. Alongside relatively recent strategies of ethnic lobbying, the old demon of racial discrimination still exists, however. Widespread rioting in 1999, following the suspicious deaths of a number of Afro-Creoles in police custody, highlighted the frustrations of this group, who are most affected by the persistence of racial stereotyping.

The generational differences in Mauritius are also marked, but may ultimately be an antidote to the long-standing divisions based on community and colour. School is a bastion of cultural mixing in a society with a large youth population, and increasing exposure of teenagers to Western media is impacting on old preconceptions. While most Mauritian girls still do not have the freedom of their Western counterparts, or even of their male peers, discotheques provide a means of socialising that was not available to their mothers.

Mauritius today is a fascinating blend of the spiritual and the material. A place where the accountant working in the booming offshore sector will take a day off to participate in a religious pilgrimage, maybe buying a herbal infusion from a stallholder at the Port Louis bazaar – who claims to know the remedies for all the world's ailments – which he will sip as he logs on to the internet, effortlessly combining "olde worlde" beliefs with an enthusiasm for all that modern technology has to offer. ❏

KAYA

Joseph Reginald Topize was born in Roche Bois in 1960 and began his singing career in the early 1980s. He called himself "Kaya" after one of Bob Marley's albums and his dreadlocks and pot-smoking image struck a chord with young islanders who readily identified with "seggae", a fusion of reggae and sega. In 1999, Kaya's death in police custody, one of several in less than two years, sparked off communal riots on a scale not seen since Independence in 1967–8. He has become a symbol of discrimination against Afro-Creoles. The president, sensing that things could turn ugly, pleaded with the nation to form a human chain around the island to symbolise solidarity among Mauritian ethnic groups.

LEFT: natural cures for all ills.

Sega

Sega goes back at least to the early 18th century when it evolved as the soul dance of the African slaves as a form of escapism from the harsh reality of their daily lives. After a long week toiling in the cane fields, they would gather around a fire drinking alambic. Once fuelled by the rum, they became less inhibited and started to sing and dance what became known as the sega.

Sega has been described as "an erotic dance that leaves little to the imagination", as "provocative in the extreme" or even as "a simulated sexual act". The movements are sensuous and the flirtation real, but however tempestuous it becomes, the sensuality is controlled and it is never obscene.

The original sega instruments were made from anything the slaves could lay their hands on. The ravan (a goatskin tambour), maravan (a hollowed out tube filled with dried seeds) and triang (a triangular-shaped piece of old iron) were played, along with anything else that could produce a sound – pots and pans, empty bottles and spoons. The ravan, maravan and triang are still played, but modern *ségatiers* also use guitars and keyboards.

The accompanying songs, often scattered with double entendres and sexual overtones, are an added amusement. In the past, these songs were also a way for the slaves to express their pent up feelings and vent their anger on their masters, whom they ridiculed in the lyrics.

Although its roots are in Africa, sega in its present form is found only in Mauritius, Rodrigues and Seychelles, and each place has its own particular version *(see page 261)*. In classical Mauritian sega, or *sega typic*, the women begin the dancing. They hold out their bright, long skirts in both hands and sway to the rhythmic music, swinging their hips to reveal a glimpse of leg, enticing the men to join them. As more and more dancers join in, shuffling their feet and swaying to the powerful beat of the drums, the dance develops into a sort of courtship drama. Both men and women try to attract a partner of their choice. The women are teasing and provocative, changing partners, until they single out their man. The men stretch out their arms as if to catch a dancer they admire or to prevent their chosen partner from escaping. When at last a pair form, the woman leans backwards while the man

RIGHT: an outdoor sega performance
at the Domaine les Pailles.

extends his body over hers, at which point the singers may encourage the dancers by shouting *"enba! enba!"*, literally "get down!" Then they swap positions and the woman dances above the man while he lies on the floor inviting her to come lower and lower.The drumbeats become more frenzied as the dancers move closer to each other – they never touch. Onlookers may be forgiven for thinking that anything could happen next. But the crescendo of the drum reaches a dramatic climax and, on a last exciting beat, ceases.

Nowadays, classical sega in Mauritius is mostly associated with the Rivière Noire area on the west coast. Public holidays are the best time to try and

catch authentic performances; you may be lucky enough to see a group of locals gathered around a fire on the beach, drinking rum or wine, and spontaneously breaking into dance.

However, if the only sega performance you get to see is at your hotel, you may well wonder what the fuss is all about. "Sega hotel", as the locals call it, is a refined, formalised version of the dance. The men wear tight breeches or trousers rolled up to the knee with unbuttoned *corsair* shirts knotted at the waist. The women wear full, brightly coloured ankle-length skirts and short bodices displaying a bare midriff. It makes a pretty sight but is often nothing to get excited about – though you may be asked to join in. ❑

CEREMONIES AND CELEBRATIONS

With such a multicultural society, the festival calendar is full all year, but it's the colourful Hindu and Tamil celebrations that draw the big crowds

So many festivals are celebrated in Mauritius that visitors are bound to see one or more in any month of the year. The majority emanate from the Indian communities and they are great and colourful occasions of religious celebration.

Cavadee (Thai Poosam) is a Tamil festival which can be celebrated any time in January or February. It is an amazing if blood-curdling sight. Tamil devotees pierce their bodies with needles; some also partake in fire-walking ceremonies. The Cavadee – a wooden arch decorated with flowers with a brass pot of milk attached to each end – is carried in a procession to the temple where it is placed before the Tamil deity, Muruga.

Holi is a raucous two-day festival held in February or March. It begins with a bonfire on which an effigy of the evil demon Holika is burnt. Men, women and children then all join in squirting coloured water and smearing red and purple powders on each other's faces and hair.

Divali is the Hindu's happiest festival. Celebrated in October or November, at the darkest period of the autumn months, it marks the victory of Rama (an incarnation of Vishnu) over the demon Ravana and also commemorates Krishna's destruction of the demon Narakasuran. Candles and simple earthen lamps are lit around houses, gardens and even at business premises to brighten the moonless night.

△ **HINDU SHRINES**
Many shrines have been built on the banks of Grand Bassin. This one is to Lord Krishna and Rahna Radi.

◁ **DANCING FOR DIVALI**
Divali celebrates the victory of good over evil symbolised by the thousands of little lights that flicker in the night.

▷ **SWORD-WALKING**
Blessing of swords before a sword-walking ceremony, another form of penance, usually enacted between April and June.

as it rarely reaches half a metre (2 ft) in length it does little harm.

Free from rats, Round Island is home to a whole community of native reptiles, including three species of skinks and two Phelsuma geckos, one of which is a Durrell's night gecko, named after the late naturalist Gerald Durrell, who made Round Island famous in his book *Golden Bats and Pink Pigeons*. Two rare types of endemic boa live here as well, but one of these, the burrowing boa, has not been seen since 1975. This island is so important that visits can only be made with special permission. However, there are plans to establish additional

ing survivors are the Mascarene cave swiftlet, Mascarene swallow, Mauritius cuckoo shrike, Mauritius black bulbul, Mauritius fody, paradise flycatcher and two types of white-eyes. The swiftlet breeds in lava tunnels but has been in decline for many years as its nest is considered a delicacy for bird's nest soup. There are, however, still 2,000–4,000 birds on Mauritius which can be seen flying in flocks over any part of the island. The heavily built swallow keeps to the dry southwest and is most active in the late afternoon when it feeds on flying insects. The only other endemic bird that you are likely to see around and about is the grey white-eye, a tiny

populations of some of the reptiles on other islands such as Île aux Aigrettes.

Surviving birds

There are 11 surviving species of land birds endemic to the islands of the southwest Indian Ocean, and seven of them are endemic to Mauritius. The best known are the Mauritius kestrel, pink pigeon and echo parakeet, for these have been the subjects of a conservation programme since the mid-1970s *(see page 91)*. The remain-

LEFT: a herd of Javan deer.
RIGHT: the yellow weaver bird, one of many colourful birds you can spot flitting around hotels and houses.

MAURITIUS WILDLIFE FOUNDATION

Formed in 1984 by Gerald Durrell and other naturalists, the Mauritius Wildlife Foundation is a charity dedicated to the conservation of the native wildlife of Mauritius, Rodrigues and their islands. It is most well known for its work on the Mauritius kestrel, pink pigeon and echo parakeet, but is also working on protecting endemic passerines and the endangered reptiles of Round Island, and Rodrigues' golden fruit bat. Several small islands have been restored by the foundation. Île aux Aigrettes, for example, has been cleared of rats and many weeds and the MWF is now in the process of replacing the missing fauna and flora.

grey bird with a white rump that travels in small flocks and is known as a *pic-pic*. You would be lucky to see any of the other birds, which are all perching songbirds (passerines), unless you specifically go to look for them in the forests of the Black River Gorges and Bassin Blanc.

The woods along Cascade Pigeons River and at Solitude on Rodrigues are home to two of the world's rarest birds: the endemic warbler, which only has about 25 pairs left and the striking yellow and orange fody with about 200 pairs.

ISLAND FLOWER

The beautiful boucle d'oreille *(Trochetia boutoniana)*, meaning earring, is the national flower of Mauritius. However, it can only be seen in cultivated sites.

The colourful birds commonly seen around the hotels and houses have mostly been introduced to Mauritius. Many of these may seem very familiar since they are common cage birds that long ago escaped from captivity and established themselves in the wild. The most prolific are the mynah bird, the elegant, crested red-whiskered bulbul, the bright red Madagascar fody and the yellow village weaver.

Coastal creatures

Nesting on the small islands around Mauritius are boobies, sooty terns and noddies, as well as several species of petrel. A wonderful sight to see is the elegant, rare red-tailed tropic bird which nests in cliffs on Gunner's Quoin, Flat Island and Round Island. But its more common smaller cousin, the white-tailed tropic bird *(paille-en-queue)* can be watched from the Black River viewpoint.

Fourteen species of whales and dolphins have been recorded around the Mascarene coasts. Spinner and bottle-nose dolphins can often be seen from the shore and in Tamarin Bay, beyond the reef. The chances of seeing dolphins on a boat trip are high and you may also see sperm whales off the west coast. A school of humpbacked whales returns to the waters between the mainland and Round Island during July and August most years, probably to breed.

At one time dugongs, or sea cows, lived in the lagoons around Mauritius and Rodrigues feeding on sea-grass. These sea beauties are believed to have been the creatures sea-weary sailors mistook for mermaids, but it didn't stop them from being hunted. Luckily, some still survive off Madagascar in the Mozambique Channel.

Fascinating flora

The native hardwood forests of Mauritius are now largely limited to the mountain tops and deep in gorges, where they could not be exploited for their timber. Only 5 percent of the island is forested, and only small areas of that are in good condition. Nevertheless, Mauritius has 685 species of native plants of which 311 are endemic and most are endangered.

It is a sobering thought that Mauritius has some of the rarest plants in the world. The palm *Hyophorbe amauricaulis* is down to its last plant, surviving in the Curepipe Botanical Garden. Rodrigues is hanging on to its last specimen of café marron *(Ramosmania heterophylla)* but we are too late for the *Pyramid pandanus*, which succumbed to Cyclone Hollanda in 1993.

Many of those that haven't survived have been supplanted by alien plants, such as the Chinese guava and *Lantana camara* that have run riot, suffocating seedlings. The familiar casuarina tree seen lining the beaches was brought from Malaysia as a windbreak and the mighty banyan tree with dangling roots, so typical of tropical forests, comes from India. ❏

LEFT: lesser noddies in a two-storey nest, Île aux Cocos.

To the Rescue

Mauritius is most famous for its birds and in particular for its extinct birds – the dodo being the best known, but there are many other birds that have vanished, including a large black flightless parrot, the largest parrot ever known, a blue pigeon, some ducks, owls, more parrots and others. Indeed scientists still argue about the numbers of species that have disappeared.

However, since the mid-1970s three birds – the Mauritius kestrel, the pink pigeon and the echo parakeet – have been rescued from the edge of extinction by a group of conservationists, led by the ornithologist Carl Jones along with Gerald Durrell's Jersey Wildlife Preservation Trust (JWPT).

The Mauritius kestrel *(Falco punctatus)* is a small falcon which lives in the forested gorges and mountains, feeds on bright green day geckos and nests in cliff holes. In 1974 there were only four wild birds, and only one pair were breeding. The rescue operation was started by breeding birds in captivity. Over several years, eggs were harvested from the last pair – every time a clutch of eggs was taken from the wild kestrels, they would lay again, increasing their productivity. Many of the young reared from harvested eggs were released back into the wild together with birds that were bred in captivity. These were fed and provided with nest boxes and protected from predators such as the mongoose and feral cats. The released kestrels began to breed well and between 1984 and 1994, 331 birds were put back into the Black River Gorges and tracts of forest that had not had kestrels for decades. Today it is believed there are between 500 and 800 birds.

Almost as rare as the kestrel, the pink pigeon *(Nesoenas mayeri)* was believed by some to be extinct. But in the 1970s a population was found in an isolated pocket of woodland near Bassin Blanc. These birds were slowly declining because rats and monkeys were stealing their eggs or they were being caught by feral cats. By 1990 there were only 10 birds left in the wild but a small population had been established in captivity and since then the captive-bred birds have been released into the wild, boosting the numbers. A programme controlling the introduced predators has also been put in

force. The pigeons have responded dramatically to these initiatives and the population has increased to more than 370 birds, but the pink pigeon still has a long way to go before it is safe.

The work with the kestrel and pigeon may have been tough but the problems were minor compared to those encountered rescuing the echo parakeet *(Psittacula echo)*. This emerald green parrot – distinguishable from the introduced ring-necked parakeet by its shorter tail, more rounded wing and darker green – had the distinction of being the world's rarest parrot, until recently. In 1987 there were thought to be only eight left, with only two females. The problem was their low breeding rate.

Working under the auspices of the MWF *(see page 89)*, conservationists tried rearing the young and eggs taken from nests that seemed doomed to failure. Many died until it was learned how to nurture them with a good diet (plenty of fresh fruit and vegetables), filtered water and scrupulous hygiene. The wild parakeets were provided with extra food and their nest sites in hollow trees improved. The nesting birds were guarded against predators and their nesting cavities regularly cleaned out and treated with insecticide, to kill the nest flies that sucked out the babies' blood. The population increased slowly and now the future looks good, with around 350 echo parakeets flying free along the Macchabee Ridge in the Black River Gorges National Park. ❏

RIGHT: once the world's rarest bird, there are now more than 500 Mauritius kestrels flying around the island – some even nesting in people's gardens.

caves and tunnels attract shoals of kingfish, crayfish and black-tip sharks.

Snorkelling

While authorities argue that safeguards and restrictions are in place to protect the lagoons, such as a ban on dynamite fishing, collecting shells and corals from the seabed and spear fishing, many islanders complain of increased pollution and impaired visibility. However, there is still an amazing marine world to be discovered just below the surface. Snorkelling is just as popular as diving. Hours of pleasure can be had gliding silently over shallow reefs to observe the many creatures which live there. Hotel boathouses provide free snorkelling equipment for their guests, though these are not always in tip-top condition. If you've been bitten by the snorkelling bug, you might want to invest in your own equipment. Good quality masks, fins and goggles are on sale everywhere.

A walk on the wet side

One way of discovering the seabed in complete safety for R1,100 is to take an undersea walk or "helmet dive". Undersea walking began in the Bahamas in 1948, but the idea was patented and brought to Mauritius in 1990. Following

TAKE THE PLUNGE

Mauritius' warm waters and rich marine life make it the perfect place to learn to dive. Dive centres attached to hotels are affiliated to CMAS (World Underwater Federation), PADI (Professional Association of Diving Instructors), NAUI (National Association of Underwater Instructors) and BSAC (British Sub-Aqua Club) and operate under strict safety rules, providing all the equipment you need and multilingual instructors.

Most dive centres offer a brief resort course designed to test your affinity with the sport. For more in-depth training, you can enrol on an intensive five-day course leading to an Open Water One certificate, followed by a number of qualifying dives. Children are specially catered for, with themed dives introducing them to the wonders of the ocean.

Experienced divers can expect to pay up to R1,300 for a day dive and R1,950 for a night dive, although packages of six and 10 dives are better value at around R7,600 and R9,600 respectively. (See Travel Tips, Activities, for a list of recommended dive centres.)

Diving accidents are rare but if you get into trouble, arrangements are quickly made to convey you to the island's recompression chamber at the paramilitary Special Mobile Force (SMF) Headquarters at Vacoas (tel: 686 1011), about an hour's drive from the coast.

the success of the first company, Captain Nemo's Undersea Walk (tel: 263 7819) in Grand Baie, others followed including Aquaventure (tel: 256 7953) at Coco Beach Hotel.

Undersea walking attracts people of every age and ability, including non-swimmers and young children. A boat ferries you to a floating dive platform inside the reef where a glass fronted steel helmet is placed over your head and rests loosely on your shoulders. Initially it feels heavy but once you are under water it

LANDING A MARLIN

The best time for catching marlin is from October to April, although big game fisherwoman, Birgit Rudolph, says "You never know when a big one is coming".

Submarine safari

To observe the colourful corals teeming with fish, and stay dry, join an hour-long submarine safari from Grand Baie (Blue Safari; tel: 263 3333). You can also hire the submarine for a private party, a night dive, or even as the venue for an underwater wedding.

Unmissable for families with young children is a trip in *Nessie*. This semi-submersible boat can be booked through hotels and tour operators and guarantees viewings of marine life gliding through a riot of ornamental vege-

becomes relatively weightless. Compressed air is then pumped into the helmet and filtered out through valves ensuring a fresh air supply and preventing the water from seeping up to your face. You can even chat to your fellow undersea walkers, and wearers of contact-lenses or glasses need not worry. Experienced guides stroll with you through a garden of spectacular coral inhabited by giant clam and flowering anenomes, and let you hand-feed the shoals of zebra fish.

LEFT: diving off *The Charming Lady*.
RIGHT: facilities for water-skiing, and other water-sports, are available all along the Mauritius coast.

LETHAL WEAPON

The stone fish *(Synancea verucosa)*, known locally as the laff, lurks like a barnacle of basalt in mud and rock, clamping its upturned mouth on whatever takes its fancy. Hollow dorsal spines emit a highly toxic poison causing excruciating pain and swelling, and days of incapacity to anyone unfortunate enough to step on one. In some cases the injury can even prove fatal. In case of injury, clean the wound and seek medical help immediately.

Wearing plastic water shoes when wading through mud and rocks is essential, not only to protect your feet from the laff's noxious spines, but also to avoid cutting yourself on sharp rocks and corals.

tation, in the comfort and safety of an air-conditioned compartment attached to the hull.

Cruising

Most hotels offer free use of hobie cats, windsurfing boards and kayaks for pottering about inside the lagoon. But to experience the real McCoy, you could spend a day sailing along the coast with an experienced crew in a luxury catamaran or yacht. Join in pulling a few ropes or just relax on deck and watch the shapes and shadows of miniature mountains unfold. Full-day tours cost around R2,350 per person including lunch and soft drinks (*See Travel Tips, Activities*).

THE SHOALS OF CAPRICORN

Initiated by the Royal Geographical Society, the Shoals of Capricorn is a major marine science research programme into shallow water environments. British oceanographers are currently investigating the massive Seychelles Mauritius plateau and the adjacent Rodrigues trench. Larger than the Great Barrier Reef, longer than the Red Sea and covering an area of around 115,000 sq km (44,000 sq miles), it is one of earth's few submerged features clearly visible from space. If you're in Rodrigues you can see the work they are doing by dropping in at the Shoals education centre next to the Fisheries Office at Pointe Monier, to the west of the capital, Port Mathurin.

Unspoilt Rodrigues

When it comes to corals, many experienced divers maintain that Rodrigues wins over Seychelles. In *Islands in a Forgotten Sea*, author T.V. Bulpin refers to the scenery outside the lagoon as "dreamlike jungles of coral reefs" while Jacques Degremont, instructor at Cotton Bay, believes the island's waters are far superior to anything he has seen in Mauritius, especially since 1998 when many Indian Ocean corals died because of the rise in water temperature caused by El Niño. Because of its southerly location, Rodrigues escaped the worst of the El Niño effect. (The 2004 tsunami had little or no impact on the waters around Mauritius bar flooding in Port Mathurin, but an early warning tsunami system for the Indian Ocean is now in place.) Today pristine sites in crystal-clear waters can be enjoyed for most months of the year outside the cyclone season.

One of the best sites for both divers and snorkellers is The Aquarium, inside the lagoon near Cotton Bay, where you need only slip over the side of the boat to see beautiful coral outcrops infested with brightly coloured reef fish. Just beyond the reef, at Aquarium Passe, lie canyons inhabited by shoals of king and unicorn fish. You may even spot some turtles.

Two hotel dive centres at Cotton Bay (tel: 831 8001) and Mourouk (tel: 832 3351) provide equipment and instruction with qualified PADI instructors. Both are affiliated to international dive associations. Rates here are slightly higher than in Mauritius, but groups tend to be smaller and more intimate. As the island does not have a recompression chamber, dives deeper than 30 metres (100 ft) are never undertaken and precautionary decompression stops are compulsory for those deeper than 12 metres (40 ft).

The range of other water sports on offer in Rodrigues is similar to Mauritius, though there is no parasailing or water-skiing because the lagoon is too shallow. Big game fishing was only introduced to Rodrigues in 1997, and is still in its infancy, but the unpolluted waters attract yellow fin tuna, dog tooth tuna, skipjack, dolphin fish, blue, black and striped marlins and sizable sailfish. With just five big game fishing boats to choose from and an entire ocean to play in, your chances of hooking "The Big One" are high. ❏

LEFT: the restored 19th-century vessel, *Isla Mauritia*, carries tourists on day trips around the coast.

The Big Ones

Big game fishing is big business in Mauritius all year round. It's no secret that the numbers of fish in Mauritian waters have dropped in recent years, and that sea temperatures have certainly been lower than usual, which most scientists are putting down to the effects of La Niña. Nevertheless, the seas are still rich in game and some of the top big fishing grounds in the world are around here.

The best season for black and blue marlin is usually from October to the end of March or April. For 16 years, Mauritius held the world record for blue marlin at 648 kg (1,430 lb). Yellow fin tuna traditionally migrate in massive shoals to Mauritian waters between March and April. They can weigh anything between 63 and 90 kg (140–200 lb). Then in September the ocean sees prolific runs of wahoo which are reputed to be the fastest moving fish in the sea, sailfish averaging at around 45 kg (100 lb) which literally fly through the air when hooked and furiously fight for their freedom, not to mention bonito, better known to the supermarket shopper as skipjack tuna. Then, of course, there are the different species of shark from blue, hammerhead, mako and tiger, to black fin and white fin.

Most of the big hotels have their own boats and there are a number of boat clubs that operate fishing excursions for tourists. The largest fleets are based at the Corsaire Club at Trou aux Biches and the JP Henry Charters at Black River, but if you're staying at Le Paradis Hotel at Le Morne in the southwest, you can get to the fishing grounds from the fishing centre at the hotel jetty, just a 20-minute ride away. The luxury craft are all equipped with ship to shore radio, trolling equipment for live and artificial lures, life-saving rafts and jackets and everything you would expect from an experienced skipper and deck hand.

If you're up to flexing your muscles with a marlin, just sit back in a fighting chair, strap on your harness and wait for the big moment. There really is nothing quite like the thrill of the chase to get the adrenalin levels pumping when a marlin strikes. These majestic, hugely powerful fish don't give themselves up easily and if they are hooked and landed, the winners pose for pictures alongside their catch.

RIGHT: a proud moment – landing a 23-kg (50-lb) yellow fin tuna.

You may prefer just to sit back and scan the ocean for signs of marlin or shark fins while the professionals prepare themselves for a fight. If you're just going along for the ride, the sun deck of any big game fishing boat is designed for a long sultry day at sea. You need do nothing more strenuous than cover yourself with high factor suncream and equip yourself with a cool drink.

As for the catch, it can be returned to the sea, but expect to pay a hefty charge since many big game fishing operators rely on the income generated from selling it to the local market. Smoke houses in the Black River area process and package marlin, which is similar in taste and texture to smoked salmon

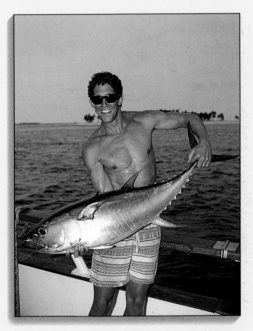

and is perfect served with a twist of lemon and black pepper. But if you really want to taste your own catch then smaller fish, such as bonito, can be cooked to order by the chef at your hotel.

If you're keen to take your prize marlin home as a trophy then a professional taxidermist can do the job for you. It might look a little out of place in your living room and you could wait up to six months for the process to be completed, but if you just want to see what one looks like, there's a fine specimen hanging from the rafters of the Blue Marlin Restaurant at Le Paradis Hotel.

Most boats take up to six passengers and a day's hire is between R24,000 and R27,000. ❑

● *For reputable organisations see Travel Tips, Activities.*

PLACES

*A detailed guide to Mauritius, with principal sites
clearly cross-referenced by number to the maps*

The most important decision you will have to make when planning a visit to Mauritius is where to base yourself. The most
established "resorts" lie on the northwest coast – in particular
Grand Baie, the island's only conventional resort, with a choice of
hotels and nightclubs, bars, shopping centres and a lively beach area.
The appeal of nearby Trou-aux-Biches focuses on the main hotel,
but between here and Port Louis, small side roads lead to a series of
more isolated hotels. These are about as close to Port Louis as you
can get, so are useful if you're in Mauritius on business.

The west coast resorts, renowned for year-round fine weather and
magical sunsets, offer some of the best diving and water sports, and are
well located if you are keen to explore. The main centres are Flic en
Flac and nearby Wolmar, and the Morne peninsula, which has some of
the island's finest beaches. Within easy reach are the wild and dramatic Black River Gorges, a perfect place for walking. Organised treks
are led by local guides and may even offer the chance to glimpse one
of Mauritius' endangered birds. The western hotels are also well placed
for forays to the rugged south coast, which provides a temporary
escape from the tourist trails of the north. Wild and windswept, it's best
to hire a car to get around and explore the isolated fishing communities, lonely beaches, rolling sugar fields and old colonial residences.

For some, the east coast may feel too isolated. People come here to
enjoy the top-class hotels, including the world famous Touessrok and
St Géran hotels, the superb beaches around Belle Mare and Trou d'Eau
Douce and the lovely offshore islands.

There is a small concentration of hotels near Mahébourg in the
southeast corner of the island – a handy spot for the airport, trips along
the unspoilt south and east coasts, and the National History Museum.

While for tourists the coast is the source of Mauritius' appeal, local
people aspire to live in the plateau towns sprawled across the centre of
the island. Though not obviously attractive, these communities show
the real Mauritius, where ordinary folk go about their daily business.

It is possible to go to Mauritius and not even visit the capital, Port
Louis, as the airport is on the other side of the island. Mauritians are
proud of the rejuvenation of the waterfront, which has brought new
restaurants and shops and boosted the nightlife. For newcomers,
however, the central market is also appealing for its chance to take
in a dose of contemporary island life.

Rodrigues requires an effort to visit, and generally attracts only
wanderers, walkers and escapists. What it lacks in sophistication is
compensated for by the warmth of the islanders; if you want a simple,
no-frills insight into remote island life, go now before things change. ❏

PRECEDING PAGES: majestic peak of Montagne du Rempart, as seen from Tamarin.
LEFT: carved wooden door of the Jummah Mosque, the island's main mosque.

PORT LOUIS

Map on page 104

The capital of Mauritius may lack obvious appeal, but the busy streets, the jumble of new and scruffy old buildings, and the old-fashioned market are worth exploring

Not so long ago, when office workers chorused "pens down at 4pm" and left the stifling heat of the capital for the cooler uplands, Port Louis simply shut up shop and went to bed. The city was as dead as a dodo and, save for late-night gambling with Sino-Mauritians and newly arrived sailors in the casino, there was nothing else to do. Since then, Port Louis has undergone something of a transformation – or, as the locals would say, a "lifting", a hand-me-down expression acquired from the British, meaning a face-lift. This is thanks largely to the development of the new Caudan Waterfront, which, with its trendy designer shops, alfresco cafés, cinemas and 24-hour casino, has become the focal point of the city – and is generally considered the main attraction for tourists.

But anyone not interested in shopping is likely to find more of interest in the rest of the city, with its jumble of new and decrepit old buildings, mosques, churches and temples, Chinese and Muslim quarters, racecourse, and above all the lively, attractive market. There is enough to keep you busy for half a day at least. Remember though, that between November and April the city can be uncomfortably hot.

Port Louis

LEFT: the shiny new Caudan Waterfront, hub of the capital. **BELOW:** old Port Louis still attracts shoppers.

History of an island port

Port Louis started out in 1722, when the infant French East India Company transferred its headquarters from the old Dutch settlement at Warwyck Bay (now Mahébourg) to what was then North West Harbour. It was renamed Port Louis after Louis XV of France. From its early days, fortune seekers descended on the city prompting an 18th-century traveller to note that it contained "a sort of scum of bankrupts, ruined adventurers, swindlers and rascals of all kinds". Those characters have long gone but, for all the modernity of air-conditioned shopping malls and fast food outlets, the past has not been completely erased.

Under the British, Port Louis developed into a major port for sailing ships, but by the late 1800s, with the introduction of the steamer and the opening of the Suez Canal, the city had lost much of its appeal, while outbreaks of disease, cyclones and fire caused many of its folk to flee to the healthier climate of the uplands.

A look across the Caudan Basin today, with its cargo and freighter ships, reminds you that Port Louis is still very much a working port and commercial centre. Many thousands pour into the city each day to work, congesting the roads with traffic and adding to the resident population of 150,000 – all packed into 10 sq km (4 sq miles). It is no surprise that Port Louis, like most modern capitals, is crowded, dirty and noisy. But the Moka mountains behind, and the sea in front, provide a resplendent setting.

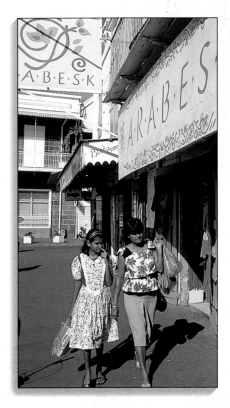

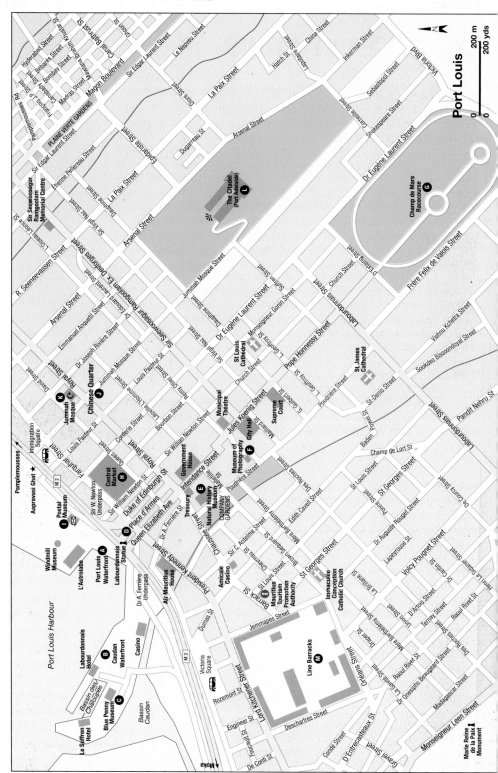

Port Louis

On the waterfront

The new waterfront development is officially divided into two sections – the large, privately run Caudan Waterfront and the smaller, government-run Port Louis Waterfront. A good place to start a walking tour of the city is from the **Port Louis Waterfront** , where you'll find several cafés and L'Astrolabe shopping mall.

The most curious sight in this area is the **Windmill Museum** (open Mon–Fri 10am–noon and 1–3pm; free). A windmill was first built on this spot by the French in the 18th century, and it was France that donated the mechanism inside the modern reconstruction and which also supplies the grain used in occasional demonstrations. The collection of old photographs and the video focus on the transformation of the waterfront.

Over on the **Caudan Waterfront** , beyond the complex of shops and restaurants, rises the vast **Labourdonnais Hotel**. Patronised mainly by international businessmen, the hotel is not a bad pit stop in the evening – particularly if you're flush with rupees from the nearby casino.

One of the best views of the city is from the sea, and you can take a **harbour cruise** from just outside the Labourdonnais. The pleasure boat chugs past a panoramic view of a delectable landfall of peaks and knolls. Looking inland, from right to left, the bulk of Signal Mountain dominates the city. Next, Le Pouce (The Thumb) rises from the south wing of the Moka Range in a "thumbs up" sign. The most distinctive peak of all, whose pinnacle looks like the cloak-shrouded shoulders of a man, comes in the form of **Pieter Both**, named after the Dutch Admiral who drowned off the coast. Closer to the city to the north is a knoll known as La Citadelle, named after the ruin of a fortress at its crest.

A museum well worth calling into is **The Blue Penny Museum** (open Mon–Sat 10am–5pm; entrance fee; tel: 210 8176). Home to a rich collection of national treasures, it exhibits fine art, old maps and sections on philately and postal history, coins, paper money, postcards and photography. Many items were formerly in the possession of private collectors.

BELOW:
old meets new.

Place d'Armes

If you cross by the subway beside the waterfront you reach the **Place d'Armes** , where you'll be greeted by the most famous landmark of the city, the bronze statue of Bertrand François Mahé de Labourdonnais. He arrived in 1735 as the newly appointed French governor-general of the Mascarene Islands and went about transforming shambolic Port Louis into a thriving sea port and commercial centre.

Some local people seem to enjoy having a chat beneath the royal palms that line the square, but the constant buzz of cars around the edge does not make the Place d'Armes a peaceful place. At the top stands **Government House**, the official centre of government. It started life as a ramshackle wooden hut, was enlarged by Labourdonnais in 1738 and later embellished by the British. In the courtyard, secured by wrought-iron gates, is a rather severe marble statue of Queen Victoria, shaded in summer by brilliant red flamboyant trees. Beyond it stands a statue of Sir William Stevenson, British governor from 1857 to 1863. To the right, on the

Reminder of a colonial past.

corner of Chaussée, the old Treasury Buildings (1883), refurbished in 2004 as the prime minister's office, provide good cover if you get caught in a downpour.

Along La Chaussée is the Mauritius Institute, home of the **Natural History Museum E** (open Thur–Tues). The museum is an apology for what was once a priceless collection of flora and fauna and you may be disappointed with the displays, which include a stuffed dodo sealed inside a dirty cabinet, some giant Aldabra tortoises, shell collections, stuffed Mascarene Island birds and a weary looking shark strung up from the rafters. It is tempting to drop a note in the Suggestion Box by the exit proposing that they start again from scratch. The **Company Gardens** next door could do with some attention too, and tend to be a haunt of prostitutes – though it is quite busy at lunchtime, when city workers take a break beneath giant banyans and bottle palms. The Kentucky Fried Chicken outlet attracts more regular custom.

Now reopened on Chaussée Street is the **Amicale Casino**, built to replace the original which rioters reduced to a heap of ruins in an arson attack in 1999 during which seven people lost their lives. Today's smoke-filled, seedy den is open to tourists but is mainly patronised by male hopefuls huddled around blackjack and roulette tables or trying their luck on the gaming machines. Further down the road, turn right for the **tourist office** (open Mon–Fri 9am–4pm; tel: 210 1545) on the 5th floor of Victoria House, St Louis Street.

A walk up Intendance Street

BELOW: multi-coloured Hindu temple, one of many on the island.

A quick stroll south from Place d'Armes along Intendance Street takes you past the rest of the city's other main historic buildings. First is the **Municipal Theatre**, which was built in 1822 and is the oldest theatre in the Indian Ocean.

Map on page 104

If it is open during the day, ask the caretaker to show you the beautiful painted dome and crystal chandeliers. During the 1930s, the citizens of Port Louis were entertained by old favourites like *Madame Butterfly* brought to them by visiting troupes from France. The theatre had virtually shut down by the 1950s but re-opened in 1994 after a massive face-lift. Seats now sell fast for modern jazz gigs, operas and plays, but it's also the hotspot for weddings and prestigious functions when big shots get invited by moneyed Mauritians.

Opposite the theatre, cobbled Rue du Vieux Conseil leads to the **Museum of Photography** ❻ (opening hours vary; entrance fee; tel: 211 1705), where you'll find one of the island's oldest displays of cameras and prints, which includes daguerreotypes as well as photographs of colonial Mauritius. All these have been collected by photographer Tristan de Breville, who fights a constant financial battle to keep his museum open.

Heading east, you reach the austere **St Louis Cathedral**. The original French church was reduced to rubble by cyclones in the 1800s. It was rebuilt twice before the present version was consecrated in 1932. To the left is the **Episcopal Palace**, a fine 19th-century colonnaded mansion. The other important church in the city is **St James Cathedral**, nearby in Poudrière Street, which looms over gardens shaded by palm trees and tumbling bougainvillaea. It was once a gun-powder store and prison under the French, before the British turned it into a church, and also saw service as a refuge centre when Port Louisiens would abandon their wooden houses on the approach of a cyclone for the security of its 3-metre (10-ft) walls.

From these two places of worship, it is only a short diversion to the gambling den of the **Champ de Mars** ❼ (also known as the Hippodrome), cradled by the

TIP

At the Café du Vieux Conseil, virtually opposite the Museum of Photography, you can enjoy a drink or snack, shaded by trees and away from the bustle of the city streets. It is open in the daytime only.

BELOW: from May to November, Saturday is race day.

A MAURITIAN NATIONAL PASTIME

In Mauritius, it is said that there are three seasons – summer, winter and the racing season. The Mauritius Turf Club, the second oldest in the southern hemisphere, was founded by Colonel Draper in 1812. He had friends in high places on both sides of the divide and, being a passionate punter, thought it only gentlemanly to bring the French and English together in an atmosphere of leisure.

Today, most horses come from South Africa and Australia and are trained in one of the island's eight stables. Race meetings are held every Saturday afternoon from the first week in May to the end of November. Spirits run high, with screams of *"Allez, allez!"* following the horses as they gallop round the course. Music is played between races as punters press round Chinese bookies to place their bets or collect their winnings, and food sellers do a roaring trade.

Many Mauritians are well versed in the international race scene. They follow the progress of individual horses closely and the use of starting stalls, photo-finish systems and adherence to Newmarket disciplines attracts jockeys from all over the world. There are even professional gamblers who try to make a living from picking a winner; most of them will have a "hot tip", but remember, despite what some may tell you, there is no such thing as a "dead cert".

Moka mountains at the eastern edge of the city. Once the training ground for French soldiers, today it is often used for Independence Day celebrations on 12 March – and the nation's most popular sport: horse racing. An invitation to the members enclosure on classic race days, like the Gold Cup or the Maiden Cup, should not be refused; you get a bird's eye view of the paddock, free rein of all facilities, which include bars and comfortable terraces and an unmissable opportunity to rub shoulders with those in the know. On non-race days, joggers replace the horses.

The Penny Black should really be called the Twopenny Blue. It was issued in Mauritius in the mid-19th century when the island was one of the first colonies to have its own post office, and has become one of the rarest stamps in the world.

Following the spice trail

If there is one place no one should miss in Port Louis, it is the covered **Central Market** (open daily 6am–6pm), known as the Bazar Central in Creole, two blocks north of Place d'Armes. Built in 2004 to replace its old tumbledown predecessor, where traders from all continents converged for more than 150 years, this attractive building accommodates over 300 stalls in rather more hygienic and pleasant conditions, yet manages to retain its traditional charm and atmosphere.

On the ground floor you can follow the locals picking out the best from the mounds of tropical fruit and vegetables, or picking up herbal remedies guaranteed to cure everything from diarrhoea to diabetes. Upstairs, Indian, Creole and Chinese traders sell T-shirts, basketware, spices and cheap clothing, and there are good views from the gallery of the bustle below. You can pick up spicy pancakes *(dal puris)*, curry-filled *samousas* and other popular Mauritian snacks for just a few rupees, perfect for a mid-morning snack or light lunch. Those with a more sensitive constitution may want to avoid them. You should probably steer clear of *bombli*, the dried salt fish with a stench that defies description.

BELOW: fresh produce for sale at the Central Market.

Philatelic passions

After the bustle of the market, you can find solace in the calm of the **Postal Museum** (open Mon–Fri 9am–2.45pm, Sat till 11.30am), which lies across the busy road from the market in the former General Post Office. This well laid-out museum contains 19th-century postal equipment such as telegraph and stamp-vending machines and a fine collection of stamps, postal stationery, original artwork and printing plates. For serious collectors there are stock books, stamp albums, mounts, magnifying glasses and tweezers and first-day covers and commemorative sets of stamps, such as the 400th anniversary of the Dutch landing which was issued in 1999.

A short walk north alongside the busy road takes you to the gardens of the **Aapravasi Ghat**, a UNESCO World Heritage Site. Once known as the Immigration Depot or Coolie Ghat, it housed the first Indian immigrants who were brought here before being farmed out to the sugar estates. Look for the 11 bronze murals showing scenes of immigrant life, including one depicting a pair of hands breaking free from chains. A poem dedicated to the Unknown Immigrant recalls how "He… turned stone into green fields of gold", a reference to sugar cane.

The Chinese Quarter

The **Chinese Quarter** ❿, encompassed in several streets to the east of the market, is the most colourful part of the city with its specialist food and spice shops and herbal remedy (ayurvedic) stores. There are plenty of eating houses called hotels, too, where fast cheap meals, such as the ubiquitous noodles *(mines)* can be slurped from bowls. A variety of snacks such as *gâteaux piments*, crispy *samousas* or the more unusual combination of fresh pineapples with hot red chilli sauce, are also sold from mobile food wagons on street corners.

The **Jummah Mosque** ⓚ in Royal Street is open to tourists only at certain times, but one of its most striking features are the beautifully carved teak doors and the ornate decorations of the outer walls. Built in around 1853 for the growing Muslim community and subsequently enlarged, it is the island's most impressive mosque. Plaine Verte, the Muslim Quarter to the north of Port Louis, is home to the annual Ghoon festival, but other than its small teahouses and tumbledown textile shops, has little to interest the visitor.

Symbols of authority

The only reason for going to **The Citadel** (**La Citadelle**) ⓛ, also known as Fort Adelaide (open daily 9am–4pm, Sat till noon), is the panoramic views of the city's amphitheatre of mountains, the Champ de Mars racecourse and the harbour. The basalt fort was named after Queen Adelaide, wife of William IV, and must rank as Port Louis' greatest white elephant. Apart from the occasional concert and a few small shops selling local arts and crafts, it never seems to wake from its apathy even when the silence is broken by the babble of tourists.

The colourful Chinese temple on the corner of Generosity and Justice streets

Map on page 104

The Jummah Mosque.

BELOW: the lively Chinese Quarter.

Map
on page
104

*There aren't too
many green spaces in
Port Louis but you
could join the locals
at the Robert Edward
Hart Gardens, south-
west of the Caudan
Waterfront, where
you'll find a rather
incongruous stone
bust of Lenin.*

BELOW:
Government House.
RIGHT:
preparing leaves for
weaving, Domaine
Les Pailles.

is worth visiting for the views of the city from the Buddhist shrine on the first floor. Another temple is the **Kwan Tee**, the oldest in town, on the roundabout south of the Caudan Waterfront, dedicated to the Chinese warrior god who fought for justice. Best of all is the **Thien Thane**, for its pagoda architecture and serene location in the foothills of Signal Mountain, on the southeast edge of town.

For some Mauritian quirkiness, wander down to **Line Barracks** 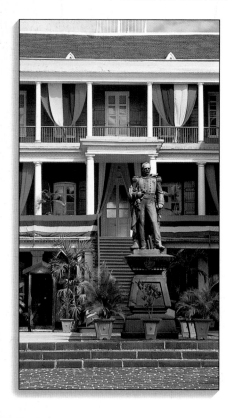 *(caserne)*, home of the Mauritian Police Force, which contains fine examples of 18th-century colonial architecture. Inside, look out for the petrified dodo and for learner drivers taking their tests. See the prison dubbed "Alcatraz" and the Golden Gates at the main entrance which caused a stir because they cost a fortune. Nearby is an incongruous blue-tiled archway marked "Gateway of Discipline" which leads to the policemen's car park.

Around Port Louis

The **Church and Shrine of Père Laval** at Sainte-Croix in the foothills of Long Mountain to the northeast is only a 10-minute drive from the city centre. Père Laval arrived as a missionary in 1841 and was soon revered for his work with the poor. When he died in 1864 his body was buried at Sainte-Croix and became the object of pilgrimage. Many Mauritians still believe in his special healing powers and every day hundreds of people of all faiths file past the stone sarcophagus that contains his remains, topped by an effigy framed with flowers, and pray for the sick. He was beatified by the Catholic Church in 1979 and is one step away from being canonised, so that it won't be long before Mauritius has its very own patron saint. An annual pilgrimage to the church takes place during the nights of 7 and 8 September. The curate's residence nearby is a superb example of colonial architecture.

About 10 minutes' drive south of the city centre and well signposted off the motorway, is **Domaine les Pailles** (open daily 10am–5.30pm; entrance fee; tel: 286 4255). With four restaurants, a casino, the futuristic Swami Vivekananda Conference Centre where cultural shows and trade fairs are held, and 1,200 hectares (3,000 acres) of grounds to explore, the estate attracts both tourists and business people seeking an escape from the brouhaha of the capital.

The most popular attraction, particularly for children, is the one-hour guided tour (by mini-train or horse-drawn carriage) which aims to inform visitors about the production of sugar, rum and other local products. The tour goes through a working reconstruction of an early sugar factory and rum distillery, as well as a spice garden and mask museum, with, of course, the ubiquitous sega show at the end. Children can also go pony trekking or splash in the pool, while adults have the option of a safari by jeep or mountain bike along 11 km (7 miles) of winding mountain tracks, spotting wild stag, monkeys and hare on the way – though the vegetation is the main attraction really.

Breathtaking views of Port Louis can be enjoyed from the peaceful setting of the Marie Reine de la Paix monument on the flanks of **Signal Mountain**, southwest of the city. In 1989 this place of pilgrimage swelled as thousands of islanders gathered for Mass held by Pope John Paul II. ❑

THE NORTH

The beach-lined north coast is the most popular on Mauritius, and has the island's only proper resort town, Grand Baie. Only one thing can lure people away from the sea: the Botanical Gardens

Map on page 114

Port Louis

Most visitors to Mauritius head for the hotels north of **Port Louis ❶**. Tourism is well established between the resorts of Balaclava and Grand Baie, which act as bookends to one of the loveliest stretches of beach on the island, with an unbroken chain of powder-white beaches and gentle, crystal lagoons. Hotels, guesthouses and private bungalows are plentiful in this area, and more hotels are also sprouting up in the less accessible areas between Balaclava and Port Louis. The coast's best-kept beaches are attached to hotels with beach loungers reserved for residents' use, but if you want to mix with the locals the public beaches at Balaclava, Mont Choisy and Pereybère are lively, particularly at weekends.

Away from the coast, the sugar-swathed lands of the north are not as scenic as the mountainous interior of the south, but the flat terrain, broken up by the gentlest of hills, is ideal for cycling, and there's something exciting about getting lost in the maze of sugar cane fields and asking for directions – only to get the reply back in Kreol, French, English or a combination of all three.

Tombs, turtles and shipwrecks

The fastest route to the northern beaches is to take the motorway – either straight to Grand Baie or Trou aux Biches, or to the turn-off for the resorts further south – but if you are in no hurry, you could opt for the longer coastal route.

Just beyond the city suburbs is **Roche Bois ❷**, where the mass of headstones in the Chinese Cemetery are bright red, the colour of good luck, and bear witness to the island's Sino-Mauritian population. But Roche Bois is also a poor Creole suburb and a byword for poverty on the island. In 1999, one of its sons, a Creole singer called Kaya, was arrested for smoking cannabis at a pro-pot public demonstration and next day died in a police cell *(see box page 78)*.

In 1615, four Dutch East India ships were swept on to the reef during a cyclone and sunk at nearby **Baie du Tombeau (Bay of Tombs) ❸**. Everyone died, including the Dutch Admiral Pieter Both who was on his way to Holland after a spell as the governor of the company. The sleepy village of Baie du Tombeau lies on the bay's southern flank, apparently turning its back on the world, and blocking its lovely, deserted beach from view. Access to the beach is not easy, but if you persist look out for the ruin of an old French fort partially hidden in shrubbery nearby.

You link up again with the Grand Baie road at the crossroads near **Arsenal** (named after a French ammunition store nearby), where you can also turn inland towards the Pamplemousses Botanical Gardens *(see page 120)*.

LEFT: lounging by the pool, Cap Malheureux.
BELOW: Grand Baie basket seller.

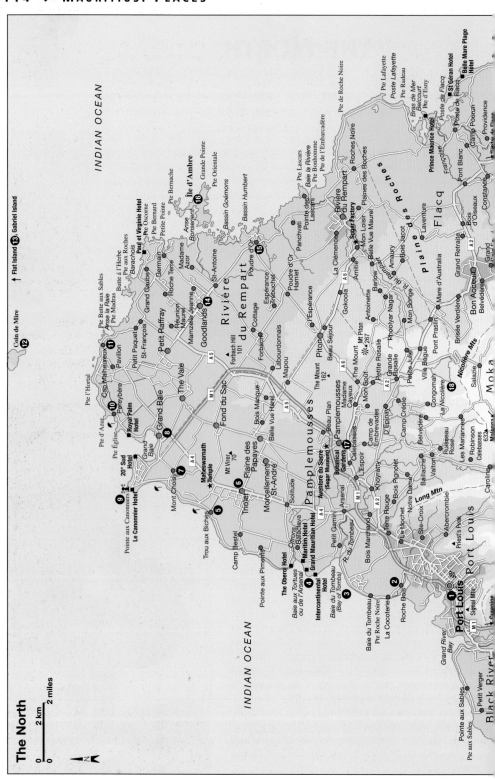

Beyond residential **Balaclava**, reached through sugar fields on the B41, is an area that is fast being developed – though passers-by will see nothing but the entrances to private drives leading to hotels such as The Grand Mauritian, Oberoi and Maritim. These neighbouring hotels flank the banks of the River Citrons, which enters the estuary forming the **Baie aux Tortues (Turtle Bay)** ❹, also known as Baie de l'Arsenal. The Maritim Hotel occupies grounds that formed part of a French arsenal at nearby **Moulin à Poudre**, where ammunition for ships was supplied for expeditions to India.

Although hotel development is strictly monitored, some locals fear that the increase in the number of hotels in this previously undiscovered area may threaten the bay, which is reputed to contain 90 percent live coral. From Grand Baie, you can take a trip on the ***Isla Mauritia*** *(see tip, page 116),* which drops anchor at Baie du Tombeau. On the way you pass Baie aux Tortues, where great armies of turtles once swam and which today is noted for its fine snorkelling.

The road finally hits the coast at **Pointe aux Piments**, where filao trees rustle in gentle breezes and life chugs on slow and unhurried on the beaches. If you can leave the pristine paradise fronting the Victoria or Le Meridien hotels, then take a stroll outside and surrender to the magic of a Mauritius sunset and watch wellie-booted fishermen wading in a shallow lagoon. Alternatively, visit the Aquarium Mauritius on the Coastal Road (tel: 261 4561 for opening hours).

Trou aux Biches

The small resort of **Trou aux Biches** ❺, with its gently shelving sands and deep blue lagoon, is a mecca for beach-lovers. It is much more sedate than its northern neighbour, Grand Baie, particularly midweek when you can glimpse snapshots of how life used to be, and still is in parts of this former fishing village. At the start of the 3-km (2-mile) beach, beside the fish landing station, fishermen huddle beneath casuarina trees gabbling in Kreol. Here you'll find a couple of restaurants and Chez Popo's supermarket where you can hire bikes and, if self-catering, buy a wide range of essentials.

The hotels all have facilities for water-skiing, windsurfing, diving and snorkelling, and will also arrange sailing and glass-bottom boat trips. At weekends the tranquillity of the lagoon is broken by the roar of an increasing number of speedboats, but the beach remains a retreat for relaxation and beach games. Old boys on bicycles sell freshly caught fish and touts sell seashells, pareos and trinkets, keeping you amused with gentle banter. There's no shortage of fruit sellers wandering along the beach and to watch them peel pineapples with their machetes is quite a spectacle.

Triolet and Mont Choisy

Triolet ❻ can claim to be the largest and longest (and perhaps plainest) village on the island. It has played a lively part in Mauritian political life since Independence, and is the constituency of Mauritius' first prime minister. The village also has the highest population of Indo-Mauritians, and is home to the biggest Hindu temple in Mauritius (just inland from Trou aux Biches police station). Built in 1857, the **Maheswarnath**

Map on page 114

The Hindu goddess Durga on her mount.

BELOW: the Maheswarnath Temple is the island's largest Hindu shrine.

TIP

You can book a full-day cruise with the *Isla Mauritia* from Yacht Charters at Grand Baie (tel: 263 8395). The price includes a barbecue lunch at Baie du Tombeau, where you get serenaded and "sega'd" by the crew. The fine old sailing ship was built in 1852 in Mallorca.

BELOW:

ferrying tourists to the *Isla Mauritia*.

Temple complex is a kaleidoscope of colour. It stands beside an enormous banyan where a placard welcomes all pilgrims.

At weekends and holidays it seems that everyone from the area toddles off to **Mont Choisy ➐** beach where turquoise seas meet a long strip of sugar-soft sand backed by a forest of casuarina trees. Matronly Indo-Mauritian mums make for the shade and unpack pots of rice and curry from great baskets *(tentes)* around which families gather to eat. Children play on a former landing strip, now a grassy football pitch, where a monument celebrates the first ever flight made by French pilots from Mauritius to Réunion in 1933. Midweek, Mont Choisy is a perfect spot for a quiet dip in the warm lagoon or a trip in a glass-bottom boat.

The Creole Côte d'Azur

Grand Baie ➑ is the island's hub of tourism, where not only hotels and restaurants, but also bars, clubs and designer shops, are strung around a huge horseshoe-shaped bay. Dubbed the "Creole Côte d'Azur" and, by Mauritian standards, brash, busy and boisterous, Grand Baie's development from a tiny fishing village to a large holiday resort seems to have dealt a fatal blow to the village atmosphere. Many shops have become supermarkets, property development is haphazard and islanders often complain of the lack of pavements, congested coast road and a rise in petty crime. Yet it remains popular with local residents, many of whom have second homes here, as well as with tourists who can find plenty of places to eat and drink. From here you can book island tours, including to Rodrigues, find self-catering accommodation and hire a car through tour operators, such as Mauritours, and many other smaller travel agents.

Much of the activity centres around **Sunset Boulevard**, a modern waterside shopping mall (closed Sun) opposite a cluster of supermarkets, restaurants and fast food stalls. You'll find a centre for big game fishing on the waterfront and facilities to book undersea walks, undersea safaris and parascending trips over the lagoon. The bay, which at times is crowded with small pleasure craft and catamarans, has no decent bathing beach; for peace and relaxation take a short stroll to the soft wide sands of La Cuvette public beach to the north of the bay, which has modern facilities including showers, toilets and changing cubicles. Just beyond the black basalt rocks to the right of the beach is the luxurious **Royal Palm Hotel** but be aware that casual beach strollers are not welcome unless they have a reservation for lunch or dinner. A good place to shop is at Super U complex a short stroll inland from Sunset Boulevard. Here, a large supermarket provides everyday goods, and the alfresco eateries are good value.

Grand Baie has more nightclubs (*boîtes de nuit*) than any other resort on the island (which draws quite a few local prostitutes to the area). For a spot of balmy nightlife try Banana Bar for drinks and live music or let your hair down at the Buddha Club, which attracts a trendy, young crowd.

Undersea walks can be booked through tour operators and hotels.

Pointe aux Canonniers

Enormous flamboyant trees, emblazoned with deep red flowers in summer, flank the road leading to **Pointe aux Canonniers** ❾, a beach-belted headland at the northern end of Grand Baie which was once used as a garrison by the French and later turned into a quarantine station by the British. Eighteenth-century cannons and a ruined 19th-century lighthouse watch over the reefs (which have caused the doom of dozens of ships) from the gardens of **Le**

BELOW:
Le Canonnier Hotel.

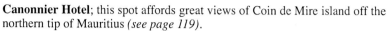

A 10-minute drive from Grand Baie to the deep cove of Anse la Raie on the northeast coast, leads to a little bridge crossing an inlet over Bain Boeuf, just after Paradise Cove Hotel. On holy days such as Ganga Asnan, Hindu women swathed in deep pink saris carry food on banana leaves to a colourful shrine right on the water's edge.

BELOW: fishing at Coin de Mire.

Canonnier Hotel; this spot affords great views of Coin de Mire island off the northern tip of Mauritius *(see page 119)*.

Hotels and shady villas house tourists and locals attracted by the tranquillity of the area. At the opposite tip of the headland from Le Canonnier is the **20° Sud Hotel**, a colonial-style boutique hotel, complete with planters' chairs and faded pictures, overlooking a swimming pool *(see Travel Tips, Accommodation)*.

Pereybère

Just 2 km (1 mile) to the north, **Pereybère ⑩** seems to be merging with Grand Baie. But the pace of life is much slower, providing a foil to the sometimes brash atmosphere of its sister resort as well as cheaper day-to-day living. Traditionally a holiday retreat for the Chinese community, Pereybère is changing rapidly to accommodate increasing numbers of foreign self-caterers, as well as holidaymakers from Grand Baie who come for a change of scene, and to stretch out on the lovely casuarina-fringed beach or snorkel in the lagoon.

A smaller version of Mont Choisy *(see page 116)*, Pereybère is swamped at weekends by islanders, who come to picnic, chat under the trees, swim, go for glass-bottom boat trips, and maybe even round off the day with an impromptu sega party. Food stalls sell hot snacks, drinks and fresh fruit (conveniently cut up into small pieces and sold in bags) and, if you're lucky, there'll be an ice cream van, too. Away from the beach, small shops provide basics and simple restaurants serve slap-up meals at knockdown prices. And if you're after a pareo, the tree-lined catwalks along the main road offer plenty of choice; prices are lower than those offered both by shops and beach hawkers.

Unspoilt coasts and sugar lands

Taking on the appearance of a country lane lined with casuarinas shading shallow bays and rocky coves, the coast road swings east to **Cap Malheureux ⑪**, 6 km (4 miles) beyond Pereybère. This, the island's most northern point, probably got its name – Cape of Misfortune – from the number of ships that foundered here. Nothing much goes on in this tranquil beauty spot, though if you get there around 4pm you will see the village wake up momentarily when fishermen bring in their catch to sell to islanders congregating beside the striking red-roofed church. There is a small beach where local kids play, just one restaurant, a general store and petrol station.

A 5-km (3-mile) drive east through sugar cane emerges at the sparkling white beaches of **Grand Gaube**, where the luxurious Legends Hotel overlooks the curvaceous bay. Or you could enjoy tasty snacks at Paul et Virginie Hotel, a short stroll eastwards.

Offshore islands

Coin de Mire, Flat Island (Île Plate) and Gabriel Island (Îlot Gabriel) all make good day trips. Depending on weather conditions, you can have a fun day out sailing around the islands, being pampered by experienced crew. Full-day tours with lunch in the luxury catamaran cruiser, *Le Pacha*, accommodating 20 to 30 passengers, leave from Sunset Boulevard in Grand

Baie. It drops anchor in sheltered bays with plenty of opportunity for snorkelling, swimming and sunbathing on deck. Other operators in Grand Baie lay on similar tours.

Coin de Mire ⑫, the closest island to the shore, is composed of layers of crumbling volcanic sandstone, making landing impossible. Getting on to **Flat Island** ⑬ is worth the effort just to pad along the lovely beaches ringed by coral reef. The same coral reef encircles neighbouring **Gabriel Island**. These last two islands once served as quarantine stations for immigrants during the cholera epidemic of 1856 which nearly wiped out the population of Port Louis. Picnic parties to Flat Island are popular and you can spend the whole day exploring the little pathways that meander round its lighthouse and cemetery.

You need permission to land on Round and Serpent islands, 24 km (15 miles) north of Mauritius, which are both designated nature reserves; but they are difficult to land on anyway because of their sheer cliffs. **Round Island (Île Ronde)** is home to many endangered species, including the rare telfair skink, two species of snake and the *paille-en-queue* – the tropic bird that graces the tail fins of Air Mauritius planes. **Serpent Island (Île aux Serpents)** is a bird sanctuary, but there are no snakes. And in case you were wondering, **Pigeon House Rock (Le Pigeonnier)**, north of Flat Island, doesn't have any pigeons either.

The "Rolls-Royce" of model ships are made at Goodlands.

Ships are the theme

From Grand Gaube the road finally draws you away from the coast and swings south to **Goodlands** ⑭. The streets in this densely populated town are usually heaving with people, who frequent the high street shops and the daily **market**. Goodlands is also home to the largest model sailing ship factory in Mauritius,

BELOW: hot Sundays in Pereybère are good for business.

Historic Marine (open Mon–Fri 8am–5pm, Sat–Sun 8am–noon; guided tours; tel: 283 9304). There is a large showroom downstairs (with many wooden objects other than ships), while upstairs you can watch the craftsmen patiently working on these mini masterpieces (weekdays only).

The road southeast of Goodlands hits the coast at **Poudre d'Or** ⓑ, an appealing village where you can linger on the headland opposite the reef where, in 1744, the *Saint Geran* foundered in a storm, a tragic incident that inspired French novelist Bernardin de Saint Pierre to pen his famous love story, *Paul and Virginie*. Some objects rescued from the wreck are on display in the National History Museum in Mahébourg *(see page 128)*. Île d'Ambre ⓰, an uninhabited island named after the ambergris once found there, is just 30 minutes' boat ride from here, and if you ask around, you should find a local fisherman to take you from the jetty at Poudre d'Or; arrange for him to pick you up later so that you can enjoy the excellent swimming and snorkelling.

The headland marking our boundary between the north and east coasts, is dominated by the wild and windy beaches of **Roches Noires** and **Poste Lafayette** studded with black volcanic rocks. They are often deserted but for men fishing in the shallows or landing their catch from boats. Be careful if you want to swim since the seas can be rough.

Botanic beauties at Pamplemousses

From Poudre d'Or the road heads inland to the **Botanical Gardens** ⓱ at Pamplemousses (open daily 6am–6pm; entrance fee), a 30-minute drive from Port Louis or Grand Baie. They are well worth a visit, even more so since their 2007 makeover, the best time being between December and April.

The 25-hectare (62-acre) gardens were renamed the Sir Seewoosagur Ramgoolam Botanical Gardens in 1988 in honour of the late prime minister, but they are still known by everyone as Pamplemousses (French for grapefruit). The village was named after a variety of citrus plant, imported from Java by the Dutch in the 17th century and which once grew in the area. Its fruit resembles a large grapefruit known as a *bambolmas* in Tamil, thought to be the origin of the French word.

You should allow a couple of hours to explore the maze of palm-lined avenues. Tour operators often combine a visit with a shopping spree to Port Louis and tend to lead groups on lightning-quick tours. The official guides will also whisk you around rather quickly for a fixed fee of R50, but they do point out the main attractions and provide interesting nuggets of information about some of the more unusual species; try to collar one of the older guides, who are likely to have worked in the gardens for years and are usually more informative. If you want to explore independently, it's a good idea to buy the guidebook (available at the main entrance), which contains a map as well as an authoritative explanation of the plant species – only some are labelled – and other attractions. There are no refreshment facilities inside the gardens, so stock up on water from the food stalls by the car park (near the motorway turn-off).

Wrought-iron gates (exhibited at the 1851 Great Exhibition at London's Crystal Palace) mark the original entrance to the gardens but the main entrance is now by the big car park on the other side. From here, guides will lead you along shaded avenues named after botanists and benefactors and show you trees such as the bastard mahogany *(Andira inermis)*, marmalade box *(Genipa americana)*, chewing gum *(Manilkara achras)* and sausage tree *(Kigelia pinnata)*.

In all, there are about 500 plant species out of which 80 are palms and 40, such as ebony, mahogany and pandanus, are indigenous to the Mascarene Islands. Among the most impressive sights are the **Lotus Pond**, filled with yellow and white flowers, and the huge **Lily Pond**. Half concealed by the floating leaves of the giant Amazon water lily *(Victoria amazonica)* this is everyone's favourite photo opportunity. The flowers of the lily open white, fade to a dusky pink by the end of the second day and then die; the unmistakable flat leaves can reach as much as 1.5 metres (4½ ft) in diameter. The talipot palm is another remarkable species. It waits 40 to 60 years to flower, then promptly dies. Ginger, cloves and cinnamon are among the many spices you can sniff out.

Mon Plaisir

The gardens' origins go back to 1735, when Mahé de Labourdonnais bought a house in the grounds, which he called Mon Plaisir. He developed the area to supply fresh fruit and vegetables for ships calling at Port Louis. In 1768, Mon Plaisir became the residence of the French horticulturist, Pierre Poivre, who planted the seeds for the specimens you see today *(see page 247)*. The present **Chateau Mon Plaisir**, a 19th-century British legacy, was recently rescued from ruin and is used as an administration office.

Near the entrance, a collection of giant Aldabra tortoises happily munch on leaves in between noisy mating sessions. Next to the pen is a reconstruction of an early sugar mill, although there isn't a scrap of sugar cane in sight.

Scenic route to Pieter Both

For one of the most scenic drives in Mauritius – where a foreground of sugar cane is framed by the quirky peaks of the Moka mountains – take the A2 from Pamplemousses towards Centre de Flacq and the east coast. En route you pass **Grand Rosalie**, where the first sugar estate was established in 1743. The plantation house is closed to the public, but you can get an idea of the lay of the land from the nearby **La Nicolière Reservoir** ⓲. The road winds uphill, giving bird's eye views of the luscious landscape, and descends through woods and sleepy villages. If the light is right, stay a while at the welcoming hamlet of **Malenga**, the nearest you'll get to **Pieter Both**, whose pinnacle resembles a man's head perched precariously on cloak-shrouded shoulders. They say that the day the head comes off some great catastrophe will destroy the island but even the worst cyclones of 1892 and 1960 have failed to shift it. From Malenga you can watch the mountain change colour and shape as sun and clouds cast shadows across its face. From here, the B34 joins the motorway at Terre Rouge. ❏

Map on page 114

TIP

Those interested in learning more about sugar cultivation and its history should visit L'Aventure du Sucre Museum on the Beau Plan Sugar Estate near Pamplemousses (open daily 9am–5pm; entrance fee; tel: 243 0660, fax: 243 9699).

BELOW: Pieter Both.

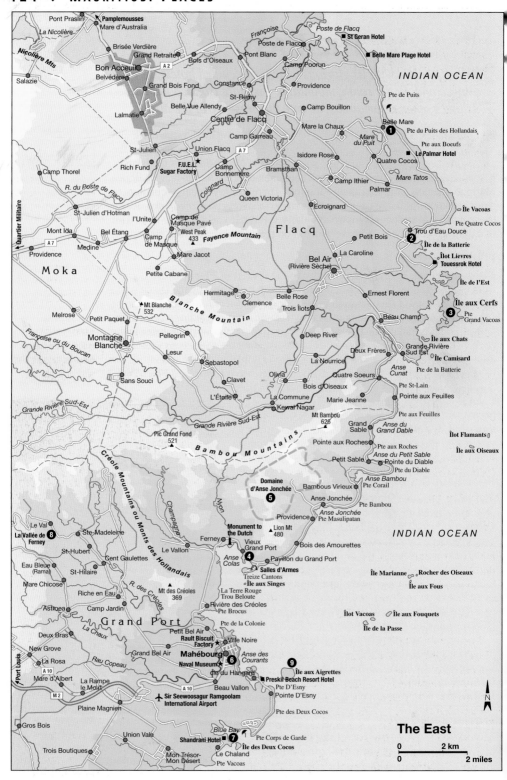

INDIAN OCEAN

Flacq

Moka

Blanche Mountain

Bambou Mountains

Créole Mountains ou Monts des Hollandais

Grand Port

INDIAN OCEAN

The East

0   2 km

0   2 miles

N

Map
on page
124

went a renaissance with the opening of an MTPA information office (tel: 480 0925), a small car park and a refurbished waterfront where enthusiastic operators are happy to ferry you to **Île aux Cerfs**. Many tourists stop at the handful of souvenir shops and simple restaurants, which make a welcome change, especially if you've been holed up in a resort for a few days. Beyond the village the pace of life has barely changed despite the proliferation of visitors to the area.

Paradise island

The **Île aux Cerfs** ❸ is a long-time favourite with Mauritians and holiday-makers. It is managed by Le Touessrok resort, just south of Trou d'Eau Douce, but it is open to the public (unlike Îlot Mangenie, which is restricted to residents only). Bear in mind however that the free car park inside the grounds of the Touessrok Hotel is reserved for golfers with a reservation at the golf course on the island. If you don't have your own transport you could join one of the full-day excursions (including by catamaran) offered by tour operators in Grand Baie. A couple of companies in Trou d'Eau Douce run a regular ferry service from the waterfront, but it's more fun to chug across the bay with one of the Creole fishermen.

Île aux Cerfs' most famous resident is a giant Aldabra tortoise thought to be 200 years old.

The island is covered in 285 hectares (700 acres) of woodland and has a golf course, lovely beaches and limpid, blue waters. You can swim and snorkel from the shore. A boathouse near the jetty provides equipment for water-skiing, wind-surfing and boating, and scattered among the trees (and even in the trees) nearby are open-air shops and restaurants. The atmosphere is relaxed, but it can get very crowded. If you want solitude, there are quieter beaches close by, and enjoyable walks can be made round the island along marked paths. In the trees beyond the jetty is a small Turtle Park.

BELOW: Touessrok diving school – lessons in luxury.

A possible trip from Île aux Cerfs is to the deep estuary of Grande Rivière Sud-Est, the longest river in Mauritius; there is a small settlement of the same name at the river mouth where you can often see bold young islanders diving into the water from the basalt cliffs, hoping to be rewarded with a few tourist rupees.

The Old Dutch Coast Road

The drive from Trou d'Eau Douce south along the B28 or Old Coast Road to Mahébourg is one of the loveliest on the island. Head inland to Bel Air where the road veers towards the coast, hitting the sea at the gorge of **Grande Rivière Sud-Est**. From here, it barely manages to keep a toehold on land as it contrives to avoid the steep foothills of the Bambou Mountains. Fishing hamlets and picturesque villages are scattered along the route.

The **Grand Port** district in the southeastern corner of Mauritius is full of historical connections since this is where the French and Dutch began their colonisation of the island. There are many ruins in the area, some dating from the 17th century, but most are in a poor state of repair. Lying in the shadow of Lion Mountain, **Vieux Grand Port** ❹ is of particular historical interest as it was the first base established by the Dutch when they landed on the island in 1598. The original Dutch fort disappeared beneath defences built by the French in

the 18th century. Now all that remains are a few blackened and disintegrating walls, but in 1997 archaeologists unearthed beakers, pottery, glass and Chinese porcelain from the 17th century. These and other finds are displayed in the adjacent **Fort Frederick Henry Museum** (open Mon–Sat 9am–5pm, Sun 9am–noon; free; tel: 634 4319), along with a model of the fort, while audio-visual displays explain the history of the Dutch East India Company and its role in Mauritius.

Along the water's edge are the caves of **Salles d'Armes**, where French gentlemen once fought duels. They are best approached by sea with a local fisherman, but you can make your own way by zigzagging through the cane fields at the northern end of Vieux Grand Port village. Further north, the **Bois des Amourettes** was a favourite haunt of French soldiers and their sweethearts. During World War II the British built a naval look-out post but all that remains are some old concrete bunkers poking through the sugar cane on the shore.

Between Vieux Grand Port and Mahébourg, you pass two memorials: one commemorating the first Dutch landing in 1598 and another marking their introduction of sugar in 1639. These memorials sat unnoticed for years, but were spruced up for the royal Dutch visit in 1998, when Mauritius celebrated the 400th anniversary of the Dutch arrival.

Domaine d'Anse Jonchée

The private nature reserve of **Domaine d'Anse Jonchée ❺** (Hunter's Domain; open daily 9am–5pm; tel: 634 5011) is the unlikely viewpoint from which to survey the theatre of conflict between the French and British navies in 1810, at the Battle of Vieux Grand Port. These days the crashing of cannon is confined to the firing of deer hunters' rifles. Once popular with private hunting parties, the estate

TIP

To see how essential oils are made from the fragrant yellow ylang ylang flowers, visit the Domaine de Ylang Ylang (open daily; tel: 634 5668), in the foothills near Vieux Grand Port.

BELOW: cane fields at Domaine d'Anse Jonchée.

is now targetting "green" tourists, who wander the 30 km (18 miles) of nature trails that run through forests of spice plants and native trees. Apart from the Javan deer reared in the 160-hectare (400-acre) reserve, you might also spot wild boar, monkey, hare and many endemic species of bird. Mini jeep safaris are also on offer. The Domaine d'Anse Jonchée is the most popular on-land attraction on the east coast, and a lot of tour groups are brought here to witness the daily afternoon visit of the endangered Mauritius kestrel, lured by the promise of food. Rustic but not inexpensive hilltop bungalows provide overnight accommodation.

Mahébourg

Named after the first governor of the Mascarenes, Mahé de Labourdonnais, **Mahébourg ❻** (pronounced Ma-y-bourg) lies on the southern shores of the immense Vieux Grand Port Bay. Under the French, Mahébourg was a busy, thriving port, which the British later linked by rail (now abandoned) to Port Louis. The names of the neatly laid out grid-style streets reflect the influence of European settlers, and there is a historical feel absent in many Mauritian towns.

These days Mahébourg is a dusty, rather run-down place, crammed with grocers' and fabric stores. Yet it has an appealing, laid-back bustle. The seafront Rue des Hollandais is done no favours by the sprawling presence of the bus station, but the area has benefited from a 2003 face-lift. The waterfront, with its memorial to the Battle of Grand Port, makes for a pleasant stroll. Multicoloured pirogues bob around the islet of Mouchoir Rouge (Red Hanky island), while, in the backstreets, life trundles slowly by; women still scrub clothes on the stone sinks at Le Lavoir, the outdoor wash-house off Rue des Hollandais. There is a lively daily market, worth visiting for exotic fruit, vegetables, herbs and spices.

Map on page 124

TIP

The Paranamour Restaurant at the Domaine d'Anse Jonchée offers both fine views and excellent food, including venison curry, grilled lobster, roasted wild pig, fresh fish and heart of palm salad.

BELOW: Mahébourg fishmongers.

National History Museum

Mahébourg's **National History Museum** (open Mon, Wed–Fri 9am–4pm, Sat–Sun and public holidays 9am–noon; tel: 631 9329), on the southern outskirts of the town, is housed in an 18th-century building. Its original owner, Jean de Robillard, turned the house into a hospital where the commanders of the French and British forces who had fought in the Battle of Vieux Grand Port convalesced side by side. The museum contains an eclectic display of exhibits from the Dutch, French and British periods. Portraits line the walls, among them Prince Maurice of Nassau, Pieter Both, botanist Pierre Poivre and "king of the corsairs", Robert Surcouf, who donated the dagger he seized in 1800 from Captain Rivington of the English ship *Kent* following an attack in the Bay of Bengal. One of the most famous relics is the ship's bell from the ill-fated *St Géran*, which sank off the northeast coast in 1744. A newspaper cutting recalls the fate of the British steamer, *Trevessa*, which sank hundreds of miles from Mauritius in 1923. The survivors landed at Bel Ombre on the south coast after 25 days in a lifeboat with nothing to eat but ship's biscuits. You can see the remains of the biscuits and the cigarette tin they used to measure water rations. Other exhibits include Mahé de Labourdonnais' four-poster bed and two wooden palanquins in which slaves would carry their masters about.

Around Mahébourg

The approach to **Blue Bay** ❼, south of Mahébourg, isn't promising as you drive past some very poor housing, but Pointe d'Esny is considered a desirable place to live, and high-walled private bungalows dot the coast. En route you pass **Le Preskil Beach Resort** hotel; a nice enough spot, with a small but pleasant beach

and views of the mountains, but unless you want easy access to the airport, it's rather an isolated place to stay. The public beach at Blue Bay, however, is worth an excursion. You can hire a glass-bottom boat here to view wonderful corals in the Blue Bay Marine Park and sail past the islet of Île des Deux Cocos, an exclusive retreat for weddings and private functions. On the other side of the bay, the **Shandrani** hotel is the height of luxury. It stands on its own peninsula in 30 hectares (74 acres) of gardens, just 6 km (4 miles) from the airport. To the west of Shandrani, at Mare aux Songes, an almost intact set of dodo bones was discovered in 1865 and the skeleton is on display in London's British Museum. In 2006 Dutch scientists unearthed more dodo bones, which will enable them to understand more about this extinct bird.

From **Ville Noire**, north across La Chaux River from Mahébourg, signs point the way to the **Rault Biscuit Factory** (open Mon–Fri 9–11am and 1–3pm; entrance fee; tel: 631 9559), where you can take a guided tour to see women baking *biscuits manioc* made from the cassava that grows in the nearby valley.

The B7 from Ville Noire runs through cane fields to the village of **Riche en Eau**. The area, literally "rich in water", was home to small family-owned sugar estates, where isolated chimneys, now listed as national monuments, mark the sites of early factories. Signs in the area lead to **La Vallée de Ferney** ❽ (open daily 9am–5pm; entrance fee; tel: 433 1050; www.cieletnature.com) where the former Ferney sugar factory has been converted into a Visitors' Centre. Wall maps and information boards highlight conservation issues, and guided walks through the 200-hectare (494-acre) valley reveal rare birds and indigenous plants thriving amid mountain-backed landscapes and bubbling streams.

Map on page 124

Île aux Aigrettes

Ecotourism is developing at **Île aux Aigrettes ❾** (open daily 9am–5pm; tel: 631 2396), a nature reserve that opened to the public in 1998. It's a 20-minute ferry trip from Preskil Beach Resort Hotel *(see Travel Tips, Accommodation)*. A guide from the Mauritius Wildlife Foundation (MWF) leads no more than 20 visitors at a time along marked paths. Look out for bands of pink pigeons *(see page 91)* breeding among flora found nowhere else in the world. The MWF has been active in regenerating the island, its main aim being to re-create a microcosm of the original coastal habitat. During World War II, much of the native forest was cleared to make room for British troops, who installed guns (still in place) as defences against a Japanese invasion. Old hands remember waiting for the enemy which never came. The old generator room has been converted into a museum and if you climb to the rooftop viewing platform panoramic views unfold across the sweeping bay and **Île de la Passe** beyond.

The rare pink pigeon now breeds happily on Île aux Aigrettes.

Among the historic ruins on this islet off Vieux Grand Port are the remains of French defences, an old reservoir and a beautifully preserved 18th-century powder magazine, complete with a harp etched into its wall. This was probably engraved by a homesick soldier of the 87th Royal Irish Fusiliers, stationed here in the 1830s. Both islets make a wonderful half-day excursion. ❑

BELOW: washday at Rivière des Créoles.

THE SOUTH COAST

The rugged south coast comes as a breath of fresh air for hard-nosed wanderers on the run from the well-trodden shores elsewhere on the island, and can be explored in a day's drive

Map on pages 132–3

Port Louis

The south coast from Bel Ombre to Riambel is currently undergoing major development to increase tourism and revive the economy of this forgotten region. The lack of tourist amenities is offset by gorgeous scenery and the sense that you are witnessing Mauritius as it used to be. Great stretches of rugged basalt cliffs assaulted by strong southeasterly winds lie against a backdrop of hills and undulating sugar fields that are part of century-old plantations. The old estates, built to withstand the southern winds, have survived better here than elsewhere. Apart from four luxurious hotels dominating sandy beaches in the west, there is scant evidence of the 20th century, let alone the 21st. But changes are afoot, heralded by the 2008 opening of Shanti Ananda Hotel, with its spacious beach-side accommodation at St Felix, mid-way along the south coast.

Rivers flowing from the central uplands to the ocean have, in many places, prevented coral reefs from gaining a foothold, depriving the area of the gentle lagoons reminiscent of the north, and swimming, except from designated beaches, can be dangerous. In the west, the Savanne Mountains (which give the district its name) rise steeply from deep coves, relegating the coast road to a narrow strip west of Souillac. The east is flatter. Here, the roads run through cane fields and over bridges spanning rivers and streams, linking shanty villages. Not a lot of tourists pass this way.

If you're driving, the south coast can easily be explored in one leisurely day – less if you're based at one of the hotels on the west coast or on the south-east coast near Mahébourg. If you have a full day to spare, you might even consider making a circular drive by taking in the route through the Black River Gorges National Park (described in The West chapter, *see page 146)*. Most hotels offer full-day tours of the south coast, which usually include lunch in an old sugar estate house.

From beach to sugar lands

Our tour begins at the western end, just south of Le Morne. Here you'll find a quiet rock-strewn beach, where fishermen sit mending their nets and children play among the trees. The first significant hamlet is **Baie du Cap ❶**, typical of many villages along the south coast: there are just a few Chinese-run *boutiks* (and a police station built by a local sugar magnate from a ship that sank offshore in the 19th century). A short distance beyond is **Bel Ombre ❷**, where at certain times of the year the only vehicles you are likely to encounter are lorries laden with sheaves of sugar cane bound for St Aubin and Savannah factories further east. Bel Ombre has long been the heartland of the south coast's sugar industry. Back in 1816, philanthropic businessman Charles Telfair, after whom

LEFT: sugar cane estate worker, with children in tow.
BELOW: braving the waves at wind-swept Gris Gris.

*Precious eggs of
the rare Mauritius
kestrel.*

TIP

In Val Riche Forest
look out for the relics
of an old mill standing
on the site of a former
sugar factory,
indigenous plants and
trees, plantations of
edible palms and
herds of deer. Book
through specialist
operators Valriche,
tel: 623 5615.

the hotel nearby is named, bought the factory. Newly arrived from England, he immediately set about turning Bel Ombre into a model sugar estate, only to incur the wrath of local slave owners who did not agree with his idea of providing proper food and shelter for slaves.

Adjoining the colonial-style Telfair Hotel is an 18-hole golf course; all that is left of the factory is the chimney. Guided nature tours, horseriding and walking trails into Val Riche Forest via Frederica, coupled with elegant haute cuisine at the splendid 19th-century Bel Ombre Château, attract golfers, environmentally conscious tourists and gourmets. Other contenders offering grand scale sanctuary, serenity and space, are the Heritage, with its enormous African-village style spa, the sumptuous Moorish-inspired Mövenpick and the Tamassa Hotel.

Driving now through swaying fields of sugar cane, a mile or so east of Beau Champ, the B10 branches inland to **Chemin Grenier**, where a minor road runs north to the water-filled crater of **Bassin Blanc**. Here, with a little patience, you may be able to spot the brilliant green echo parakeet and Mauritius kestrel. (Bassin Blanc is also accessible on foot from the Black River Gorges National Park.)

Beaches versus "green tourism"

The B9 coast road to the west of **Pointe aux Roches ❸** fringes a public beach; the area to the east is dominated by the Shanti Ananda Hotel. If you would like to combine beach activity with "green tourism", the 2,400-hectare (6,000-acre) St Felix Sugar Estate offers speed zip wire rides over the Rivière des Galets. More sedate activities on offer include archery and guided nature tours through the estate.

Meanwhile, the coast remains beautifully rugged, although it is not without its dangers due to an absence of coral reef. Further east, **Pomponette** is known for its treacherous currents, and most locals head for the safer **SSR Public Beach** just before the peaceful hamlet of **Riambel** (from the Malagasy word meaning "beaches of sunshine"), where the Cap Sud restaurant provides simple meals.

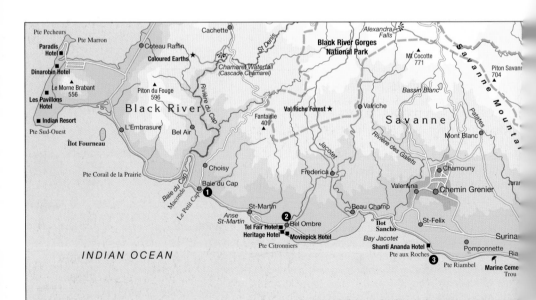

Souillac

The largest settlement on the south coast is **Souillac ❹**, which lies on an inlet where the rivers Savanne and Patates form an estuary (about 30 minutes' drive from Le Morne on the west coast). At the height of sugar production in the 19th century, steam ships loaded cane from nearby estates and shunted along the coast to Port Louis, but the port fell into decline when road and rail replaced the steamers. In the 1990s, substantial improvements were made to the old port area, prompting the town's designation as a "tourist village". While such a billing owes more to optimism than reality, it is worth stopping off to explore the handful of sights that are scattered around the bay.

On the western side a road turns off to Souillac's **Marine Cemetery**, one of the most beautiful in Mauritius. Who knows what graves were washed out to sea over the years, but in 1957 people reported seeing hundreds of skulls and human bones littering the cemetery as a result of a tidal wave. Meanwhile, constant erosion of the sea wall threatens even more damage to graves, many of which date back to the early 19th century. One of the oldest tombs is that of Thomas Etienne Bolgerd (1748–1818), a Souillac bigwig and owner of 500 slaves who was captured by the British in 1809 and released in exchange for some goats. The most famous member of the d'Unienville family, Baron Marie Claude Antoine Marrier d'Unienville (1766–1831), is also buried here, as is Robert Edward Hart (1891–1954), the country's most celebrated poet and writer.

Next stop is the old **port** area, where the most evident improvement is the restoration of a 200-year-old sugar warehouse, part of which is now occupied by **Le Batelage** restaurant, where tourists on organised trips are often fed and watered. The shady terrace on the quay at the front provides good views over the river, now so tranquil after years of inactivity.

Not far from the seafront, a road runs 5 km (3 miles) inland through cane fields to the **Rochester Falls**, which tumble from the Savanne River from a height of 10 metres (33 ft). Constant erosion has fashioned the basalt rock into upright columns, and young boys enjoy scaling the jagged cliffs before diving into the cold fresh water. It's also a great place for a swim. Taxi drivers will take

Harvesting the canes.

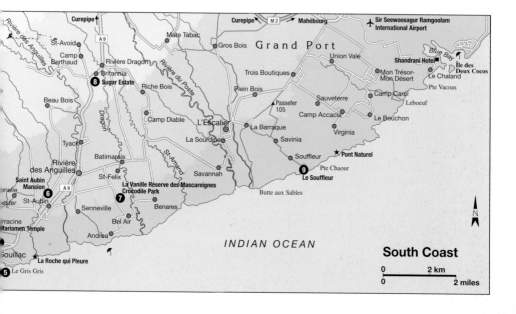

INDIAN OCEAN

South Coast

0   2 km

0   2 miles

you there (and wait to take you back), but you can also hoof it. The track weaves uphill for about 15 minutes before descending to the falls.

On the way, you pass **Terracine**, one of the island's earliest factories, dating back to 1820. It closed down in 1947 but the chimney, a national monument, stands as a reminder of its sugar-producing days. Right next to it, the colourful Mariamen Temple, which remains quiet for most of the year, bursts into life in December and January when it is taken over by Tamil fire-walking and body-piercing Cavadee ceremonies *(see page 80)*.

Gardens, culture and black magic

Heading for the heart of Souillac, the first place of interest is **Telfair Gardens**, just across the road from the bus station. Shaded by gigantic Indian almond trees and banyans, the gardens are a favourite spot among the locals who come here to pass the time of day while kids, quite oblivious to the skull and cross bones signs, swim off the rocky coast. The cemetery is visible across the bay.

From here it is a 10-minute stroll to the **Robert Edward Hart Museum** (open Mon, Wed–Fri 9am–4pm, Sat–Sun 9am–noon; tel: 625 6101), the former home of Souillac's most famous son. The half-Irish, half-French poet and writer lived alone in a charming little coral-built bungalow, known as La Nef (The Nave), which contains manuscripts, books and personal belongings. Hart churned out work in English and French and his efforts were recognised in both English and French literary circles with an OBE, and a gold medal from the Académie française. He was obviously inspired by the beauty of his surroundings, and you can understand why when you see the golden beach pounded by ferocious seas at the rear of the house.

BELOW:
Rochester Falls.

If you continue along the road from La Nef you reach **Le Gris Gris ❺**, the most southerly point of Mauritius, more like the windswept coast of Scotland than the gentle shores of a tropical island. Some say it is called Gris Gris because black magic (*gris gris* in Kreol) used to be performed here. If you walk along the yawning sandy beach and allow your imagination to run riot, you can pick out the figure of a sorcerer scored out of the rock, who appears to be holding a cauldron. Up on the headland, where weather-beaten casuarinas attest to the ferocity of the winds, a 15-minute walk along a small path leads to a rocky outcrop called **La Roche qui Pleure** (The Crying Rock), so named because the sea which cascades around it gives the impression that it is weeping. (A monochrome photograph of La Nef illustrates the uncanny similarity between the silhouette of this rock and the profile of Robert Edward Hart.)

Saint Aubin and colonial-style living

One of the highlights of a south coast tour is a visit to the area's colonial homes. Many are off-limits to the public but tour operators offer a full-day guided tour that starts at Domaine les Aubineaux, a former tea planter's residence in Curepipe, with tea-tasting in the grand living room, and finishes with lunch at the residence of **Saint Aubin ❻**, built in 1870, on the A9 5 km (3 miles) northeast of Souillac. The visit provides a leisurely glimpse of colonial life, with relaxation on the broad verandahs, a tour of the vanilla and anthurium plantations and a stroll through spacious grounds.

The full-day guided tour includes transport to the **Bois Cheri tea factory**, 10 km (6 miles) inland. Although tea is no longer produced in large quantities, the factory is worth visiting to see how it is processed and packaged. You will

Map on pages 132–3

Packing tea at the Bois Cheri factory.

BELOW: plantation house at the Saint Aubin estate.

Map on pages 132–3

TIP

The Hungry Crocodile restaurant in La Vanille Crocodile Park has an interesting menu. If you're not tempted by the idea of crocodile croquettes, you can always opt for a croc-free *croque monsieur*.

BELOW: off to work.
RIGHT: feeding time at La Vanille Crocodile Park.

also be driven to a hilltop tea pavilion overlooking a lake surrounded by neat tea fields. Here, you can sample plain, vanilla- or bergamot-flavoured tea, and go for a stroll on the hillside from where there are magnificent views of the coast.

Well worth considering for the contrast in scenery are sojourns at **Andrea** and **L'Exil**, former seaside and hunting lodges respectively of Franco-Mauritian sugar barons. You can stay overnight or for a few days in the beautifully renovated lodges, set in exceptional locations. Andrea opens onto a grassy-sloped clifftop where surf beats on the boulder-strewn mouth of Rivière des Anguilles. L'Exil overlooks the Rivière Savanne and has panoramic views of the nature reserve of Combo, where a guide will point out endangered plant and animal species.

Alternatively you could book a guided day tour of the area direct at Andrea (tel: 576 0555); it includes lunch at one of the lodges and transport, although there's nothing to stop you from just turning up at Andrea for a drink if you're in the area or visiting the Crocodile Reserve *(see below)*.

Happy snappers

You don't need to be on an organised tour to visit **La Vanille, Réserve des Mascareignes Crocodile Park** ❼ (open daily; entrance fee; tel: 626 2503), signposted right off the road running through the large village of **Rivière des Anguilles** (on the banks of the river of the same name). The park occupies a valley that features about the closest thing you'll get to tropical rainforest, which is why Owen Griffiths, an Australian zoologist, chose the area to farm Nile crocodiles. The stud of the estate and four females were brought from Madagascar in 1985, and the mating process produced little critters who grew into man-eating monsters. They are kept in secure enclosures, waking only at feeding time to snap mighty jaws with a sickening thud on freshly killed chicken.

A nature trail meanders through the forest, past squads of giant Aldabra tortoises, wide-eyed Mauritian fruit bats, wild boars, macaque monkeys, an insectarium and a host of luminous green geckos and chameleons. (Be sure to douse yourself with plenty of insect repellent before you visit.)

Heading north along the A9, you pass the manicured lawns and pineapple plantations of the **Britannia Sugar Estate** ❽, the south's last significant sugar plantation. It is still very active, with a pristine estate village of stone-built homes and a school.

If you are heading towards Mahébourg, you can follow the little-used B8, which branches east from Rivière des Anguilles. About midway, at **L'Escalier**, a road runs south to **Le Souffleur** ❾, a blowhole fashioned in a dramatic outcrop of rock (due to erosion it is now more a cloud of spray than the fierce jet of water that shot skywards until the 1970s). If you walk along the coast you'll get a clear view of the break in the coral reef that allows the sea to rush up against the cliffs. There's also a striking *pont naturel* (natural bridge) which formed when the roof of a sea cave collapsed. Le Souffleur is accessed via the grounds of the Savinia sugar estate, and to visit the blowhole you need to ask permission from the estate office (near the L'Escalier police station). ❑

LA VANILLE CROCODILE PARK & NATURE RESERVE
← KM.

SUGAR: FROM CANES TO CRYSTALS

Despite rapid developments in the tourism and textile industries, the giant sugar estates are still the country's third biggest employer

Until recently, over 90 percent of the arable land of Mauritius was given over to the cultivation of sugar. With the diversification of agriculture and expansion of the tourism and textile sectors, sugar production is no longer the country's number one earner. Many sugar workers have hung up their overalls and handed in their machetes, opting instead for more comfortable employment in offices, factories and hotels. Nevertheless, mechanisation has ensured that sugar production continues to play a major role in the economy and there are perks for those who have remained loyal to the industry. Sugar estates provide housing, hospitals and free medical facilities, free school transport and plenty of leisure and sporting activities. Many have scholarship schemes and sponsor the training of workers and their families in technical schools.

Mauritius produces the best unrefined sugar in the world and most of it is exported to the European Union. One important by-product is *bagasse* or cane fibre, which is used to fire boilers in the factory and any excess burned to generate additional electricity for sale to the national grid. Another is molasses, used in the production of vinegar, drugs and perfumes, while cane spirit is used to make rum. Nothing goes to waste; even the scum from the purification process contains essential nutrients which are fed back into the soil, and the long green leaves of the cane are used for animal feed.

△ **GREEN FIELDS**
Just over half of Mauritius is owned by several giant sugar estates; the rest is shared among 30,000 individual farmers or "planters".

△ **THE NO. 1 RUM**
One by-product of sugar: Green Island, the island's best-selling brand of rum, is made from cane spirit.

△ **CANE CUTTER**
Although much of the work traditionally undertaken by labourers is now being done by machine, teams of cane workers toiling in the fields are still part and parcel of the Mauritian landscape.

◁ **CUTTER'S HUT**
During the sugar harvest, many cane workers live in houses by the fields, like this one near Mahébourg.

CRUMBLING GIANTS

Sugar cane was introduced to Mauritius by the Dutch who brought it over from Jakarta in 1639. By the time the British came in 1810 thousands of acres had been planted with sugar cane. For generations sugar was the lifeblood of Mauritius. People got rich on it, fought over it and died for it. It wasn't until the 1980s, with the progressive centralisation of the sugar industry, that the number of sugar estates began to dwindle. Of the hundreds of factories that once thrived across the island, only a few are left. But the ruins of the old sites remain, and the chimneys – which have been designated national monuments – are dotted all over the countryside.

To see how the brown sludge from the crushed canes was transformed into sugar crystals, before mechanisation took over, visit the early sugar mill reconstructions at l'Aventure du Sucre or at the Domaine les Pailles, a 10-minute drive south of the capital.

▽ **HARVEST TIME**
Between June and December the air is thick with the sweet scent of molasses as cane is cut and loaded into lorries.

△ **OX POWER**
The first sugar mills used ox-driven crushers to extract the cane juice, but by the mid-19th century, animals had been replaced by machines.

▽ **THE END PRODUCT**
After a lengthy purification process cane juice is transformed into various sugars, from fine caster to thick molasses.

◁ **HARD LABOUR**
Before the advent of tractors and lorries, cane bundles were transported from the field to the factory on ox-drawn carts.

THE WEST

*In the west, the main attractions are the beaches at Flic en Flac
and Le Morne, but inland the mountains of the Black River area
provide the best place on the island for hikers and birdwatchers*

Map
on page
142

Port Louis

Soon after leaving the uninspiring suburbs and industrial installations of
Port Louis, the quirky angles of the Corps de Garde, Rempart and Trois
Mamelles mountains and, in the distance, the solid hammer head of Le
Morne Brabant peninsula, stay with you as you travel southwards, offering a
range of rewarding views unmatched in other parts of the islands. The A3, which
runs the length of the 50-km (30-mile) coast, meanders inland south of the capital, with side roads periodically offering access to the sea, but from Tamarin the
road hugs the coast. The glistening beaches of Flic en Flac, Wolmar and Le
Morne and their turquoise lagoons remain tantalisingly hidden from view.

Suburban Port Louis and beyond

It is all too easy to speed through the suburbs of Port Louis as you make a bee-
line for the obvious attractions of the coast, reachable in about 30 minutes, but
there are a few places that might attract your attention along the way.

Heading out of Port Louis along the A1, before the A3 branches off to Flic en
Flac, you pass through **Grande Rivière Nord-Ouest**, notable for the iron
bridges that span the river of the same name, and for the ruin of an 18th-century
hospital. There are splendid views over the river at the point where the B31
leads coastwards to **Pointe aux Sables ❶**. The beach
here is mediocre by Mauritius' standards, but attracts
a crowd due to its proximity to the capital. Note that
the resort has a seedy reputation due to its popularity
with local prostitutes; the beach and overall scene is
more pleasant at the point than in the village itself.

The B31 links up with the B78 (just before it rejoins
the A3), which veers west to **Pointe aux Caves ❷**. A
climb to the top of the early 20th-century lighthouse
here provides good views of the mountains and coast.

Back on the A3, the road continues southwards
bisecting a wide and fertile plain and separating the
plateau towns from a picturesque coast of low cliffs.
At the busy village of **Bambous ❸**, with flamboyant
tree-shaded avenues and pretty dwellings, ask for
directions to **St Martin Cemetery**, nestling in cane
fields north of the village. Here, 127 identical tombstones are the final reminder of 1,580 Jewish wartime
refugees from Eastern Europe. Having been refused
entry to Palestine by the British in 1940 because they
were considered "illegal immigrants", they were
transported to Mauritius. They were well received,
but conditions in their refugee camp, where they were
kept until the end of the war, were poor. After the war,
many started new lives abroad but their families still
return to Mauritius to pay their respects to those who
never made it back home. There are also some beautiful Tamil tombs in the cemetery.

LEFT: harvesting
salt in the Black
River estuary.
BELOW: view from
Le Morne road.

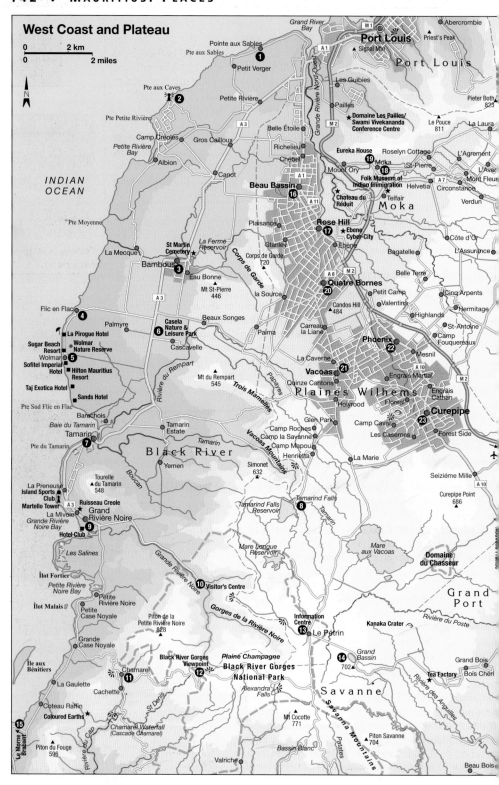

West Coast and Plateau

0 | 2 km
0 | 2 miles

INDIAN
OCEAN

Grand River
Bay

● Abercrombie

M1

Port Louis
● Priest's Peak

P o r t   L o u i s
▲ Signal Mtn

● Pointe aux Sables
Pte aux Sables
● ①
Petit Verger ●

A 1

Les Guibies ●
Pailles ●

Pieter Both
823

Pte aux Caves
● ②

Petite Rivière ●

Domaine Les Pailles/
Swami Vivekananda
Conference Centre

Le Pouce
811

● La Laura

M 2

Pte Petite Rivière ●

A 3

Belle Étoile ●

Grande Rivière Nord-Ouest

Mount Ory ▲

L'Agrement ●

Camp Créoles ●
Petite Rivière Bay

Gros Cailloux ●

Richelieu ●

Chébel ●

Eureka House ★
● ⑲
Moka ●
Folk Museum of ● ⑱
Indian Immigration

Roselyn Cottage ●
St-Pierre ●

L'Aver ●

Albion ●

Canot ●

A 1

Helvetia ●

Mont Fleu ●
Circonstance ●

Pte Moyenne ●

La Mecque ●

St Martin
Cemetery ★
Bambous ● ③
Eau Bonne ●

La Ferme
Reservoir

Plaisance ●

Beau Bassin
⑯

Stanley ●

Château du
Réduit ★

Telfair ●

Verdun ●

M o k a

Côte d'Or ●
L'Assurance ●

Mt St-Pierre
446

Corps de Garde
720

A 11

Rose Hill
⑰

Ebène ★
Cyber City

Bagatelle ●

Belle Terre ●

Flic en Flac ●

A 3

la Source ●

Ebène ●

Palmyre ●

Beaux Songes ●

Casela ● ⑥
Nature &
Leisure Park

Cascavelle ●

Palma ●

A 8
M 2

Quatre Bornes
⑳

Petit Camp ●

Valentina ●

Cinq Arpents ●

Hermitage ●

La Pirogue Hotel ■
Sugar Beach ■
Resort
Wolmar ●
Sofitel Imperial ■
Hotel
Taj Exotica Hotel ■

Wolmar ■ ⑤
Nature Reserve
Hilton Mauritius ■
Resort

Sands Hotel ■

Carreau ●
la Liane
La Caverne ●

Candos Hill
484

Highlands ●

St-Antoine ●

Camp ●
Fouquereaux

Barachois ●

Rivière du Rempart

Mt du Rempart
545
Trois Mamelles

Quinze Cantons ●

Phoenix
⑫ ⑫

Mesnil ●

A 10

Baie du Tamarin
Tamarin ● ⑦
Pte du Tamarin ●

Tamarin
Estate ●

Tamarin

Vacoas
Mountains

Vacoas
● ㉑

Engrais Martial ●

M 2

La Preneuse ●
Island Sports ■
Club
Martello Tower ■
La Mivoie ●
Grande Rivière
Noire Bay

Tourelle ▲
du Tamarin
548

Ruisseau Creole ●
A 3
Grand
Rivière Noire
⑨

Yemen ●

Simonet ●
632

B l a c k   R i v e r

Camp Roches ●
Camp la Savanne ●
Camp Mapou ●
Henrietta ●

Glen Park ●

Holyrood ●

P l a i n e s   W i l h e m s

Floreal ●

Engrais ●
Cathan

Camp Caval ●

Les Casernes ●

Curepipe
㉓ ●

Forest Side ●

Hotel Club ■

Les Salines ●

La Marie ●

Mare
aux Vacoas

Seizième Mille ●

A 10

Île Fortier ●
Petite Rivière
Noire Bay

Île Malais ●

Petite Rivière
Noire ●

Petite
Case Noyale ●

Mare Longue
Reservoir

Tamarind Falls ●

Tamarind Falls
Reservoir

⑧ ●

Curepipe Point
686

Domaine
du Chasseur

Grande
Case Noyale ●

Piton de la
Petite Rivière Noire
828

Visitor's Centre ⑩

Gorges de la Rivière Noire

Rivière du Poste

Kanaka Crater ●

G r a n d
P o r t

Île aux ●
Bénitiers

Chamarel
● ⑪
Cachette ●

St Denis

Black River Gorges
Viewpoint
⑫

Plaine Champagne
Black River Gorges
National Park

Information
Centre
⑬ Le Pétrin ●

Grand
Bassin
702

Grand Bois ●
Bois Chéri ●

La Gaulette ●

Grande Rivière du Cap

Coteau Raffin ●
Coloured Earths ★

Alexandra
Falls ●

⑭ ●

S a v a n n e

Tea Factory ●

Le Morne
Brabant
⑮

Chamarel Waterfall
(Cascade Chamarel)

Piton du Fouge
596

Mt Cocotte
771

Piton Savanne
704

Bassin Blanc ●

Valriche ●

Patates

Savanna Mountains

Rivière des Anguilles

Beau Bois ●

Flic en Flac

The name of the village **Flic en Flac ❹** is Dutch in origin and is thought to derive from "Fried Landt Flaak", meaning "Free and Flat Land"; later, under the influence of the French, this evolved into Flic en Flac. Most visitors don't waste too much time wondering about etymology but head straight for the beach.

If Grand Baie is the Creole Côte d'Azur then Flic en Flac is the Creole Costa del Sol, with a concentration of small seafront hotels, shops, restaurants and bars backed by concrete apartment complexes spreading inland to replace the sugar plantations of yesteryear. But it's a popular choice for self-caterers, independent travellers and islanders themselves (many of whom have weekend homes here), lured by the nightlife, a superb beach and public transport giving easy access to Port Louis, the Plateau Towns – just a 45-minute bus ride away – and the Black River Mountains.

At the entrance to Flic en Flac is a small clutch of bars and cafés, together with the resort's main hotel, **Villas Caroline**, which overlooks the northern reaches of the enormous beach. Soft, powdery sands shelve into the lagoon, where people windsurf and swim. Further along the main road ubiquitous casuarina trees back the beach, where the sand is packed hard enough for cars to drive on. Sunsets here are often a hypnotic vision of feathered clouds flecked with silvery-peach hues. On weekdays it is quiet, with just a couple of food stalls. But on weekends, the resort springs to life as locals descend from all around, and at the end of the day, great groups of islanders wait in orderly queues for the homebound bus.

Flic en Flac is a haven for divers, windsurfers and snorkellers. Unlike Grand Baie, no speedboats disturb the waters with wash thrown up from their bows, and the best dive sites in Mauritius lie off this part of the coast *(see page 93)*. One of the best places in Mauritius to learn is the **Pirogue Diving Centre**, while more experienced divers will find interesting opportunities at Villas Caroline *(see Travel Tips, Accommodation)*.

Less than 2 km (1 mile) south, **Wolmar ❺** is really an extension of Flic en Flac. The original hamlet has now been completely swamped by a handful of very smart hotels, which include the **Sugar Beach** resort, **La Pirogue** (complete with casino), the **Sofitel Imperial**, the **Hilton Mauritius Resort**, the most luxurious on the west coast, **Taj Exotica** and **Sands Resort Hotel**. These hotels certainly have better facilities than anything you'll find in Flic en Flac.

South to Tamarin

Casela Nature and Leisure Park ❻ (open daily 9am–5pm; entrance fee; tel: 452 0693) focuses on fun, and "green tourism". Sitting on the flanks of Rempart Mountain on the A3 just south of Flic en Flac, the extensive grounds include walkways over delightful ponds, a petting farm, a mini-zoo, dozens of aviaries containing 142 species of birds from all over the world – including the rare pink pigeon and Mauritius kestrel – fishing, mini golf and a restaurant overlooking the west coast's rolling, cane-clothed countryside. Guided tours include photo safaris for sightings of antelope, ostrich, deer, zebra and wild

Map on page 142

Thirst-quenching beach snacks.

BELOW: sailboards for hire on La Pirogue beach.

boar, exciting nature escapades by mountain or quad bike, and rock climbing. Unmissable for a humbling and exciting experience is the popular attraction of walking in the wild with lions and cheetahs, accompanied by expert guides.

Pressing southwards, the massive mound of Le Morne Brabant appears to rise over Tamarin Mountain, while inland the horizon is dominated by the bulk of Rempart and the Black River mountains. Some 6 km (4 miles) south of Casela you hit the coast and **Tamarin ❼**. The village, overlooking a tranquil bay, is showing encouraging signs of development as a quieter alternative to Flic en Flac and its cheap *pensions* provide a good base for exploring the southwest.

The Tamarin Hotel right on the beach has brought new life to the area, with jazz nights on Thursday, while the Riverland Sports Centre, with its large pool, tennis courts, gym and pleasant restaurant, welcomes day visitors. The area is also the focus of Mauritius' first Integrated Resort Scheme (IRS) and an example of how sugar barons are turning their lands over to real estate development. Under the scheme foreigners can buy property for the first time, albeit in designated areas and for a minimum investment of US$500,000. In 2007, luxurious villas and an 18-hole golf course were completed at Tamarina Golf Estate, making Tamarin a fashionable place to holiday.

There is a good unspoilt beach but the coral reef is subdued by fresh water that flows from the central highlands via the Rempart and Tamarin rivers. The waters are famous for the black and long-beaked dolphins, and local people run dolphin-spotting tours from the bay. Between June and August waves can reach over 2 metres (6 ft) and the bay is also popular with surfers.

The area around Tamarin is one of the west coast's most scenic. In summer the River Tamarin is lined with scarlet-blossomed trees, and at any time of year,

BELOW:
high-speed antics.

Map on page 142

especially in the late afternoon, there's definitely a romantic feel about the place. If you're a photographer this is the best time to capture the reflections of Tamarin Mountain on the river and watch the pencil-thin surf rolling in.

The River Tamarin starts at the **Tamarind Falls** ❽, where a reservoir near the small village of Henrietta on the central plateau *(see page 155)* supplies water for irrigation and to a hydroelectric power station some 250 metres (820 ft) below. Also known as Les Sept Cascades, the falls tumble over seven stepped cliffs through a deep narrow gorge. The best way of getting there, particularly if you're an adrenalin junkie, is with Vertical World (tel: 697 5430 or 251 1107), who provide ropes and harnesses to abseil your way down. Beginners are first given lessons on how to abseil on dry cliffs before taking the plunge. Intermediate and hard-core enthusiasts can try their skills negotiating 45-metre (145-ft) drops into ponds and smaller waterfalls followed by a strenuous hike back to the top.

Other ways of getting to Tamarind Falls are from a rough track from Henrietta or hiking from Le Pétrin in the Black River Gorges National Park *(see page 146)*, but neither option is recommended unless you go with a qualified guide.

Black River area

Vast rectangular pans, where salt is extracted from sea water by solar evaporation, lie alongside the A3 south of Tamarin en route to **Grande Rivière Noire** ❾, at the estuary of the eponymous river that tumbles through some of the most rugged areas of Mauritius. The Rivière Noire (Black River) area is sparsely populated, with no proper towns, only small villages and hamlets. Once regarded as the poorest region in Mauritius, with a predominantly Afro-Creole population, the area now has an influx of cash-rich expatriates building luxurious homes there.

During the winter months locals gather the cherry-red fruits of the Chinese guava bush that grows in profusion on the steep-sided slopes of the Black River Gorges. The fruit are great as a Vitamin C-packed snack, while the bushes make a handy hiker's balustrade along the slippery trails.

BELOW: flamboyant tree in full bloom.

MARTELLO TOWERS

Overlooking the public beach of La Preneuse, 2 km (1 mile) or so south of Tamarin, is the best-preserved Martello Tower in Mauritius. The tower is one of five such fortifications that were constructed on the coast of Mauritius by British soldiers in the 19th century; three remain, all on the west coast: one in Pointe aux Sables *(see page 141)*, another at La Harmonie, and one at Les Salines just south of Grande Rivière Noire. The tower at La Preneuse is open as a museum (tel: 493 6648).

The towers were built to withstand gunfire and have walls that are an impressive 3 metres (11 ft) thick on the seaward side. They included a powder magazine and store, living quarters for 20 men, and revolving cannons on the roof. They were veritable fortresses, entrance to which could be made only by a ladder that was let down from high up the building so that attackers would find it almost impossible to enter.

The name comes from Mortella Point in Corsica, where British soldiers first came across such a tower during the French Revolution. Between 1796 and 1815 the British went on to build around 200 Martello Towers in Britain and throughout the Empire – in places as far flung as Bermuda, Ireland and the Ascension Islands.

Black River Gorges Viewpoint.

BELOW: the Chamarel Falls are particularly impressive after heavy rains.

Contrasting sharply with the laidback lifestyle of Grande Rivière Noire village and its traditional eateries and stores, which are strung out along the A3, is the gleaming Ruisseau Creole complex with its designer shops and restaurants. Just a stone's throw from the main road of Grande Rivière Noire village is the west coast's centre for big game fishing, where trips can be arranged through **JP Henry Charters**. If staying elsewhere, your hotel should also be able to arrange a trip for you. Between September and March, marlin, sailfish, yahoo, yellow fin tuna and various species of shark migrate to the warm waters around Mauritius *(see page 97)* and feed just beyond the reef where the seabed falls abruptly to a depth of 600 metres (1,970 ft).

Black River Gorges National Park

Much of the beauty of the west lies inland, and nowhere more so than in the southwest corner of Mauritius, where the rugged mountains once provided a hideaway for *marrons* (runaway slaves), who lived in isolation, safe in the knowledge that their masters would never find them. The good news for visitors is that these mountains are now easily accessible via the **Black River Gorges National Park**, which was officially opened in 1997 in an attempt to preserve what is left of the island's disappearing native forests. The 6,575-hectare (16,250-acre) park offers something for everyone, from dedicated walkers to those who just fancy a scenic drive and a break from the beaches. This green heart of Mauritius is not a place to spot wildlife on a grand scale, but you could spend days tracking down the 150 endemic species of plants and nine endemic species of birds, including pink pigeons and Mauritius kestrels. While you may be lucky enough to spot these two endangered species, you are more likely to see the graceful white tropic bird, cuckoo shrike and Mauritius blackbird.

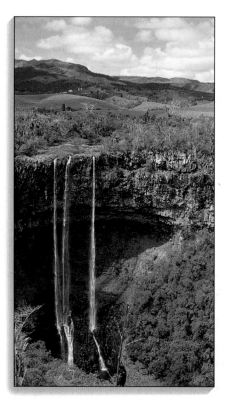

From the west coast you can access the northern area of the park by taking the new road which leaves the A3 just south of Grande Rivière Noire village, near the **Pavillon de Jade Restaurant**, which serves the best Chinese food in the area. This leads through sugar fields to a picnic and parking area just 5 km (3 miles) inland, where a **Visitor Centre ⑩** provides walking maps and information on the condition of the trails. From here you can explore the lower slopes of the park or follow the boulder-strewn Grande Rivière Noire for a strenuous 16-km (10-mile) uphill trek on the "Parakeet" and "Macchabee" trails, which link the Gorges area with the Plaine Champagne.

The other way to get to the Black River Gorges is to drive south from Black River to Grande Case Noyale, and then turn inland and upwards to the forested plateau of **Plaine Champagne**, named after the creamy white flowers of the privet that call to mind the white froth of champagne. This route leads to Le Pétrin, the park's other visitor centre *(see page 148)*, but is also better suited to those interested merely in a scenic drive.

Coloured earth at Chamarel

From Grande Case Noyale the road winds steeply through the forested foothills to the village of **Chamarel ⑪**, offering glorious views down to the coast; if you are heading downhill, be sure to test your brakes first.

The Chamarel area is known for its coffee, but the reason most people come here is the waterfall and the curious geological phenomenon the village is famous for.

Chamarel Waterfall (Cascade Chamarel) tumbles from the St Denis river into a large crater, and at 83 metres (272 ft) it is the highest waterfall in Mauritius. About 1 km (½ mile) further on are the **Chamarel Coloured Earths** (open daily 9am–5pm; entrance fee). Geologists are fascinated by this unique rolling landscape of multicoloured terrain, thought to have been caused by the uneven cooling of lava, now fenced off and beautifully landscaped with viewing platforms and timber walkways. Interestingly, the colours never fade in spite of torrential downpours. East of Chamarel village, nestling in a verdant valley is **La Rhumerie de Chamarel** (open Mon–Sat 9.30am–5.30pm; entrance fee; tel: 483 7980). Bundles of cane are cut daily and brought to this state-of-the-art distillery where *fangourin*, a sweet non-alcoholic juice, is extracted, fermented and turned into high-quality rum. Guided tours include rum tasting and the shop sells unusual Mauritian-made handicrafts and gifts, such as candles, honey, salt from Tamarin and a range of designer clothing and accessories.

From the waterfalls, you can continue southwards through sugar cane via a tortuous road to the south coast emerging at Baie du Cap *(see page 131)*, or backtrack to Chamarel village and push eastwards.

Black River Gorges views and walks

The road east of Chamarel running high up across the Plaine Champagne is narrow and lined with scrubby vegetation, offering fleeting chances to admire the scenery. It has no verge and only the occasional stopping place, though there are a couple of designated viewpoints. Most people stop at the **Black River Gorges**

Map on page 142

TIP

Before booking a hiking, rock climbing or abseiling excursion, do confirm that your guide is a fully qualified first-aider, that drinks and first-aid equipment are carried at all times and that emergency procedures exist in case of accident or sudden illness.

BELOW: Chamarel's coloured earth.

BELOW:
shrine of Lord
Krishna and Radha
Rani, Grand Bassin.

Viewpoint ⑫, where there's usually a snack van and a man selling freshly cut fruit in the car park – the only source of refreshments for miles. A few miles east, a track runs a short way to the **Alexandra Falls**, with less extensive views down to the south coast, and you can hear the falls more than you can see them.

Just east of the Alexandra Falls the road veers suddenly north taking you to **Le Pétrin Information Centre** ⑬, the first port of call for those approaching the Black River Gorges area from the plateau towns and the best access point to all areas of the park. Next to the Information Centre is the **Pétrin Native Garden**, a mini showcase of native species, including many medicinal plants. Among the plants are the national flower, the *boucle d'oreille* (earring), the quirkily named *patte poule piquant* (prickly chicken legs), used for stomach upsets and liver problems, the *pots de chambre du singe* (monkey chamber pots) and the umbrella-shaped *bois de natte* tree, often draped with tree ferns, wild orchids and lichens.

Grand Bassin

Located 2 km (1 mile) east of Le Pétrin and surrounded by forests infested with monkeys, the water-filled crater of **Grand Bassin** ⑭ attracts crowds not so much for its natural beauty but for its religious significance. The volcanic crater is known among Hindus as Ganga Talao, and is dominated by Mauritius' tallest sculpture, of the Hindu god Shri Mangal Mahadev, which stands 32 metres (108 ft) high. Legend has it that the lake contains nocturnal fairies, but it was after a Hindu priest dreamed that it was linked to the sacred River Ganges that Grand Bassin became a place of pilgrimage for the annual Maha Shivaratree festival. In February, thousands of Hindus dressed in white walk from all parts of the island and converge on the lakeside to make offerings at the colourful

grand houses hidden behind high hedges in nameless streets around the centre and in the suburbs of **Floreal** and **Forest Side**. Curepipe has the dubious distinction of having the highest rainfall on the island, and on rainy days, which is most of the time, the buildings look depressingly grey. The town's most attractive public buildings are clustered in a compound on Elizabeth Avenue near the market. Of most interest are the 1920s **Carnegie Library**  and the impressive Creole-style **Town Hall**, which overlooks a statue of *Paul et Virginie*, central characters of the 18th-century romance inspired by a shipwreck off the Île d'Ambre.

Most people come to Curepipe to shop. **Currimjee Arcades** (on the corner of Royal Road and Chasteauneuf Street), is not particularly large, but has a few good clothes shops downstairs. The arcades were extended to include a first-floor shopping area, **Galerie des Îles** (tel: 670 7516). This pleasant collection of boutique-style shops sells designer cashmere pullovers and jewellery, modern art, crafts, souvenirs and home accessories. Spend time browsing here before taking a break in the casual bistro-type eaterie on the terrace overlooking the main street. **La Sablonnière**, in Pope Hennessy Street, a classic example of colonial architecture complete with miniature Eiffel Tower, has been turned into a shopping emporium. The high-ceilinged rooms echo with the chatter of tourists who arrive daily, deposited by taxis and tour coaches, to buy "duty free" oriental carpets, objets d'art and furnishings. For serious shopping you'd do better to go to Floreal shopping complex where you can purchase quality garments made from raw imported materials, such as cashmere, cotton and silk.

The **Botanical Gardens** , in the west of town, are not as big or as impressive as the Pamplemousses Gardens, but are perfect for a quiet stroll.

The most famous local attraction is **Trou aux Cerfs** , a 300-metre (980-ft) diameter crater. Formed as a result of volcanic activity millions of years ago, it is now choked with silt, water and dense vegetation. The crater is a 15-minute walk or a short taxi ride from the centre of town. The view stretches beyond the blanket of buildings to the spectacular mountains, which so far have remained untouched by developers.

To the southwest of Curepipe along the A10 at Nouvelle France, **Domaine du Chasseur** (open daily 11am– 3pm; reservations only; tel: 577 0269) is an appealing escape to the hills around town, especially if you're into hunting: several hundred deer and wild boar roam acres of beautiful countryside, and guns and ammunition are provided. You can eat in the rustic lodge-style restaurant, and quad and mountain biking are also on offer.

Heading south

The plateau towns are a good starting point for a drive south through the Black River Gorges National Park. Either take the B3 from Quatre Bornes south through Glen Park and La Marie to Le Pétrin, or the B70 from Curepipe to La Marie where you turn left for Le Pétrin. If you're short of time, you can get a taste of the area by driving just past the village of Henrietta, where touts will show you a viewpoint overlooking Tamarind Falls *(see page 145)*, a 15-minute hike along a rough downhill path. It's better to go with a specialist operator, such as Yemaya Adventures (tel: 752 0046 or 754 4234). ❏

Maps:
Area 142
Town 152

Curepipe's origins go back to the 18th century. The popular theory is that it was the halfway point where soldiers and travellers crossing the island would stop to rest and clean or "cure", in French, their pipes.

BELOW:
star-crossed lovers,
Paul et Virginie.

RODRIGUES

*This island is remote, laid-back and rugged. Its beauty
lies in its simplicity and, though it may not be able to compete on
the tropical beach front, its marine environment is hard to beat*

Map on page 158

Hidden in a lagoon almost twice its size, Rodrigues is the smallest of the Mascarene trio. Lying 560 km (350 miles) east of Mauritius and shaped like a plump fish, the island is just 18 km (11 miles) long and 8 km (5 miles) wide. A hilly ridge runs along its length from which a series of steep valleys extend to narrow coastal flatlands. The appeal of Rodrigues, as discovered by Prince William and friends during a holiday in 2004, lies in its rugged and simple beauty. There are stunning coves and deserted beaches. You can fish in shallow lagoons, dive and snorkel the reefs and enjoy magnificent walks through casuarina forests. The people are warm and welcoming; in spite of being cut off from the rest of the world, they survive with a cheerfulness born of optimism.

Rodrigues welcomes visitors who are unbothered about swift service and five-star trappings. Currently, the island has just four hotels and a growing number of guesthouses. Tourists from Réunion and Mauritius come here on 3- or 5-day packages that include the flight and half-board accommodation. Those who have more time can take a cabin on the *Mauritius Pride* or the *Mauritius Trochetia,* which make regular crossings to Rodrigues *(see Travel Tips).*

A pint-sized capital

Rodrigues was occupied in 1726 by the French who established a tiny settlement at **Port Mathurin ❶**. They imported slaves from Mozambique and Madagascar and settlers from French-occupied Mauritius, increasing the population to just over 100 in 1804. The town, laid out in grid style in 1864 by the British, had many streets named after local administrators. In 2006 they were officially renamed in a fit of autonomous zeal, but people still use the old names.

At last count, Port Mathurin numbered 5,390 inhabitants. The capital may be bereft of monuments, but a wander round will give you a taste of Mascarene Island life at its most leisurely. A good place to start is the jetty where a memorial stands to Rodriguan volunteers who fought in both World Wars. It's worth hauling yourself out of bed early for the **Saturday market** in Wolphart Harmensen Street (formerly Fishermen Lane). Many of the islanders set off from their villages in the hills at midnight to set up stalls (trading starts at around 6am) or to be the first to bargain for the best fruit and vegetables. By 10am most people have packed up and gone home. Parts of the market are given over to touristy knick-knacks, but bottles of home-grown chilli and chutneys and fruit and vegetables sell like hot cakes.

There is no tourist strip as such and most shops, no more than corrugated iron shacks with handwritten nameplates nailed to the door, are concentrated in the

LEFT: the *Mauritius Pride* docking at Port Mathurin.
BELOW: walking the pet pig.

Baskets for sale at Port Mathurin market.

block bounded by Rue François Leguat, Rue de la Solidarité and Rue Hajee Bhay Fateh Mamode. A few shops in Rue Max Lucchesi sell more unusual gifts and lethal home-bottled chillis, but for a great range of island handicrafts call at the **Careco Workshop** (open Mon–Fri 8am–3pm, Sat 8am–noon; tel: 831 1766) at Camp du Roi at the back of town. Careco employs 30 disabled people who make and sell original souvenirs. An apiary also produces the clear and distinctly flavoured Rodriguan honey. The workshop is a tourist attraction in its own right and tour operators feature it on every itinerary of Port Mathurin.

The main artery of the town is Rue de la Solidarité (formerly Jenner Street), one block back from the waterfront, that starts from the island's only petrol station to the west and and continues over a footbridge, built to replace the Winston Churchill Bridge which collapsed in 2006, to the bus terminus in the east. At the western end of Rue de la Solidarité, tucked between shops, is the tiny six-minareted **Noor-ud-Deen Mosque**, built for the few descendants of the first Muslims who arrived in 1907 as textile merchants. In the same street is **La Résidence**, the former Island Secretary's house and now the Rodrigues Tourism Office (tel: 832 0866), with the original wide verandah shaded by a gnarled Indian almond tree.

A short stroll east leads to the Anglican **Saint Barnabas Church**, surrounded by gardens and trees. Most Rodriguans are Catholics and the little **Saint Cœur de Marie Church** in Rue Mamzelle Julia sees a regular congregation. Crossing the footbridge over the River Cascade you stumble across the spot where Rodrigues' first settlers, led by François Leguat, set up camp in 1691.

Further up river towards Fond La Digue, the latanier huts of the 1940s once occupied by "women of easy virtue" have been replaced by Port Mathurin's

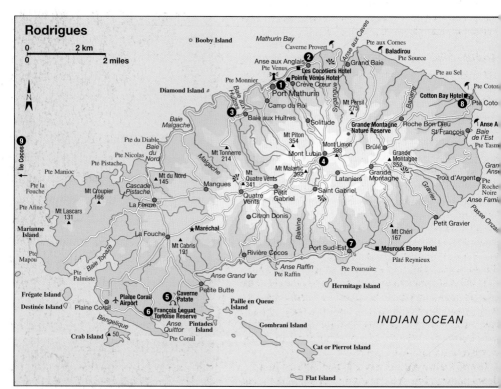

only hotel, the simple, Creole-style **Escale Vacances**, set in a deep-wooded valley overlooking the river. There are some lovely walks from here (some uphill) along jungly boulder-strewn tracks – sturdy shoes are advisable.

Around Port Mathurin

In 1761 a British fleet arrived and camped on a strip of beach at **Anse aux Anglais ❷** (English Bay) east of Port Mathurin and, meeting with little opposition from the handful of French inhabitants, stayed for six months. The Englishness of Rodrigues was compounded in 1901 when cablemen from the Eastern Telegraph Company (later Cable & Wireless) laid a submarine telegraph cable linking the island with Mauritius, thus completing the line of communication between Australia and Europe. There are good views across Port Mathurin from the headland where French and British astronomers recorded the Transit of Venus in 1761 and 1874.

A cluster of small guesthouses overlooks the beach at Anse aux Anglais and at low tide the lagoon is a favourite haunt of groups of fisherwomen, known as *piqueuses ourites*, who make a living spearing octopus, which they hang out to dry in the sun. A stiff uphill climb from Anse aux Anglais, via the tranquil beach-side bungalows of well-to-do Rodriguans and Mauritians at Caverne Provert, leads to a fairly flat area where acacia trees border the road. From the headland are resplendent views over **Grand Baie**. You can follow the road up from Grand Baie beach until it peters out to a narrow uphill track towards the sweeping deserted beach at **Baladirou**. A less strenuous way of getting there is to take a 40-minute boat ride along the coast from Port Mathurin.

Just 2 km (1 mile) west of Port Mathurin is **Baie aux Huitres ❸** (Oyster Bay), an enormous bay surrounded by hills and thick casuarina forest. For the best views, drive up to **Allée Tamarin**, a hamlet at the back of the bay.

Inland from Port Mathurin

Port Mathurin's bus station and taxi stand are a boon for independent travellers and a handy location to start a journey inland, around fearsome hairpin bends, to the spine of the island where little villages overlook the north and south lagoons.

You can jump on a bus, thumb a lift or drive yourself to the Meteorological Station on the windswept **Pointe Canon** for panoramic views over Port Mathurin and the lagoon. Here a cannon, erected by British troops during World War II, points out to sea and is oddly juxtaposed beside a white statue of the Virgin Mary, La Reine de Rodrigues. If you're around on 15 August, the approach road and hills are a riot of colour with islanders trekking towards the statue to celebrate the Feast of the Assumption.

The forest at **Solitude** is 2 km (1 mile) south of Port Mathurin on the Mont Lubin road. Bounded by deep valleys and thick with eucalyptus trees, the forest also has small copses of jamrosa and mango trees which provide food for the Rodriguan fruit bats that swoop down to feed on them at dusk.

Mont Lubin ❹, a busy little village of tumbledown shops, gives the impression of being at the top

Map on page 158

The last Transit of Venus occurred on 8 June 2004. For anyone interested in astrology, the Pointe Venus Hotel (tel: 832 0104), overlooking the headland where the two previous observations took place, is not a bad place for star gazing.

BELOW: hanging the octopus out to dry.

of the island, but the highest point is actually nearby Mont Limon at 398 metres (1,289 ft). Most visitors drop in at the **Women's Handicraft Centre** to watch women weaving baskets from vacoas leaves and perhaps buy one of the finished articles on display, before making their way to Pointe Coton and the beautifully isolated beaches of the east *(see below)*.

Heading westwards on the Mont Lubin road, it's worth making a detour to Rodrigues' biggest church at **St Gabriel**. The church was built by locals in 1939 under difficult conditions. Specially trained donkeys carried most of the sand from the coast to the heights of St Gabriel and voluntary helpers, including women and children, brought cement, lime, blocks of coral, corrugated iron and timber up narrow mountain paths. It can be visited any time, but for a splash of colour, music and singing, get there in time for 9am Mass on Sunday.

The 5-km (3-mile) stretch of twisting road between the hamlets of Petit Gabriel, Quatre Vents and Mangues, is peppered with glimpses of translucent blue lagoons and scenes of rural life.

The next main settlement after Mangues is the large and noisy village of **La Ferme** which has a small stadium where Pope John Paul II held mass during his visit to Rodrigues in 1989. You need to pass through La Ferme to reach **Cascade Pistache** (2 km/1 mile west of the village), an enormous crater hewn out of granite surrounded by grassy hills. The waterfall that tumbles into Rivière Pistache is particularly beautiful after heavy rains. Alternatively, take the newly opened road northwards from La Ferme to Baie du Nord for a scenic 9-km (5-mile) coastal drive back to Port Mathurin, passing isolated homesteads swathed in poinsettias, hibiscus and marigolds, and causeways filled with mangroves at Baie Malgache.

BELOW: exploring the rocky maze of the Caverne Patate.

VOYAGES AND ADVENTURES

The first settlers on Rodrigues were a band of Huguenots (all men) led by François Leguat. Fleeing religious persecution in France, they set sail from Holland in search of their own island paradise. Travellers' tales drew them to the Mascarene archipelago and, in 1691, they landed on the uninhabited island of Rodrigues. They lived for the next two years on "very wholesome and luxurious foods which never caused the least sickness".

During his stay, François Leguat wrote the island's first guidebook, *Voyages and Adventures*, a classic tome documenting the island's unique flora and fauna. In it he describes how the beaches were covered with tortoises weighing over 136 kg (300 lb) so that he literally used their shells as stepping stones to reach the sea. Leguat's name would have sunk into oblivion were it not for the opening in 2007 of an amazing reserve named after him, the **François Leguat Tortoise Reserve** at Plaine Caverne. Conservation programmes to restore Rodrigues' native habitat are paying off here with the planting of thousands of endemic plants plus a colony of more than 500 giant Aldabra tortoises shipped over from Mauritius. Explore caves with qualified guides and visit the only museum devoted to Rodrigues' history, fauna and flora.

RÉUNION

This may be a Gallic outpost, but you won't find

scenery or a local culture like this in France

Réunion, born three million years ago as a result of an undersea volcanic eruption, consists of two great volcanic mountain masses. The oldest, in the northwest, covers two-thirds of the total area of the island and rises to form the Piton des Neiges which, at 3,000 metres (9,840 ft) is the highest peak in the Mascarenes. Over time, the Piton des Neiges, an extinct volcano, collapsed and eroded to form three caldera-like valleys or cirques.

Réunion has its share of popular beaches, but the biggest thrill for tourists is taking in the beauty of the verdant cirques and the eerie landscape of the volcano. The island cannot compete with Mauritius in terms of beaches and luxury hotels, but it has many more conventional sightseeing opportunities in the shape of museums, sugar factories, and well-preserved colonial and creole architecture. Many people come just for the adventure sports, which are the big thing here – from trekking, mountain biking and horse riding, to kayaking, canyoning and paragliding.

Eighty percent of Réunion's visitors are French. They see the island as an extension of the motherland and feel comfortable with the left-hand drive Renaults and Peugeots, the smooth roads, the out-of-town hypermarkets, and the bistros and boulevards. They feel at home in the Novotels and mountain gîtes and can even bring their dogs with them, and of course everyone speaks French.

The tropical warmth and breathtaking scenery are intoxicating and the Réunionnais are an attractive, gentle people. A fascinating mélange of Malagasy, European, Chinese and Indian, they are taking inspiration from their counterparts in Mauritius and rediscovering their heritage.

Réunion remains a well-kept secret in the English-speaking world and, for the discerning traveller, in many ways it is the most fascinating of the Mascarene trio. ❑

PRECEDING PAGES: breathtaking sights: up in the clouds of the Commerson Crater; down by the wave-beaten, rugged coast.
LEFT: aerial view of marshland near St Paul.

THE RÉUNIONNAIS

The melting-pot phenomenon is seen more clearly in Réunion than anywhere else in the Western Indian Ocean

The culture and people of Réunion can be defined in one word – *métissage*. The overriding importance of the French language and culture throughout most of the island's history has meant that religious and ethnic differences were always subordinate to the notion of integration with the mother country. The assimiliationist tendency that characterised the period from 1946 to 1981 hindered the emergence of a separate Réunionnais identity but today the inhabitants happily juggle several identities and recent years have seen a cultural and religious resurgence among Réunionnais of Tamil, Muslim and other non-Christian minorities.

The foundations of society

The first inhabitants of Réunion were a few exiled Frenchmen and a handful of Malagasy. The birth of their Franco-Malagasy children heralded the beginning of a process of ethnic mixing that has always characterised Réunionnais society.

In the 17th century, more settlers arrived in dribs and drabs from Europe and Asia and pirates relocated to what was then Bourbon from their old haunts in Madagascar. With the development of coffee cultivation, and the importation of slaves from East Africa and Madagascar, 18th-century Bourbon became a society where blacks outnumbered whites. During this period the Kreol language was in its formative stage. Some whites, however, became pauperised as the subdivision of landholdings between siblings forced the less fortunate to the higher regions, to farm the inhospitable terrain of Les Hauts. In 1830 land concessions were made for Salazie, and in 1840 for Cilaos, but Mafate, the largest of the cirques, was still too difficult to access.

The 19th century saw the arrival of sugar cane culture in Réunion – Charles Desbassyns introduced the first steam powered machinery

– and other *grands blancs* or powerful white families joined them to form the island's plantocracy. By mid-century cane had become the island's principal crop. On 20 December 1848 slavery was abolished, and many of the new free men established themselves in Les Hauts as blacksmiths and charcoal makers. Among

the indentured workers subsequently imported to Réunion were Malagasy, Indians and Chinese. A few Comorians and Yemenis were also brought.

Towards the end of the 19th century, free immigrants began to arrive from Cantonese- and Hakka-speaking regions of China. They gravitated into hawking and shopkeeping in the north and south of the island respectively, establishing community networks for themselves and schools for their children. Traders arrived from Gujarat and Bombay over the same period. This last wave of chiefly commercial immigrants adopted a dualistic pattern of socialisation: absorbing one culture while

LEFT: "Petit blanc" from Salazie.
RIGHT: Bois Rouge Tamil Temple, St-André.

retaining another. To this day, these communities are perhaps the most self-enclosed and distinctive within a largely integrationist culture.

Social realities

Today, almost three quarters of Réunion society is composed of *métis* – persons of mixed origins. There are few signs of racial antagonism although a few white families still wield an economic influence disproportionate to their numbers. They are the remnants of the large landowning class, some of whom

> **PRICK UP YOUR EARS**
>
> The term *z'oreilles* (lit. ears), used for the French living on Réunion, is said to originate from the habit new arrivals had of cupping their hand behind their ear as they attempted to understand the Kreol language.

have moved into banking and import/export businesses. Their numbers have been swelled by professionals and senior civil servants, including many recent arrivals from France. Their luxury homes are in the best quarters of St-Denis and St-Pierre, and they keep holiday villas in cool Cilaos or Hell-Bourg for the summer and often have a beach-house at St-Gilles that they use in winter.

The less well-off whites, or *petits blancs*, who have been living in Les Hauts for generations, have evolved into a tight-knit but distinctive community. Their attachment to the traditional agricultural and handicraft occupations of their forebears, their small stature, characteristic facial

features and eyes of a particular shade of blue, make them highly visible. There is perhaps a greater social gulf between these country dwellers and the urban professionals of St-Denis than between the whites and *métis* of the capital who inhabit the same cultural space.

The Réunionnais today are differentiated less by colour than by creed. The descendants of Indian traders, most of whom are Muslims, are known as *z'arabes*. Almost a quarter of all Réunionnais are of South Indian descent. Their forebears were mostly Tamil-speaking Hindus. Freed from the enforced Catholicism of the colonial period, many Tamils are rediscovering their religious roots. This group are also called Malabars. The largely Catholic Chinese of Réunion are increasingly intermarrying, and may not be a distinctive community for much longer.

The newest constituent of society are the *z'oreilles* or metropolitan French, who help to run the modern state as bureaucrats, teachers and the like. The status of Réunion as a *département* of France means that any EU national can apply to work and live on the island, just as the Réunionnais have the right to travel to, work and stay in France. The plum posts occupied by the *z'oreilles* sometimes provoke resentment among the Réunionnais, just as the metropolitans occasionally give vent to less than charitable assessments of the laid-back approach of the islanders.

Despite the preponderance in Réunion of individuals of mixed ethnicity, the African origins of a significant proportion of the population are clearly evident. Descendants of these Afro-Creoles are sometimes known as *cafres* (from the Arab *kafir* or heathen), but it is a term that can cause offence.

Society as a whole is characterised by dependence: the population is young – almost half is below the age of 25 – and unemployment in Réunion has been as high as 37 percent. A significant proportion of the population relies on social security payments from France. The evident disparities between the haves and have nots have created latent tensions that occasionally erupt: in February 1991 riots in Chaudron, a run-down suburb of the capital, brought these social problems into sharp relief.

Keep an eye open in the cirques, gorges and around cliffs for the spectacular white-tailed tropic bird *(paille-en-queue)*, which has a long, streaming tail and is the island's national bird. Petite Île, just off the south coast and Réunion's only satellite island, has a breeding population of at least 300 pairs of common noddies and up to 300 non-breeding lesser noddies, who have recently been joined by a fairy tern.

Colourful geckos

Apart from the many nocturnal house geckos that you see darting about the gardens and houses, the island has two brightly coloured

each side, its distribution has been split by lava flows from the volcano, creating different races of the same species. You can sometimes spot them lurking around the tourist kiosks up there.

The beautiful green, blue and red panther chameleon from Madagascar is the only introduced species that is protected; it can be found around St-Paul.

Tamarinds and orchids

Cultivated land bearing sugar cane reaches as high as 800 metres (2,600 ft) above sea level, then gives way to verdant mixed forest which becomes a dwarf heath as you move up to the

endemic day geckos that are worth looking out for. Funnily enough, the only place you will see the stunning green, red and white Manapy day gecko is on a walk through Manapany on the south coast. There you will see them all over the place, basking on banana leaves, scuttling up coconut palms and the pandanus, or screw pine. The Réunion day gecko, however, is a much more difficult species to find as it lives high up in the forests of the northeast and east. A blue-green colour with red stripes down

higher elevations. There are more than 60,000 hectares (148,000 acres) of natural forest on the island, looked after by the Office National des Forêts (ONF), and the endemic tamarind of the acacia family, alongside an island bamboo called the *calumet*, is quite a common sight. Epiphytes, including a wide variety of orchids (seven of which are unique to Réunion), and ferns grow in abundance on trees that lend their physical support.

Some of the introduced plants are a menace, such as the goyavier from Brazil, which runs rampant in the forest undergrowth. But its guava-like red berries are rich in vitamin C. ❏

LEFT: Réunion's national bird, the white-tailed tropic bird, is easily distinguished by its two long tail plumes.
RIGHT: wild lupins at Mafate.

ISLAND OF ADVENTURES

The spectacular landscape of Réunion is punctuated by trails, craters, peaks, rivers, forests and waterfalls, tailor-made for a vast array of outdoor pursuits

Experiencing the great spectacle of the interior uplands of Réunion can take as little or as much effort as you choose. Whether you take it easy and fly across the island in a helicopter or take a stroll along a nature trail, or prefer the challenge of hiking along a Grande Randonnée *(see pages 186–7)*, testing your nerve abseiling down a waterfall, or paragliding off a mountain ridge, you will discover mystery in its isolation, magic in its inaccessibility and power in its grandeur.

The cirques, mountains and plains providing the magnificent terrain for such activities were formed at different stages of the island's volcanic development over many thousands of years. Originally the Piton des Neiges (3,609 metres/11,840 ft) was the summit of a massive volcanic dome that collapsed around it and then was eroded to form the three great amphitheatres of gorges, waterfalls and ridges known as the cirques – perfect for canyoning, white-water rafting, rock climbing, hang-gliding and paragliding.

Les Hautes-Plaines, comprising the Plaine-des-Palmistes and the Plaine-des-Cafres, form an open landscape of forests and pastureland between the extinct volcanic landscape and the active Piton de la Fournaise. They are criss-crossed with mountain-bike tracks, hiking paths and horse-riding trails. The higher Plaine-des-Cafres is the gateway to the volcano *(see pages 217–21)*.

Be prepared

The best time to take on any arduous, lengthy activity, such as hiking, horse trekking or mountain biking, is during the cooler and drier months of May to November when mountain temperatures hover between 12°C (54°F) and 18°C (64°F) during the day but can drop to near zero at night. The Maison de la Montagne et la Mer will give you a general update of weather conditions, which can change very rapidly, or if you

understand French, you can phone the meteorological office *(see Travel Tips, Activities)*.

It's important that you are aware of your own level of fitness and stamina before starting any activity and stick to rules of basic safety. Helicopters frequently survey the cirques and should you be injured or in trouble you can send a dis-

tress signal by raising both arms in a V shape. Every year, scores of people, mostly suffering from broken bones or twisted ankles, are rescued in the cirques.

For overnight stays en route, there are several types of accommodation, ranging from *gîtes de montagne* (mountain huts or lodges), to *chambres d'hôtes* (B&Bs) and youth hostels. Campsites are rare, but there are a number of *abris* (shelters) on trekking routes. The shelters consist of only a roof so you need your own tent and sleeping bag.

Many places provide meals and at several of the *chambres d'hôtes*, a *table d'hôte* is offered when all the guests sit down to a meal together

LEFT: paragliding off a mountain ridge.
RIGHT: negotiating the rapids.

with the host. Reservations must be made in advance for all accommodation through Maison de la Montagne et de la Mer *(see box below)*. There is usually a grocer's shop *(épicerie)* in the villages *(îlets)* scattered around the interior, selling a basic range of foods, but not in all of them.

Up, up and away

The cirques and mountains are an awesome sight, especially from the top, and you can experience the sensation of flying between the peaks in a helicopter *(see page 220)* or smaller still, in a microlight. One or two people can fly in a

microlight round a choice of the cirques, Piton des Neiges, or the volcano. Bookings can be made through Felix ULM Run (tel: 0692 87 32 32) or Les Passagers du Vent (tel: 0262 42 95 95), both to the north of Le Port, before St-Paul.

To fly like a bird with only the rush of wind in your ears has to be one of the greatest thrills, especially over, within and around such dramatic scenery as Réunion's. The best hang-gliding and paragliding spots are Piton Maïdo on the edge of the wild and secluded Cirque de Mafate, from the top of Piton des Neiges and the Hauts de St-Paul, where protected from the strong winds, the conditions are perfect for

MAISON DE LA MONTAGNE ET DE LA MER

Whether you spend a day or a week in the cirques and mountains, Maison de la Montagne et de la Mer, whose office is in St-Denis *(see Travel Tips, Activities)*, can assist you with whatever you would like to do. Knowledgeable, English-speaking staff will advise on hiking routes, can arrange mountain accommodation and provide guides if necessary. They can also organise horse-trekking trips, canyoning, mountain biking, hang-gliding and many other mountain sports, and stock the Institut Géographique National's 1:25,000 scale maps (4401 RT to 4406 RT), and the ONF's walking guides.

To ensure safety in the mountains, the organisation has

drawn up the *Ten Commandments of the Crafty Papangue*:
● Never venture alone into the mountains.
● You must be fit to take full advantage of the mountains.
● For peace of mind, arrange your tour through Maison de la Montagne et de la Mer.
● Good shoes, warm and waterproof clothing ensure comfort.
● To avoid accidents never take unmarked paths.
● If you do get lost, stay calm.
● Know the distress signal – arms held up in a V.
● Never leave a wounded person alone. Wait for help.
● If you don't know the mountains, take a guide.
● Always keep the mountains litter free.

beginners, too. Contact Azurtech (tel: 0692 85 04 00) in St Leu, and Parapente Réunion (tel: 0262 24 87 84) in St-Leu, which also offers training sessions.

Rivers wild

Streams cascading over ridges and waterfalls powering off the mountains provide ideal conditions for the hair-raising sport of canyoning. For daredevils only, in a well padded wetsuit, canyoning means abseiling down waterfalls and torrents in the heights of the cirques. Try Îlet

ADRENALINE RUSH

For hiking, rock climbing, canyoning and trekking to Réunion's volcano, contact adventure sports specialists Cilaos Aventures, tel: 0692 66 73 42. Prices start from €35 per person.

Mountain bike challenges

Seven large areas of the island's magnificent interior have been devoted to mountain biking (VTT), and marked tracks, approved by the French Cycling Federation, total nearly 700 km (435 miles). These areas, each with their own steep challenges and beautiful views, include Maïdo, Entre-Deux, Cilaos, two at Hautes-Plaines, St-Philippe and Ste-Rose. Suitable bikes can be hired from companies such as Rando Bike (tel: 0262 59 15 88) and VTT Réunion (tel: 0262 38 01 97).

Fleurs Jaunes and Îlets du Bois Rouge in the Cirque de Cilaos or Trois Cascades. As the slopes become less steep, rivers, such as the Rivière des Roches, provide exciting conditions for kayaking; and there are plenty of rapids, such as those of the Rivière des Marsouins, for whitewater rafting. Companies specialising in river sports are Austral Aventure (tel: 0262 32 40 29) in St-Gilles-les-Hauts and Alpanes (tel: 0692 77 75 30) in St-Denis. These companies will organise mountain climbing expeditions as well.

LEFT AND RIGHT: more adventurous ways to explore Réunion's heights and depths – canyoning, mountain biking or horse trekking.

Trekking on horseback

Viewing the beauty of Réunion at your own pace from the back of a horse has to be an enriching experience – for an hour, a day or for several days, with tent and meals included in the price. With Ferme Equestre du Grand-Etang *(see pages 222–3)* you can ride a three-day circuit through the Forêt de Bébour-Bélouve (tel: 0262 50 90 03), and with Centre Equestre Alti-Mérens (tel: 0262 59 18 84) you can go on a two-day ride to the volcano. The horses in Réunion are the gentle Mérens breed brought over from the Pyrénées in France, on which even a beginner will feel at ease. *(For more details on adventure sports, see Travel Tips, Activities.)* ❏

Hiking along the Grandes Randonnées

Réunion is a walker's paradise, in spite of what novelist Walter Besant had to say about it when he walked to the Piton des Neiges in 1863. His tramp in the tropics may have been "a time of bruisings, and barkings of the skin, of tearings and scratchings, of dirt, discomfort and disaster", but today there are more than 1,000 km (620 miles) of well-marked trails across the island, mostly maintained by the Office National des

Forêts (ONF) and ranging from an hour's easy walk to a challenging week-long hike.

There are several organisations that will help you plan your route, book accommodation in advance and provide guides, the main one being Maison de la Montagne et de la Mer (see page 184). Maham (tel: 0262 47 82 82) in Hell-Bourg (see page 228) provides a package tour with guide, meals and accommodation that includes seven days of hikes of varying levels. If you are not familiar with the island, hiring a local guide-pei (native guide) through the tourist office is a good idea. Not only will you be in safe hands but they enjoy sharing their in-depth knowledge of their native land. On the other hand, a good locally available

book is Topo-Guide, "a trekkers' bible" which covers eight one-day walks of varying levels along the Grandes Randonnées (GR R1 and GR R2), illustrated by extracts from the IGN maps.

The opening of GR R1 in 1979 made trekking less hazardous than in Besant's days. The 60-km (37-mile) trail encircles Piton des Neiges through the three cirques of Salazie, Cilaos and Mafate. No visit would be complete without spending at least one night in the cirques, if only to wake at sunrise and gaze upon deep mysterious valleys clothed in magnificent forests. The air is clear and sharp and rouses even the weariest walker to experience a world of soaring, spectacular peaks.

The 150-km (93-mile) GR R2 crosses the island from the north to southeast. It starts from La Providence just outside St-Denis, links with the GR R1 at Marla in the Cirque de Mafate, and continues through diverse landscapes of rugged mountains, fertile plains, volcano and humid forest to St-Philippe. The following are some ideas for hikes that take in the Grandes Randonnées and last from half a day to as long as you would like.

La Roche Écrite. One of the most popular walks starting from St-Denis, it takes you south to La Roche Écrite (2,277 metres/7,470 ft). The trail passes through Réunion's various stages of vegetation from humid lowlands and tamarind forests with an abundance of rich flora to the almost denuded summit of La Roche Écrite itself.

If you're on limited time, the return trip can be done in one full day, but overnighting at the gîte at Plaine-des-Chicots will enable you to wake early to complete the final ascent to the ramparts of La Roche Écrite where you can experience the best views of Réunion's two highest mountains, Piton des Neiges (3,609 metres/11,840 ft) and Le Gros Morne (2,991 metres/9,813 ft) and the cirques of Mafate and Salazie to the right and left.

Most people drive inland from St-Denis on the D42 to Le Brûlé and park in the car park at Mamode Camp, about 5 km (3 miles) along the Route Forestière (RF1). From here the trail is clearly signposted, rising gently through forests of cryptomeria and eucalyptus and lush areas of wild flowers and fruits and endemic bamboo (Nastus borbonicas). Continue southwards, crossing two ravines surrounded by forests of mixed evergreens or bois de couleurs and tamarinds to reach the gîte at Plaine-des-Chicots, where you can stop for the night. From here it is another 1½-hour trek southwards to La Roche Écrite through landscape that changes to a plateau of lichen and moss.

You'll pass two intersections on the way but you should ignore both and keep to the marked path; the first on the right after about 45 minutes leads to La Mare aux Cerfs, a small watering hole noted for dawn sightings of Réunion's deer, which you could make a detour to on the way back. The second leads to Caverne Soldats. Continue on for another 25 minutes to La Roche Écrite.

Mafate. The most isolated of the cirques, no roads penetrate its rim. Mafate is wild and peaceful, only disturbed by the sound of the odd helicopter coming in for a closer look. But there are plenty of trails criss-crossing the cirque that offer a challenging choice, from a simple, but not so interesting, three-hour walk along the Rivière des Galets to more difficult day-long walks. Alternatively, you can stay in Mafate trekking from *îlet* to *îlet* and overnighting in mountain *gîtes*.

The *îlet* of Dos d'Ane on the D1 is a handy starting point for a couple of days of trekking along the GR R2. This trail descends steeply for two hours taking you down to the Rivière des Galets, which flows from the slopes of Le Gros Morne through a huge valley of *bois de couleurs* and meets the ocean at Le Port on the northwest coast. The trail crosses the river several times before it forks off to the left, leading to the *îlet* of Aurère, a good two-hour climb. Here you can stay at M Georget Boyer's *gîte* (tel: 0262 55 02 33) – basic, but breakfast and an evening meal are provided.

The next day you can do a four-hour hike to Le Bélier on the edge of the Cirque de Salazie, along either the Scout path, or the shorter, but more dramatic, direct path. This descends to the bottom of a ravine before climbing up to the top of the Grand Rein ridge, then down again and along the Route Forestière for the last leg.

Grand Place, past the turn-off to Aurère, is a good *îlet* to make your base for a few nights if you would like to spend several days exploring Mafate, as many of the trails pass through here.

Salazie. Hell-Bourg *(see pages 228–9)* at the end of the D48 has plenty of places to stay and is where you can start a hike to the Piton des Neiges, lasting about 5½ hours. The Gîte de la Caverne Dufour offers basic but hospitable dormitory-style accommodation at the foot of the mountain. From there it is a 1½-hour climb to the top, best started before dawn before the clouds descend.

Starting from Hell-Bourg, the trail climbs steeply to the Terre Plate, a wooded plateau where trails turn off to Manouilh, mineral springs on the edge of cliffs, and lead through woods of cryptomeria. You join the GR R1 towards the Piton des Neiges, skirting the edge of the Forêt de Bébour and crossing heathland, called *les branles*, until you reach the *gîte*.

Cilaos. The GR R1 winds and climbs its way west from Cilaos to Marla in the Cirque de Mafate. The six-hour hike goes via the Cascade de Bois Rouge and Col du Taïbit (2,082 metres/6,831 ft). If you want to try to do it in a day, start from the trailhead on the Îlet à Cordes road, 6 km (4 miles) west of, and accessible by bus from, Cilaos. Alternatively,

you can do a round walk to the Cascade de Bois Rouge in around two hours.

The volcano. Starting at Pas de Bellecombe or from the RF5, an alternative to climbing the Piton des Neiges *(see pages 217–21)* is to follow the GR R2 along the southern ridge (l'Enclos) of the volcano to the Nez Coupé du Tremblet. This five-hour hike, which passes through the magnificent Plaine des Sables *(see page 219)*, has been graded as not too difficult but you could just go halfway by returning at Foc-Foc where the trail forks. Here the main section of the GR R2 continues steeply, and is slippery in parts, down through dense and humid forest to Basse Vallée on the south coast – at least a seven-hour hike. ❑

LEFT: spoilt for choice.
RIGHT: walkers at Grand Étang.

PITON DE LA FOURNAISE: "PEAK OF THE FURNACE"

In 1801, explorer Bory de St Vincent described the volcano as "immense, tumultuous, bloody and majestic". He was inspired by it, but many feared it

Piton de la Fournaise, an "Hawaiian-type" shield volcano, is one of the most active on earth. It has erupted at least 153 times since 1640. In 1778, it added notably to the size of the island by pouring millions of tonnes of lava into the sea; in 1786 the explosion was so loud that it was heard in Mauritius; the following year "the sky turned red and the ocean turned into a boiling cauldron as fire met water".

Piton de la Fournaise has two main craters. The highest one, Bory, has been inactive since 1791, while the active Dolomieu manages, for most of the time, to confine its eruptions to within the enclosure. On 8 April 1977 the islanders witnessed the sheer power of their volcano when for five days the Dolomieu spewed red fire from its molten heart. Lava rolled down the mountainside destroying 20 houses and a petrol station at Ste-Rose on the east coast, only to stop just before the doorstep of a church and harden into a black mass.

Then on 20 March 1986 the Dolomieu crater exploded again, spitting out great gobs of lava which flowed at the rate of 100,000 cubic metres (353,100 cubic ft) per hour reaching temperatures of up to 1,160°C (2,120°F). The lava flow trickled down to the coast, sizzling as it sank into the sea, extending the island's land mass by several hectares.

On 9 March 1998, yet another spectacular eruption, this time lasting for 196 days – the longest in the 20th century – caused panic and excitement as blood-red fire fountains turned into rivers of lava. They flowed down to the Tremblet area only to peter out beside a shrine to St-Expédit on the RN2, 7 km (4 miles) north of Pointe de Tremblet (*see pages 207–8*).

▷ **SOME LIKE IT HOT**
Any volcanologist will tell you that all live volcanoes, no matter how predictable, should be treated with caution and respect.

△ **COASTAL EXTENSION**
Pointe de la Table was where the lava flow from the 1986 eruption came to rest, extending the east coast here by several hectares.

△ **CIRQUE DE CILAOS**
Stream cutting through volcanic basaltic rocks en route to the Cirque de Cilaos, visible in the distance.

◁ **VOLCANO FACTS**
Find out everything about volcanoes and see footage of recent explosions at the Maison du Volcan in Bourg-Murat.

FOUNTAINS AND RIVERS OF FIRE

Like the volcanoes of Hawaii, Piton de la Fournaise is a shield volcano. It produces spectacular fire fountains and churns out rivers of basalt lava, which flow over great distances. Because the lava is so fluid it trickles easily downhill without piling up, which explains why shield volcanoes are not steep. Around the Piton de la Fournaise you'll find two types of solidified lava flow which have been given Hawaiian names: *pahoehoe* (pronounced pa-hoy-hoy) and *aa* (ah-ah). *Pahoehoe*, which looks like coils of rope, is smooth and easy to walk on. This type of lava cools slowly and remains viscous for a while, allowing the gases to ooze through a steadily solidifying "plastic" skin. In contrast, *aa* flows quickly and solidifies into sharp angular chunks of lava called scoria, which can ruin your shoes.

DRAMATIC SEAS
ust south of L'Étang-Salé les ains, the RN1 cuts through jagged expanse of black va rock with views of ashing waves and water ts, known as *souffleurs*.

LUNAR LANDSCAPES
he area around the volcano d following the lava flows own to the coast is an eerie oonscape of twisted basalt rmations – a truly triguing facet of the island.

◁ SOLIDIFIED LAVA FLOW
A river of lava runs through the Grand Brulé forest and into the sea.

▷ OUR LADY OF LAVA
In 1977, the volcano disgorged its molten lava into the coastal village of Ste-Rose, miraculously coming to a halt at the doorstep of the village church.

PLACES

A detailed guide to Réunion, with principal sites
clearly cross-referenced by number to the maps

I f you've just flown in from Mauritius, the contrast in landscapes comes as a shock, confounding the idea of being on yet another Indian Ocean island. Instead of the low-lying fields and long stretches of beach that characterise the latter, you'll find awesome volcanic craters, rugged coastlines and lush gorges. Roland Garros, as modern as any airport in "la métropole", as the mainland is called, fully complements the Gallic spirit of the capital, St-Denis, with its brusque, business-like beat and traffic-packed boulevards. Apart from some attractively restored buildings and a couple of interesting art collections, however, there is not much to see or do here. Most people head straight for the west coast between St-Paul and St-Pierre where all the beaches are, but no trip to Réunion would be complete without a visit to the volcano and at least one of the cirques.

Thanks to the good roads, getting around is easy, either in a hire car or on the comfortable public buses. A smooth coastal highway goes all the way around the island and it's possible, though not necessarily advisable, to get round the island in a day. The stretch of road that runs between St-Denis and St-Paul, known as the Corniche, cuts a coastal route round powerful mountains towards the fashionable beaches of St-Gilles-les-Bains, but it is often choked with commuting cars. If you're not in a hurry you can take the high road that runs along the ridge. It's slower and more winding, but fantastically picturesque.

St-Gilles-les Bains, the self-styled "St-Tropez of the Indian Ocean", is a buzzing resort on the west coast. It's a good place to base yourself if you want to be by the sea, with plenty of bars and restaurants and all the facilities you need for water sports, but it does get crowded. At the far end of the island's western beach stretch is St-Pierre, one of Réunion's most pleasant towns and another good base, being within easy reach of the southeast coast and about an hour from Piton de la Fournaise.

The east coast areas around the town of St-André and the sleepy corner of St-Philippe are often neglected, but deserve more than a brief stop to explore the inland forests, volcanic wastelands, rugged seascapes and walking trails.

There's no doubt that the island's greatest assets lie inland. At the heart of the country you'll find mysterious mountains, jagged peaks and gorges, rivers and waterfalls, extinct craters, isolated villages and a temperamental volcano. For an altogether different experience, Hell-Bourg, at the eastern edge of the Cirque de Salazie, is a popular base for trekkers and adventurers. It is the starting point of the Piton des Neiges climb, and has some of the best preserved creole architecture on the island. ❑

PRECEDING PAGES: locals on the beach at St-Gilles-les-Bains.
LEFT: sailing tours office in the port of St-Gilles-les-Bains.

ST-DENIS

Map on page 196

Sometimes called "Paris of the Indian Ocean", St-Denis is more like a provincial capital. Many people come just to gather information, but it's worth pausing to look at the lovely creole architecture

St-Denis

When French governor Regnault founded St-Denis in 1669, he chose a sheltered spot on the uninhabited north coast. Life for the first 77 inhabitants was dull and, save for the odd pirate or two who dropped by, fairly uneventful. Even when the headquarters of the French East India Company was transferred from the old capital, St-Paul, in 1738, the town still had little going for it, in spite of a hundredfold increase in population. Successive governors tried to turn the new capital into a maritime and military base, but it ended up as neither, and by the late 1950s the infrastructure was so poor that even tourists had a job finding a place to stay.

All that's changed, and St-Denis has transformed itself into a reasonably sophisticated capital of 191,000 people, and these days offers much that you'd expect from any major town in metropolitan France. The difference, of course, is the tropical setting. Splendid renovated creole homes, often with grand wrought-iron gates and lush gardens, are one of the chief attractions for casual visitors. And while the restaurants may look typically French, you'll find *carri* (curry) and unfamiliar vegetables such as *chou chou* on the menu; as well as dozens of small creole eateries offering all the local delicacies, such as *samousas* and *bonbons piments* (fritters).

Spending a day in St-Denis will give you plenty of time to stroll the streets, visit the major sights, and book accommodation in the interior if you need to. But two words of warning: St-Denis is not a cheap city, and there are better things to do and see elsewhere. If you want to base yourself on the coast, you would do better to plump for St-Gilles, Boucan-Canot or St-Pierre.

The waterfront

Your first glimpse of St-Denis will most likely be from the air. The plane descends into Roland Garros airport 11 km (7 miles) east of the city, sweeping past dark mountains that must have struck awe into the hearts of the early settlers. Hemmed between the Rivière des Pluies and the Rivière St-Denis, the city spreads upwards on to the flanks of La Montagne where modern apartment blocks and luxurious houses have replaced the shanty town of the 1950s.

A good place to start is at the shaded waterfront promenade known as the **Barachois Ⓐ**. The area, once an inlet for unloading ships, had an adjustable jetty affixed to the shore by a set of iron chains, which was raised or lowered above the sea to allow passengers to disembark; according to the writer T. V. Bulpin, they "had to leap upon it with some display of acrobatics, with the thought of sharks if they slipped". The contraption was rendered useless during cyclones, and the iron pier that later replaced it was equally ineffectual,

LEFT: La Préfecture.
BELOW: filigree woodwork is a feature of creole houses.

To order a bottle of the local Bourbon beer ask the barman for "un dodo".

so the inlet was eventually filled in and planted with palm trees. Nine cannons face out to sea, placed there to symbolise St-Denis' supposed days as a military base. They are among Réunion's many coastal cannons that were either salvaged from shipwrecks or bought for decorative purposes by various governors.

Le Barachois is as chic as St-Denis gets, overlooked from across the busy Boulevard Gabriel Macé by Hôtel St-Denis and a handful of cafés and restaurants. Several former French East India Company warehouses survive here, in Place Sarda Garriga, with their facades still intact. One houses the town's oldest restaurant, the **Roland Garros** *(see Travel Tips, Restaurants)*, named after the famous aviator who was born in the capital. Nearby at 5 rue Rontaunay is **La Maison de la Montagne et de la Mer** (tel: 0262 90 78 90), where you can ask for advice, plan walking itineraries, book *gîtes* and so on. The huge relief model of Réunion on the wall conveys the island's dramatic topography, and provides plenty of inspiration to explore the cirques and volcanoes. You can buy IGN walking maps, books, crafts and a lot more at the **Caze de la Montagne** inside.

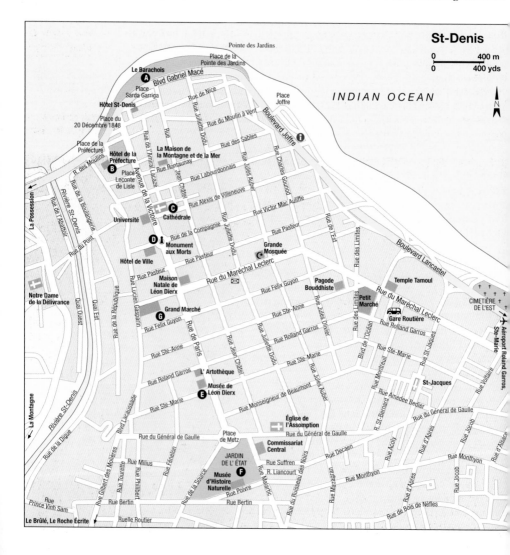

An architectural tour

A walk inland, south along Avenue de la Victoire, leads to some of the city's finest buildings. First is **Hôtel de la Préfecture** , an attractive colonial mansion overlooking pretty gardens. It began as a humble coffee warehouse, grew into the headquarters of the French East India Company and later became the official governor's residence. In 1942 it was occupied by Free French Forces, who arrived to rid the island of its Vichy sympathisers, closely followed by General de Gaulle. Later visitors included Giscard d'Estaing and Jacques Chirac. The Préfecture is closed to the public.

In the adjacent square, now used as a car park, a **statue of Mahé de Labourdonnais** stares solemnly out to sea. It was here that important announcements from the motherland were made, including the abolition of slavery in 1848. Labourdonnais is best remembered in Réunion for treating the island as a rather forgotten satellite when he was governor of the Mascarene Islands.

Three blocks beyond, past an uncharacteristically unobtrusive branch of McDonald's in a converted warehouse, is the 19th-century **Cathédrale** . It has some interesting bas-reliefs of St-Denis, but is not a beautiful building. The square at the front, with vast, twisted trees and 19th-century iron fountain, is more attractive.

As you head south, on the right in quick succession are several more notable colonial buildings, including the **Université**, built in 1759, but the best old buildings are still to come. The towering **Monument aux Morts** , which commemorates the death of over 1,000 Réunionnais who fought in World War I, marks the start of **Rue de Paris**, lined with some of the capital's grandest creole homes. Poet and landscape artist, Leon Dierx (1841–1912), was born in one of them, and the **Musée de Leon Dierx** (open Tues–Sun

Map on page 196

In 1913 Roland Garros (1888–1918) became the first pilot to fly across the Mediterranean. Taken prisoner during World War I he escaped only to die in action a month before it ended. His statue stands outside the Hôtel St-Denis in Place Sarda Garriga.

BELOW: St-Denis Cathédrale in 1832.

TIP

Parking is not normally problematic in St-Denis. You may be lucky enough to find a space in Place Sarda Garriga. There is also a car park by the Grand Marché on Rue du Maréchal Leclerc, where you can park for one hour for free. There are also spaces by the Jardin de l'Etat.

BELOW: *Jeune femme au divan* by Berthe Marisot (1841–95).

9.30am–5.30pm; entrance fee; tel: 0262 20 24 82), in a fine colonnaded mansion just up the road, displays his work alongside original sculptures and engravings of rather more famous artists such as Cézanne, Gauguin, Renoir and Picasso, as well as work by other Réunionnais artists. Unfortunately, the museum earns money by lending its best works to foreign museums, but there is normally at least one Gauguin or Picasso piece on show. Next door, in another superbly restored 19th-century villa, regular exhibitions of modern art are held in the former Maison Mas, now **L'Artothèque** (open Tues–Sun). •

A lesson in natural history

Rue de Paris ends at Place de Metz and the **Jardin de l'Etat ❻**. A golden age blossomed under botanist Nicolas Bréon, who came to Réunion in 1817 with a collection of European trees. From his continued expeditions to far flung places, he brought back the seeds with which to produce one of the most interesting botanical collections in the Indian Ocean. Two busts of green-fingered giants attest to the gardens' importance: Pierre Poivre who founded the Pamplemousses botanical gardens in Mauritius *(see page 120)* and Réunion-born botanist, Joseph Hubert, who brought back some useful spices from his travels. Labels cater to those interested in plants, while shady benches, the small café and space for *boules* are the main attraction for most locals.

The centrepiece of the gardens is the **Musée d'Histoire Naturelle** (Natural History Museum; open Mon–Sat 10am–5pm; entrance fee; tel: 0262 20 02 19), in the former Palais Législatif. The themed sections inside show how fauna survived before the arrival of humans, how it suffered under them and the measures that can be taken to protect already threatened species. Upstairs, a

wander through the town. For many people, St-Benoît simply marks the Route Nationale's junction with the N3, which heads up to the high plains and volcano *(see page 217)*. If all you want is a taste of the interior, you could take the D53, which runs 15 km (9 miles) along the course of the **Rivière des Marsouins** to Takamaka and the lovely **Cascade de l'Arc-en-Ciel** (and hydroelectric complex).

Ste-Anne ❺, 5 km (3 miles) beyond St-Benoît, would seem an unlikely place to feature in a film if it weren't for its church, whose intricate, Baroque-style stonework must have appealed to François Truffaut: he used it in *La Sirène du Mississippi* (1968), starring Catherine Deneuve and Jean-Paul Belmondo. The church dates from the 19th century, but the extraordinary carving was done in the first half of the 20th century by a group of Tamil craftsmen.

From Ste-Anne the road winds inland to the foothills of the volcano, crosses the 1893 suspension bridge over the Rivière de l'Est, and then descends to the small fishing town of **Ste-Rose** ❻. In 1809, British men o' war tested the town's defences just before they took the island from the French; on the waterfront there is a monument to Commodore Corbett, second-in-command of the British fleet, who died in one of the skirmishes. Ste-Rose is constantly under threat from the volcano which, in April 1977, twice disgorged its molten lava into the next village of **Piton Ste-Rose** ❼, destroying some 20 houses. People watched entranced as the lava flowed around the church, now known as **Notre Dame des Laves**, without destroying it, and instead hardened to form a thick black girdle – still visible today – around the building. Newspaper cuttings inside the church reveal that some villagers saw their lucky escape as "God's miracle". Local artist, Guy Lefèvre, made the stained-glass windows.

Next to the church is the flower-bedecked **Vierge au Parasol** ❽, moved from its original site south of Bois Blanc *(see below)* for its own protection following a lava flow in 2005. The shrine was erected by a 19th-century landowner who believed that it would protect his vanilla plantation from the fury of the volcano.

For the calm and quiet of a spectacular seascape, follow the signs south from Piton Ste-Rose for 3 km (2 miles) to the turn-off for **Anse des Cascades** ❾. Here, waterfalls tumble from towering cliffs into a shaded bay where fishermen sell their catch on the jetty. The secluded restaurant makes a perfect lunch stop and at weekends the cool forests of coconut trees are popular with picnickers.

Volcanic wasteland

By far the most dramatic coastal scenery of Réunion can be seen along the next stretch of road to St-Philippe as the RN2 negotiates the southeast corner of the island, skirting an immense volcanic ravine known as **Le Grand Brûlé**, formed by the lava flow from Piton de la Fournaise and Les Grandes Pentes (The Steep Slopes). Every now and then, barren wastes of solidified lava indicate the progress of previous eruptions. Just inside the ravine, soon after **Bois Blanc**, pilgrims still lay flowers on the lava wastelands where the Vierge au Parasol once stood.

There are several red shrines to St-Expédit *(see*

Map on pages 202–3

TIP

About 2 km (1 mile) south of Ste-Suzanne is the 30-metre (98-ft) Cascade Niagara, a mini version of the Niagara Falls and a good place for a dip. Go midweek unless you are happy to share the pool with plenty of locals, for whom this is a popular picnic place.

BELOW: Vierge au Parasol – the Virgin with the Umbrella.

TIP

Treks to the lava flows are not for the faint-hearted, but if you do decide it's for you the Café du Volcan, just before Puits Arabe, is a handy pit stop where an information board shows distances and times. It's right beside a shrine to St-Expédit, which features the decapitated heads of saintly figures.

BELOW: one of hundreds of red shrines to cult figure, St-Expédit.

below) in the area. One lies right beside a **lava flow** ⓾ *(coulée de lave)* whic cut off the RN2 in 1998, turning the area into an instant tourist hot spot.

If you stay on the coast road you'll be treated to more moonscapes of hard ened black lava at **Puits Arabe** ⓫, where information boards (in French describe the sequence of events which resulted in the evacuation of 500 peopl as lava flowed in four stages between the 19 and 30 March 1986, coating th slopes of **Takamaka** above the village before stabilising itself just 300 metre (980 ft) from the road. You can scramble for 200 metres (650 ft) over the solid ified lava to **Pointe de la Table**, where another lava flow from the same erup tion extended the island by 25 hectares (62 acres) into the sea; or opt for lengthier 5-km (3-mile) trek northwards towards **Tremblet**, crossing cliffs wher an 18th-century lava flow is a good example of the structures of cooling.

St-Philippe to St-Joseph

Rugged, ragged and fierce best describes the south coast, where screw pines tor by warm winds watch over wild seas beating against black basalt cliffs. Th sleepy little town of **St-Philippe** ⓬ is a good place to break after your journey through the volcanic wastelands of the east coast and stock up on supplies if yo need to. It has some interesting examples of creole architecture and, in additio to a helpful tourist office, there are roadside eateries that provide ready-packec baguettes and other snacks – perfect fodder to take on a walk up into the hills

West of town, tracks head inland from Mare Longue, Le Baril, Basse-Vallé and Langevin, some of them running all the way up the flanks of the volcanc If you aren't keen on the idea of a major hike, the forest inland from **Mar Longue**, just west of St-Philippe, is easy to explore. Here, the forest spreads ove

ISLAND SAINT: ST-EXPÉDIT

St-Expédit is a relative newcomer to the world c sainthood and probably reached such heights mor through folklore than by holy deeds. He started out as Roman soldier, was made a martyr for his Christian belief and was revered in Germany and France for his power t produce fast solutions. In the 1930s, those powers wer put to the test when a Réunionnais woman keen to leav Marseilles prayed that a boat would appear to take he home. Whether or not it was thanks to convenient sailin schedules, she soon arrived clutching a statue of St Expédit, and his reputation for prompt action spread.

In the 1960s, blood-red shrines to St-Expédit appeare in cemeteries and caves, along the roadsides and besid statues of the Virgin Mary. Viewed with suspicion by th Catholic clergy, St-Expédit has achieved cult statu because many locals call upon him to do good or harm

The biggest shrine is at Mare Longue at St-Philippe i the south, but there are more than 300 elsewher containing burned-down candles, flowers, fruit o cigarettes as inducements to expedite a problem or t thank St-Expédit for his intervention. Some shrines contai beheaded statues, presumably the work of unhappy locals but most bizarre are those draped in underwear.

About 4 km (2½ miles) south of St-Leu along the Avirons road is **Stella Matutina** (open Tues–Sun 9.30am–5.30pm; entrance fee; tel: 0262 34 16 24), a former sugar factory and now a fascinating museum devoted to the history of sugar production and agriculture on the island. If you aren't interested in all the machinery, you can take refuge in the history room hung with original maps and oil paintings of sugar barons.

Kelonia (formerly known as Ferme Corail; tel: 0262 34 81 10), 2 km (1 mile) north of St-Leu on the RN1, reopened in 2007 following major refurbishment as a research and educational centre for the study of hawksbill and green turtles. Guided visits include turtle spotting in large tanks, but the centre itself is of historic significance since it is home to two of the oldest lime kilns in Réunion. Be aware that although commercial breeding of turtles was banned in 1998, you may still find turtle products on sale, which manufacturers claim were produced before the ban.

Virtually opposite the Kelonia, the D12 runs uphill to Les Colimaçons and the **Conservatoire Botanique Jardin de Mascarin** (open Tues–Sun 9am–5pm; entrance fee; tel: 0262 24 92 27). This magnificent outdoor museum, which contains 4,000 botanical species, offers an insight into Réunion's remarkable flora and is landscaped into themed gardens of rare indigenous and endemic plants, plants introduced by early settlers, a collection of palm trees, an orchard of local fruits and an eye-popping enclosure of cacti. But the pièce de résistance is the 19th-century villa, fully restored and filled with colonial furniture. You can also visit the stables, hunting lodge and the old family kitchen, which now serves as a cafeteria. Next door to the gardens is the church of Les Colimaçons, which offers spectacular views over the reef-fringed coastline.

To reach St-Gilles-les-Bains, you can choose between the winding inland route via St-Gilles-les Hauts (and the fascinating Musée de Villèle: *see page 214*), and the faster coastal route.

Map on pages 202–3

The beach stretch

St-Gilles-les-Bains ⓴, dubbed the "St-Tropez of the Indian Ocean", is the hub of Réunion's holiday scene, attracting hordes of local and French holidaymakers. This is the best place on the island in which to soak up the sun, enjoy all the pleasure of the sea, or just lie back and recover from a hard mountain trek. If that's all too sedate, then plenty of canyoning and paragliding operators are on hand to book the jump of a lifetime down Réunion's ravines and gorges. At night, the restaurants, bars and clubs that line – and spill on to – Rue Général de Gaulle come alive. The cast of characters, from old-fashioned hippies to trendy young locals, is attracted by the blend of Gallic chic and creole insouciance that oozes from the restaurants and bars.

One reason St-Gilles' broad, sloping beach is so popular is that it has white, albeit rather coarse, sand. The focus of activity is north of the Ravine St-Gilles: it is here that most people gather to watch the sunset, something of a local tradition. South of the ravine, the beach is not so nice but more peaceful – backed by holiday homes and *pensions* rather than loud bars and restaurants. The port in the mouth of the ravine is packed

BELOW: heading for the beach.

with boats belonging to game fishing and scuba diving operators. Half a dozen game fishing boats depart on day trips to hook blue marlin, sailfish, tuna and sea bream; October to May is the best time. If you're a first-time diver, enquire at Bleu Marine Réunion (tel: 0262 24 22 00), which also offers special packages for children.

Loulou's bakery is a local institution.

If you have a car, park first and then walk to the beach, which is hidden from view by the shops and restaurants along Rue Général de Gaulle. Parking is not always easy, though. There are a couple of small car parks on Rue Général de Gaulle, but they are often full. A good place is the patch of ground just before the bridge crosses the ravine.

Just five minutes' drive north of St-Gilles-les-Bains, **Boucan Canot ㉑** is a smarter, smaller and more laid-back resort than its neighbour. Unlike St-Gilles, most of Boucan Canot's cafés and restaurants are by the beach, so it's easier to potter off for a drink or snack in between stints on the sand. The sandy beach is clean but small, and can get crowded at weekends. Drivers should note that the main drag is one-way (north to south), and that the only place to park is either at the north or south end of the seafront.

A glimpse of times past

The **Musée de Villèle ㉒** (open Tues–Sun 9.30am–noon, 2–5pm; guided tours; tel: 0262 55 64 10) in St-Gilles-les-Hauts is the former family seat of the Desbassyns dynasty. Built in 1787, the house's most famous resident was Madame Desbassyns, a coffee and sugar producer and notorious matriarch, who is said to have inflicted horrific punishments on her slaves. The colonial mansion now houses memorabilia and family portraits, maps of slave ship routes and fine

Below:
body surfers at
St-Gilles-les-Bains.

(2,070 metres/6,973 ft) from where there are absolutely staggering views of the huge ravine of **Rivière des Remparts**. From these heights, the river appears as a thin pencil line flowing southwards to St-Joseph. A challenging Grande Randonnée (GR) trail runs along the banks of the river from the coast and links up with the RF5 just beyond the Nez de Boeuf viewpoint; the 30-km (18-mile) trek is rather easier north to south than vice versa.

Next stop is **Cratère Commerson ⓓ**, where an observation platform perches over a 120-metre (380-ft) deep crater, a few paces from the road. The extinct crater, named after French botanist, Phillibert Commerson, who discovered it by accident in 1771, is a dramatic sight. Most breathtaking of all, however, are the views across the crater's 200-metre (650-ft) diameter towards the jagged ridge of Cilaos cirque.

However, the view that is likely to remain etched on your memory for longest is the one from the top of the Rempart des Sables ridge where the road begins its dramatic descent into the **Plaine des Sables ⓔ**. An information board describes the landscape that spreads below you – an utter wilderness of raw beauty and incredible wide-angle views of corroded lava, ground by the elements into fine black gravel and restrained by massive mountain ramparts and distant peaks. As the road descends across the eerie reddish-brown landscape, pockmarked with bizarre rock formations, the only signs of life are sparse bushes of gorse, heather and lichen and a trail of moving cars, before it climbs briefly to end at the parking area at Pas de Bellecombe. The track across the Plaine des Sables is unpaved but smooth and easy to follow; even so, drive slowly to avoid skidding, and be particularly careful in wet conditions.

A walk around earth's fire

Pas de Bellecombe is also the starting point of several walking routes to and around Piton de la Fournaise. In an unmanned shelter by the car park a few displays provide information on the geology and fauna and flora of the area. Most useful, however, is the relief model of the volcano which shows the routes (and distances) of the various walking trails. You don't really need a map for the more well-trodden circuits, such as Pas de Bellecombe to Cratère Dolomieu, but for more involved trekking you should invest in the IGN 1:25,000 series map 4406RT Piton de la Fournaise. You can buy this at the Maison de la Montagne et de la Mer in St-Denis, or pick it up at the Maison du Volcan in Bourg-Murat.

There is also a list of rules for walkers. The most important ones to heed are a) don't go alone, b) tell someone where you have gone and c) take water and food. The only refreshments and toilets in this remote spot are found at the **Gîte du Volcan**, about 10 minutes' walk along a path from the car park. If you're driving, the track to the *gîte* branches left off the main track just before you reach the car park.

For the full experience you should consider doing the 13-km (8-mile) circuit, a "medium" classified trek, which takes about four and a half hours. (Alternatively, you could choose to do just part of the route; for example, the return walk to Formica Léo takes

Map on page 218

BELOW: spectacular views across Commerson crater.

TIP

To witness a volcanic sunrise, make an overnight booking for the Gîte du Volcan (tel: 0262 21 28 96), a short walk away from Pas de Bellecombe. Lovely topiaried gardens provide cool comfort and you can order drinks and snacks with mountain vistas thrown in for free. Book through the Maison de la Montagne et de la Mer in St-Denis (tel: 0262 90 78 78).

BELOW: eerie moonscape of the Plaine des Sables.

about 40 minutes). Make sure you pack some energy-giving snacks and plenty of water. Provided you don't wander off the marked paths, heed the danger warning signs and wear the right clothes, you can't go wrong.

A stepped pathway winds its way down the 200-metre (650-ft) cliff to the bottom. On the way down take a good look at the plants that grow on the cliff face – beyond there is nothing but layers of lava from across the ages decorated with splodges of white paint that mark the entire route. The first landmark on the volcanic floor is the rather undramatic scoria cone of **Formica Léo ❻**. From here the path continues about 2 km (1 mile) to **Chapelle de Rosemont**, a hollow volcanic mound which looks like a small cathedral complete with a door and window – hence the name. This is a good place to rest and decide which of the two available paths you want to take. For the more strenuous route take the right-hand fork, which will lead you directly up a steep slope to the extinct 2,632-metre (8,636-ft) high **Cratère Bory ❼**. Caution should be taken on the potentially unstable paths. The left-hand fork leads you to an easier route that snakes gently northwards along the contours of the volcano to **La Soufrière** (2,530 metres/8,300 ft), the northern wall of the active **Cratère Dolomieu ❽**; you can normally smell sulphur emissions here. There is another choice of routes here: one carries on along the rim of both Dolomieu and Bory before heading back to Pas de Bellecombe; the other, shorter route cuts straight across to Cratère Bory.

There is a whole series of other walks to do. One of the easiest is the 9-km (5½-mile) walk north along the rim from Pas de Bellecombe to **Nez Coupé de St- Rose** and back. Another is the 8-km (5-mile) circular route from the Rempart des Sables to **Morne Langevin** – you should allow about three hours for this relatively easy but scenic route.

A BIRD'S-EYE VIEW

Réunion's scenery is awe-inspiring whatever angle you look at it from, but the aerial views you get from a helicopter of Piton de la Fournaise, and the Cirque de Salazie and Cirque de Mafate (see following chapter), are hard to beat. These tours may be expensive, but they are worth every euro. Pilots fly in and out of deep ravines and hover precariously over isolated hamlets and the cirques, allowing plenty of time for photographs, before heading east to the volcano.

Depending on weather conditions helicopters, seating up to eight passengers, take off at 7am, 8.15am and 9.30am. The price includes transfer from your hotel, individual headphones and commentary (in French). You should try to book at least 72 hours in advance since these flights are extremely popular.

Hélilagon (tel: 0262 55 55 55) fly over the entire island from Roland Garros Airport or from l'Eperon heliport near St-Paul for €285 per person. Corail Helicopters (tel: 0262 22 66) operate a 25-minute flight from Pierrefonds Airport to the volcano for €180. Individual tailor-made trips, ideal for professional photographers, can be organised through Felix ULM (Base ULM de Cambaie, St-Paul; tel: 0262 43 02 59) in specially equipped two-seater microlights.

Among the other much longer routes you could opt for, are treks along sections of the Grande Randonnée R2, which crosses the island (IGN 1:25,000 series map 4406RT Piton de la Fournaise). One of these follows the southern edge of the volcano to **Nez Coupé du Tremblet** before descending to Pointe du Tremblet on the east coast. Another heads south from Pas de Bellecombe on the GR2, across the so-called Plateau de Foc Foc to link up with the **Vallée Heureuse** and the Gîte de Basse Vallée, before continuing all the way to the town of Basse Vallée on the coast.

Map on pages 202/3, 218

Not so plain plains

The High Plains (Hautes Plaines) that separate Piton de la Fournaise and the three cirques may lack volcano-style drama but are still well worth exploring. Centred around La Plaine-des-Palmistes (named after the palm trees that no longer grow there) and La Plaine-des-Cafres in the west, these upland areas reveal magnificent mist-enshrouded forests, waterfalls, lakes and mountains: in short, perfect terrain for tranquil walks, scenic drives and more active pursuits such as horse riding and mountain biking. The route described below runs in a north–south direction from the coast. A number of villages on the way, such as Le Vingt-Troisième (23rd) and Le Dix-Neuvième (19th) have been named unimaginatively after their distance in kilometres from the sea, but at least they're handy landmarks.

From St-Benoît, the RN3 meanders through sugar cane fields before hitting a series of switchbacks that lead to a viewpoint at **L'Echo ㉔**, which offers fine views north towards the coast and the ocean. Before the road winds up to L'Echo, about 12 km (8 miles) from St-Benoît a track runs 6 km (4 miles) west

Gorse, heather and lichen are the only plants to sprout from the black earth.

BELOW: at the rim of the Formica Léo.

Mountain gîtes dotted around the interior provide basic accommodation for walkers, but book in advance.

BELOW: hosing down the horses after a day's trek.

to **Grand-Etang** ㉕, a lake in a most stunning spot at the foot of an awesome ridge. To prolong the pleasure, you can follow the path right around the shores of the lake; there's a waterfall just off the path near the southern shore.

Beyond L'Echo, 20 km (12 miles) from St Benoît, you hit **Le Premier Village** ㉖, often referred to as **La Plaine-des-Palmistes**, a popular holiday retreat, particularly in January and February. Even so, the area remains a comparatively untouched agricultural heartland where the red-berried goyavier fruit has become so important that every summer there is a festival in its honour. Attractive wooden houses are very characteristic of this area; you'll see them featured on postcards and posters. La Plaine-des-Palmistes is a centre of operations and you may want to stop here to make use of the tourist office in Rue de la République which can supply details of accommodation and walks, ranging from gentle to strenuous, in and around the forests of Bébour *(see page 223)*.

Horse riding and forest walking

To the northeast of Le Premier Village, a dozen gentle Merens horses wait at the **Ferme Equestre du Grand Etang** (RN3 Pont-Payet; tel: 0262 50 90 03), to take even the most inexperienced rider for a pleasant half-day's trek. A morning with Rico Nourro, a former farmer who turned his love of the outdoors into a going concern, should not be missed. His enthusiasm is infectious as he leads groups of riders along rocky narrow pathways to the stunning lake of Grand-Etang where the horses take a break and splash about in the cool water. The trek takes you along a nature trail, passing through a garden of traditional medicinal herbs and citrus orchards where you can help yourself to fruit without getting out of the saddle. Rico believes in giving all his clients a hands-on experience,

ing the centre of the three cirques. To the south, Col du Taibit (2,082 metres/ 6,832 ft) and the peak of Le Grand Bénare (2,896 metres/9,499 ft) divide Mafate and Cilaos cirques, providing another stunning spectacle. You can hike along the rim of the cirque to Le Grand Bénare, but it's tough going, and you'll need to allow six–seven hours to do the return trip.

Map on page 226

For gentler walking, or a place to keep the kids happy, stop at **Parc du Maido** (open daily 9am–5pm; entrance fee; tel: 0262 32 52 52), a recreational centre about 15 minutes downhill from the viewpoint. You can go mountain biking or pony trekking through the tamarind forests, which are dotted with picnic sites, or stay put and try your hand at archery.

Easy-going Salazie

The name Salazie comes from the Malagasy word *salazane*, which means a "stake" or "post", and probably stems from the three peaks of Le Gros Morne, which stand like sentries at the far southwestern corner of the cirque. The first European settler, a certain Monsieur Cazeau, lived in a home-made hut and made a name for himself by surviving on nothing but pumpkins during a 43-day period of rain. "When it rains at Salazie," noted one visitor in 1863, "it does rain…in a steady, business-like European way."

The ultimate high – paragliding over the Cirque de Mafate.

It still rains in Salazie, making it the most verdant of the cirques. These days the 25 villages carry on the farming traditions introduced in the 1840s, growing watercress, tobacco, coffee beans, apples and an abundance of *chou chou*. The lime green, pear-shaped vegetable *(see page 177)* is fêted each May in a three-day carnival that attracts many visitors to the colourful stalls groaning with local produce. It's a jolly affair with local music groups and a Miss Chou Chou contest.

BELOW: the cirques are strewn with isolated hamlets.

It does not take long, having left St-André behind on the coast, to get a taste of Salazie as you enter the luxuriant, tree-clad gorge of Rivière du Mât, where soaring peaks and dozens of pencil-thin waterfalls fill the space above you. Some of the latter are mere trickles of water – but not the **Voile de la Mariée ❸** or "Bride's Veil", which positively cascades into the Rivière du Mât just beyond the village of Salazie. If you're driving take advantage of the handful of stopping places along the route to admire the scenery safely. The road is winding but mostly flat as far as Salazie; after that the climb is virtually continuous. There isn't much to Salazie, though it has a few shops and places to eat, and also a tourist office (in the *mairie*). For breakfast on the hoof, you can pick up freshly baked brioches, croissants and pastries at the *boulangerie* in Rue Père Boiteau.

Close to the Voile de la Mariée, the D52 branches off west and snakes for 34 km (21 miles) through the heart of the cirque to **Grand-Ilet ❹**, a hamlet overshadowed by the peak of La Roche Ecrite. This is a base for treks into Mafate cirque, and has a handful of cheap *chambres d'hôtes*. Most walks kick off from **Le Bélier**, a hamlet 3 km (2 miles) south of Grand-Ilet (accessible by road), and follow the GR1 and GR2; one route penetrates south into Cilaos cirques *(for details on long treks, see pages 186–7)*. Alternatively, you can carry straight on to Hell-Bourg, a 30-minute

Decorative open-fronted extensions, known as guetalis, *are a common feature of traditional creole houses.*

winding drive above Salazie. There are two stunning viewpoints worth stopping at – one at **Mare à Poule d'Eau**, and the other at **Le Point du Jour**, just at the entrance of Hell-Bourg, at 892 metres (2,926 ft). La Roche Ecrite is right in front of you and you can see Le Bélier up in the hills to the left.

Delightful Hell-Bourg

Hell-Bourg ❺ – named after a certain Governor de Hell rather than the domain of sinners – is a slow-paced, delightful village and a pleasant place in which to spend a couple of days. There are several things to see inside and just outside the town, and walkers can join up with the GR1 here, too. To cater for the steady flow of visitors, Hell-Bourg has a handful of small hotels, and there are a few small food shops and restaurants on the main street, **Rue Général de Gaulle**, as well as a helpful tourist office (tel: 0262 47 89 89).

There are some lovely creole houses in Hell-Bourg, some of them brightly painted and with luxuriant gardens shaded by bamboo, orange trees and ferns like parasols. Note in particular the decorative little kiosks known as *guetalis*: strategically placed at the edge of gardens overlooking the street, they allowed the occupants to watch passers-by without being seen themselves. The name comes from the French verb *guetter*, which means "to watch out for" or "look at".

For a close look at a traditional home, visit **Villa Folio** (open 9am–11.30am, 2–5pm for guided tours; entrance fee; tel: 0262 47 80 98), almost hidden among its lush gardens opposite the church in Rue Amiral Lacaze. Built in 1870, the tiny villa belongs to Jean-François Folio, a descendant of Réunion's earliest settlers. The house is typical of the times and offers a rare insight into creole life, when much of one's time was spent on the verandah. The two small pavilions at the back used to be the kitchen and servants' quarters and a *guetali* that served as a reception area for friends who'd drop by for drinks made from the local rum and spices. The house contains original furniture, including a 19th-century English four-poster bed complete with canopy – hijacked, so the story goes, from an East India ship by corsairs.

The discovery of medicinal springs near Hell-Bourg, in 1831, drew the sick to its healing waters for over a century. A landslide in 1948 reduced them to ruins which you can see today by taking a pleasant 15-minute walk west of the defunct Hôtel des Salazes (a former military hospital), in Chemin du Cimetière.

Some of the casualties of the landslide were buried in the **Cemetery**, at the north end of Chemin du Cimetière. This is perhaps the most picturesque cemetery on the island, framed by luxuriant bamboo and verdant cliffs behind. Hidden among the graves of settlers, soldiers and aristocrats is a grey mound of rock with a simple iron cross, said to contain the headless corpse of a Mr Zett, a bandit and rapist, who terrorised the area in the early 1900s. To ensure he would not rise again he was decapitated and his head despatched to St-Denis *(see page 200)*. Glasses of rum and cigarettes are sometimes placed around the grave to appease what's left of him.

If you'd rather hook a trout than a lost soul, follow the signs to **Parc Piscicole d'Hell-Bourg** (open daily

BELOW: the picturesque cemetery at Hell-Bourg.

Map on page 226

8am–6pm; tel: 0262 47 80 16), near the Relais des Cimes Hotel. This freshwater trout farm provides bait and line, and you can have your catch cooked to order in the restaurant. For more active pursuits head for the waterfalls at **Les Trois Cascades**, about 1 km (½ mile) south of Hell-Bourg, which provide ideal conditions for canyoning. And if hanging on a rope in a wet-suit in the thundering crash of a waterfall doesn't set your pulse racing, have a go at white-water rafting and career at breakneck speed to a calm lagoon.

For the best views of Salazie cirque, head northwest out of town along the D48 towards **Ilet à Vidot**. Rising to 1,352 metres (4,436 ft) from the centre of the cirque is the hump-shaped **Piton d'Enchaing ❻**. You can follow a very challenging section of the GR1 to the peak either from Hell-Bourg or Ilet à Vidot, but take plenty of supplies. You'll need to allow at least five hours to go there and back from Hell-Bourg. A more popular trek is south to the top of **Piton des Neiges ❼**. The best option is to stay overnight at the Gîte de la Caverne Dufour, and then head on up to the summit first thing, before the clouds have descended *(see page 187)*.

Cirque de Cilaos

Cilaos is named after a runaway slave called Tsilaos, from the Malagasy *tsy laosana*, meaning "the place one never leaves" – and you probably won't want to after you've negotiated the 262 hairpin bends along the RN5, the only access road from St-Louis on the south coast. Following the course of the Rivière Bras de Cilaos, the RN5 climbs steadily to the entrance to the cirque at **Le Pavillon**. Early travellers were confined to palanquins as the only means of transport to continue their journey beyond Le Pavillon, along narrow roads which at each twist and turn open up new vistas of cloud-capped mountains and isolated villages dotted along the deep ravines.

The town of **Cilaos ❽**, at 1,220 metres (4,000 ft), is similar in many ways to the French alpine resort of Chamonix, its twin town. It's an excellent starting point for hikes and walks, with a few things to entertain you in the town itself.

Cilaos' 6,000 inhabitants are mainly the descendants of 19th-century settlers from Normandy and Brittany, who dreamed up evocative names for the peaks that surrounded them, including Les Trois Dents de Salazes (Salazie's Three Teeth) or Le Bonnet de Prêtre (The Priest's Bonnet). These days, the local people make a living through tourism and farming, though the area is also known for its embroidery, wine and lentils.

In **Rue Père Boiteau** in the town centre there are some beautifully restored bijou creole houses: notable examples include a pink and grey house called Soledad, across the road from the Stamm pharmacy; the salmon-pink, 80-year-old restaurant called Chez Noé (which serves good goat massala curry); and Cilaos' oldest house, painted in blue and white.

Worth visiting is the **Musee du Peuplement** (Settlers' Museum; open Mon–Sat 10am–noon, 2.30–6.30pm, Sun 9.30–11.30am, 1.30–4.30pm; entrance fee; tel: 0262 31 88 01). Allow an hour for a guided tour of this fascinating museum, which will introduce you to the first settlers' way of life and illustrate the plight of runaway slaves.

BELOW: the spa resort of Cilaos, also a good base for hikers.

The Cilaos red is a sweetish, full-bodied table wine made from the Cot grape.

Ever since **thermal springs** *(thermes)* were discovered in 1819 by a goathunter, Cilaos has been a health resort attracting the sick and infirm, who would make the long journey up from the coast. In 1948, a cyclone destroyed the springs but the **Etablissement Thermal d'Irenée-Accot** is still active (Route de Bras Sec; open daily 8am–noon, 2–5pm; closed Wed pm and in June; tel: 0262 31 72 27). Whether you've got digestive problems, rheumatism or arthritis, the waters from the same thermal springs can help put it right. If you're after sheer indulgence, or a restorative after a long trek, treat yourself to a sauna or massage, have a work-out in the gym and then flake out in the jacuzzi.

The best places to buy the local wine are Cilaos and nearby Bras Sec. Locals sell cheap bottles of Cilaos wine along the roadside, but it is often of inferior quality. Export-quality wine produced and bottled under hygienic conditions can be bought at the **Chaie de Cilaos** in Bras Sec (34 Rue des Glycines; open Mon–Fri 9am–noon, 1.30–4pm; entrance fee; tel: 0262 31 79 69), where you can also learn about local wine-making methods and enjoy a wine-tasting session. Modern methods using stainless steel vats are used, but the process of pressing, fermenting and bottling in makeshift cellars has not changed in years.

Many of the area's skilled embroiderers work from home and are concentrated in **Palmiste Rouge**, south of Cilaos on the CD240, but a handful come to work at the **Maison de la Broderie** (open Mon–Sat 9am–noon, 2–5pm, Sun 9am–noon; entrance fee; tel: 0262 31 77 48) in Rue des Ecoles, which was founded in 1953 by the sisters of Notre-Dame-des-Neiges. A large number of the designs originated in Brittany, but today workers struggle to keep up traditional procedures and patterns *(see Travel Tips, Activities).*

BELOW:
threshing lentils.

Stretching your legs

The tourist office is at 2 Rue Mac-Auliffe (open Mon–Sat 8.30am–12.30pm, 1.30–5.30pm, Sun and public hols 9am–1pm; tel: 0262 31 71 71), where evening slide shows are held followed by wine tasting. Here you'll find every map and walking plan imaginable and details of accommodation and adventure sports available in the cirques, as well as a huge relief map of the whole island. And if you have ever wondered what a palanquin looks like, there's an original one on display.

For one of the most straightforward walks from Cilaos, requiring four hours for the return trip, turn left at Route de Bras Sec and follow the signs north to **Roche Merveilleuse**. (It is also possible to drive along the RF11.) No real effort is needed to climb the rock and the views from the summit are great. From left to right you will see the village of Bras Sec, perched on a plateau overlooking the cirque, followed by Palmiste Rouge and Ilet à Cordes where the best lentils are grown. Access to the Roche Merveilleuse is through the **Forêt du Grand Matarum**, noted for the local *tamarins-des-hauts*, Japanese cryptomerias and Réunion's only oak trees. Marked paths weave through the forest.

For a more ambitious hike, head west to Marla in the cirque of Mafate *(see page 187)*, which is more easily reached from Cilaos than anywhere else. Other possible walks from the town are along the GR2 to Bras Sec and beyond to Palmiste Rouge.

In the area around the hamlets of **Îlet Fleurs Jaunes** and **Îlets du Bois Rouge** canyoning is the latest craze. The sport is enough to scare the pants off you as you abseil off cliffs into water-filled gorges, but at least a guide goes with you, and life-jackets, harnesses, helmets and jump suits are provided. ❑

Map on page 226

BELOW: freshly painted houses and flower-filled gardens give Cilaos an alpine feel.

SEYCHELLES

The islands' reputation as a tropical paradise is well earned

and preserving the environment is a crucial concern

The Seychelles islands are the oldest ocean islands on earth – a micro-continent that was isolated millions of years ago, evolving its own flora and fauna, from which man, and indeed all land mammals, were absent. Seychelles' human history began just a few hundred years ago. In 1609 a small landing party of English sailors made the first recorded landing in Seychelles. They had left England in March the year before, and sailed past the Cape, through the Mozambique channel, calling in at the Comores and Pemba, north of Zanzibar. They stumbled upon Seychelles by accident, but were glad they did. The boatswain, one Mr Jones *(see box page 245)*, declared the islands "an earthly Paradise".

Seychellois are proud of their spectacular country, and happy to share it with visitors. They have a certain reserve on first acquaintance, but when relaxed are incredibly warm and generous. They love to talk, make music and create delicious creole dishes, and throw open their homes and the bounty of their table to those they come to know.

This is a young nation, dealing with the inevitable problems a small and isolated island population faces when struggling to keep up with the outside world. The characteristic "mañana" syndrome is in some conflict with the need to modernise and perform to the standards of a faster, busier world beyond the coral beaches.

But it's precisely this relaxed attitude to life that appeals to visitors who come here in search of a stress-free environment and unrivalled natural beauty. If all you want out of your holiday is sun, sea and sand, there are other, cheaper tropical destinations. But if you are prepared to pay extra to enjoy unique flora and fauna and loll on some of the best beaches in the world, look no further. Many changes to the landscape have occurred since 1609, but there are so many beauty spots that still fit Bo's'n Jones' definition of "an earthly Paradise". ❑

PRECEDING PAGES: gaily painted wood, a splash of Seychelles colour to take home; St Pierre Islet, off Praslin; red-footed boobies on Cosmoledo, in the Outer Islands. **LEFT:** local fisherman, Mahé.

THE ORIGIN OF SEYCHELLES

An Indian Ocean Atlantis, Seychelles has the oldest
and only granitic ocean islands in the world

The Seychelles islands can be divided into five main groups: the granitic islands, the Amirantes, the Alphonse Group, the Farquhar Group and the Aldabra Group. The 40 islands that make up the granitic group are the world's only ocean islands built from the stuff of continents. All other isolated ocean islands

are made up of coralline or volcanic rocks, both of which have grown out of the ocean. The main islands of Seychelles are different. Their rocks have never been completely submerged. They were formed from material ejected from deep within the fabric of the earth some 750 million years ago, perhaps in a frozen, lifeless wasteland close to the South Pole.

For millennia, the rocks of Seychelles were a part of Pangaea, the ancient super-continent that once encompassed all the world's land masses. Some 200 million years ago, the forces of continental drift tore Pangaea apart. It split into Laurasia (modern Europe, Asia and North America) to the north and Gondwanaland

(South America, Africa, Antarctica, Australasia and the Indian subcontinent) to the south. Seychelles at this time lay near the point where Madagascar, India and Africa were linked.

As the process of continental drift continued, about 125 million years ago, Madagascar, Seychelles and India broke away as one land mass. Madagascar became an island around 90 million years ago, drifting away with its own unique assemblage of wildlife. Then 65 million years ago, Seychelles drifted from the western coast of India.

It may not be pure coincidence that the birth of the world's only oceanic fragments of continental rock coincided with the death of dinosaurs. There are many dinosaur extinction theories. Many scientists believe that their disappearance was caused by the earth's collision with a comet that struck the Yucatan Peninsula in Mexico, sending shock waves through the globe and triggering volcanic activity at the opposite side of the earth. A second theory suggests that a vast comet broke up on entering the earth's atmosphere, major fragments of which hit the Yucatan, and 12 hours later, as the earth turned, struck the Indian ocean. Other scientists believe that extinction was not instantaneous, but the result of an extensive period of volcanic activity in western India, close to the point where Seychelles was once attached to the subcontinent.

Isolated in mid-ocean, this new microcontinent was one land mass, covering an area of around 300,000 sq km (116,000 sq miles) — roughly the size of Britain and Ireland combined. Today, all that remains are the peaks of the highest mountains. The combined forces of erosion, sea level change and the sheer weight of coral growth (forming what geologists term a carbonate platform) have submerged all but 250 sq km (100 sq miles) of granite, less than one thousandth of its original extent, creating the archipelago we see today.

Though superficially similar to the other granitic islands, Silhouette and North Island are younger and made up largely of a type of volcanic rock called syenite. Silhouette was born rapidly and dramatically, the result of an eruption that probably occurred on land. Limited outcrops above the surface today make it difficult to determine with certainty, but it is probable that the volcano's crater lies southeast of La Passe, now almost entirely eroded away and submerged. This volcano erupted many times and Silhouette may have towered 3,000 metres (10,000 ft) or more at one time. At Pointe Zeng Zeng, you can see the only volcanic ash above sea level in Seychelles, while fingers of basalt reach out from the island to Mahé and can be seen at Glacis and elsewhere.

The Amirantes is a linear chain of coral islands and atolls that rises no more than 3 metres (10 ft) above sea level. Volcanoes once rose out of the ocean, but as they died and were reclaimed by the sea, coral growth maintained contact with the surface. Farquhar Atoll, south of Seychelles, must also have witnessed volcanic activity at one time. It is believed that while the granitic group was a micro-continent, Farquhar may have been a nano-continent (a tiny fragment of continent).

Aldabra, Assumption, Cosmoledo and Astove in the southwestern corner of Seychelles are different again. These islands of the Aldabra group

On the edge of the Seychelles Bank lie the much younger islands of Bird and Denis, thought to have emerged about 4,000 years ago when the sea level dropped as a result of a change in ocean currents. These currents stirred the waters causing a shift in the average local sea levels. Mahé's sea level, for example, is now 5 metres (16 ft) below the level in southern India. It is thought that the sea level change that revealed Bird and Denis exposed the Amirantes group at the same time.

are raised coral islands. In fact Aldabra is the largest raised atoll in the world. Unlike the usual low-lying coral atolls, they rise to up to 8 metres (27 ft) above sea level. This appears to go against the conventional wisdom that the volcanic basement of coral atolls is contracting and sinking. However, it may not be so much that the land has risen, rather that the sea level has fallen.

The cycle continues today. The biggest fear is that global warming and the rise in sea levels may spell disaster for low-lying coral islands. Signs of beach erosion can be seen throughout Seychelles and nowhere more than in the coral islands, which could disappear if present trends continue. ❑

LEFT: Aldabra channel.
ABOVE: geologists are still trying to work out the precise origins of Farquhar Atoll.

Decisive Dates

EARLY DISCOVERERS

851 Arab traders probably visit Seychelles. An Arab manuscript of this date refers to the "high island" beyond the Maldives.

961 Arab charts drawn up on which Seychelles referred to as Zarin (Sisters).

1502 On its way to India via Mozambique, Vasco da Gama's expedition sights the outer islands, which later became known as the Amirantes.

1609 A ship from the English East India Company trading fleet visits Mahé, making the first recorded

landing. Nevertheless, Seychelles remains un-occupied for more than 100 years.

Late 17th century Piracy is rife in the area. Pirates probably use Seychelles as a base.

FRENCH POSSESSION

1742–90 Seychelles' strategic position on the route to India arouses French and British interest. The French establish a settlement.

1742 Lazare Picault leads an expedition to chart the islands northeast of Madagascar, reporting to Mahé de Labourdonnais, the French governor of nearby Mauritius.

1744 Picault returns to Seychelles to collect more information and names the main island Mahé.

1756 Nicholas Morphey claims Mahé for France.

1770 A settlement is created on Ste Anne island.

1771 Pierre Poivre establishes a spice garden on Mahé.

1778 A 15-man garrison is established at L'Etablissement du Roi (later Victoria).

1786 The colony now comprises 24 military personnel, five civilians and 122 slaves. Its income is derived from provisioning ships. A legal system is introduced.

1790 In the wake of the French Revolution, the Seychelles settlers create a Colonial Assembly to run the colony.

THE WAR YEARS

1794–1803 Anglo–French rivalry in the region makes life difficult for the tiny colony. Seychelles becomes a haven for French corsairs. The pragmatism and smooth tongue of Commandant de Quinssy ensures Seychelles actually profits from the Napoleonic wars.

1794 First capitulation to the British signed by de Quincy. In all, it is renewed seven times.

1801 French political deportees arrive.

1803 Population comprises 215 white residents, 86 coloured residents and 1,820 slaves. Cash crops include cotton, maize, sugar and rice.

BRITISH CONTROL

1815–1901 Somewhat reluctantly, Britain assumes control of Seychelles. Still subservient to Mauritius, the colony declines until the arrival of liberated Africans boosts the economy.

1815 Seychelles ceded to Britain by Treaty of Paris.

1818 The population of 7,500 prospers from the cultivation of cotton.

1822 Price of cotton falls. Many planters return to Mauritius.

1835 Slavery is abolished.

1840 The population reaches 5,400. The first coconut plantations are established.

1841 L'Etablissement is renamed Victoria.

1860s Coconut oil is almost the sole export.

1861 Arrival of first of 2,500 liberated Africans.

1862 An avalanche of mud lands on Victoria. At least 70 people are killed.

1875 Ex-Sultan of Perak arrives, first of many political prisoners exiled here by Britain.

1880 General Gordon visits and suggests Seychelles was the Garden of Eden.

1891 Vanilla becoming an important cash crop. Other exports include copra and cloves.

1901 The population reaches 19,000.

substantial help from both superpowers without having to commit himself to either.

There were several attempts to oust René by force. The most dramatic of these took place in November 1981, when 50 mercenaries arrived on a Royal Air Swazi flight posing as a charitable organisation bringing toys for local orphaned children. Beneath the toys, however, hidden in secret compartments of their luggage, were guns and ammunition. The mercenaries were led by "Mad Mike" Hoare, whose previous exploits had included installing Mobutu as president of Zaire. They passed undetected through customs, until an official discovered a bunch of bananas in the case of a French tourist, the only non-mercenary on the plane. The importation of fresh fruit into Seychelles is illegal and the customs officers decided to give the luggage of the last two passengers a more thorough check. On discovery of a gun, all hell broke out. The mercenaries took over the airport and after a shoot-out escaped to South Africa in a hijacked plane, where they were promptly arrested. Mancham maintained that the plot had nothing to do with him, and commented wryly that the coup "had been foiled by a bunch of bananas".

Mancham remained in exile in London for 15 years. In 1992, with the resumption of multiparty democracy, he returned and rivalry between the DP, as it was now known, and the SPPF, resumed. In 1993 the first multi-party presidential election since independence in 1976 was held. But it was René who triumphed with 59 percent of the votes cast.

Meanwhile, a third force was emerging. At the 1998 elections, the Seychelles National Party (SNP) gained more votes than the DP, but still fell short of the number of votes cast for the SPPF. Once again René was elected president of the Seychelles Republic. René managed to get re-elected for a third time at snap presidential elections held in August 2001. Mancham and his DP party declined to stand at this election but Wavel Ramkalawan of the SNP doubled his share of the vote. At the next National Assembly elections in December 2002, SPPF took 22 seats, while SNP took 11. Mancham's DP, however, received just 3 percent of the vote and was wiped out. In 2003, René announced

his retirement and James Michel his successor as president of Seychelles.

Just as Quincy had done centuries earlier, Albert René used craft and guile to steer a course through the changes taking place in the world. Both have left their indelible marks as they led their small country through times of great change.

Seychelles today

Modern-day Seychelles is a middle-income country with low unemployment and a good standard of living. Carefully controlled tourism and tuna fishing, industries virtually non-existent a generation ago, dominate the

economy. With such a small population, the benefits of these sources of income have been profound. The traditional agricultural way of life is now just a distant memory of the older generation. Old habits such as washing clothes in streams and walking with heavy loads on the head are disappearing, replaced by the use of washing machines and cars.

The future remains uncertain, with an economy based on two industries that can be fickle. A severe shortage of foreign exchange also clouds the horizon and the government has struggled to balance its budget. Nevertheless, Seychelles is a prosperous nation and appears destined to remain so. ❏

LEFT: Victoria clock tower in 1856.
RIGHT: pro-Mancham election poster.

time, Mauritius, Réunion and Seychelles developed their own accents and patterns of speech. Today, despite the inevitable local differences, all the islanders can generally understand each other's forms of Kreol. *(For more information on language, see page 23 and the box on page 258. A list of useful Kreol words and phrases appears on page 377.)*

Religion

Most Seychellois are Roman Catholics. Going to church is a social event, as well as a spiritual occasion, and an opportunity to get dressed up. The women compete in their colourful outfits,

Pentecostals and Jehovah's Witnesses. In Victoria, there is a Hindu temple and an Islamic mosque, while in recent years, the Bahá'í faith has become quite popular.

Family relationships

The Seychellois have a relaxed approach to marriage. It is common practice for couples to *kantmenm zot an menage*, in other words live together informally, often producing large families. It is not unusual for a man to drift away (a practice known as *marse marse*), set up a new relationship and father other children. Often, in later years, the wanderer returns to

while older men wear long-sleeved white shirts as a mark of respect. You won't see anyone in shorts or skimpy beachwear, which are considered disrespectful. First holy communion is a major landmark in the life of a young Seychellois, and it is not unusual to see processions of little girls in frothy white lace dresses and formally attired little boys arriving at the cathedral in Victoria.

Other Christian sects are also represented, including Anglicans, Seventh Day Adventists,

LEFT: bicycles are an efficient form of transport for girls-about-town and policemen on the beat.
RIGHT: old couple outside their creole home.

an earlier partner, to end his days in a more committed relationship. The reunited couple may even go so far as to have an elaborate and expensive wedding, with their children as pageboys and bridesmaids.

Many households are extended families consisting of a mother with her children, usually including an adult daughter or two with their children, maybe even a granddaughter with hers. Children in such households tend to grow up with a great respect for their mothers, but less for their errant fathers, perhaps reflected in the traditional mourning period for parents: 18 to 24 months for a mother, nine to 12 months for a father.

Exorcising ghosts

Like the Malagasy people of Madagascar, the Seychellois have a healthy respect for ghosts and departed spirits, and death is treated very seriously. Modern Seychellois are perhaps no more superstitious than other peoples, but old traditions from Africa and Madagascar are still, to some extent, followed alongside Catholic rites. People still hold vigils at home for deceased loved ones, laying the body out in the best room of the house, withe the head pointing towards the mountains and the feet towards the sea. In flickering candlelight, a solemn procession of visitors, family, acquaintances and the idly curious pass by the open coffin and sprinkle the body with holy water. The closest family and friends spend the whole night beside the body, but they certainly don't sit in silence. They play cards or dominoes, and make as much noise as possible to scare evil spirits away from their loved one and prevent them from stealing the body and turning it into a *dandosya* or zombie.

Funerals have always had a huge turn-out, though sleek black hearses have now replaced the traditional handcarts that once conveyed the dead to church. A long trail of mourners follows the coffin and buses are often hired to bring the many guests to church.

GHOSTS AND SUPERSTITIONS

The Seychellois revel in a good ghost story. Certain islands are said to be haunted: Ste Anne by a cruel French woman who had a slave girl beaten to death; Long Island by a Creole girl who drowned her child; Moyenne by an eccentric Englishwoman who lived there with her dogs.

They are also renowned for their superstitions and sayings linked with good and bad luck, death and evil. It is said, for example, that bad luck will follow if you sweep the house after sunset; that a kestrel found roosting in the eaves of your house is a portent of death in the family; and that an unfamiliar call or voice in the dark should go unanswered – it could be a zombie.

Gris gris

For generations, this blend of folklore, black magic and traditional medicine played an important part in people's day to day lives. Black magicians were once quite influential people and the power of *gris gris* was greatly feared by the Roman Catholic Church and by colonial administrators, who tried to stamp it out. It certainly still goes on, but like so many traditions, it is losing the hold on people's lives it once had.

ABOVE LEFT: harvesting cinnamon.
ABOVE: "beating" an octopus.
RIGHT: playing the makalopo.

PRESERVING NATURE

The natural history of Seychelles echoes the ancient land link between Africa and Asia; much of it is still preserved in relatively pristine condition

Islands are laboratories of evolution. Nature's experiments have been going on for a longer period in Seychelles than in any other group of ocean islands, so it is no surprise that such a unique assemblage of flora and fauna should have evolved here. The roots of some species can be traced back to Africa, Madagascar, Asia and even to Australasia, originating from a time when all these land masses were linked in the supercontinent of Gondwanaland, before continental drift cast them apart.

Bats, tortoises and turtles

Seychelles was isolated in mid-ocean long before mammals appeared on earth. No mammals ever reached here by natural means except for those with the power of flight, namely the bat. Of the two endemic species, the sheath-tailed bat and the Seychelles fruit bat, the latter is by far the most common. It is one of the few creatures to have benefited from the arrival of humans and the consequent proliferation of fruit trees. Not so beneficial from the bats' point of view is the culinary speciality, curried fruit bat, a local favourite which often pops up on restaurant menus. Despite the Seychellois' taste for them, however, bats remain very common and their noisy squabbling in the trees at night is one of the islands' characteristic sounds.

With no mammals for competition, Seychelles became the last Kingdom of Reptiles. The estuarine crocodile was an early casualty of human settlement, but the giant tortoise still thrives. Aldabra has the world's largest population, with around 87,000 animals. Giant tortoises occupied islands across the Indo-Pacific for millions of years, safe from the mammals that came to dominate the continents. Their waterproof exoskeletons, their ability to survive for weeks without food and the female's inbuilt mechanism for storing sperm made them ideal candidates for ocean transport. The luck-ier ones that had been swept away by the tide from the shores of the mainland were washed up on remote tropical islands. This happened rarely enough for unique island races to evolve. Sadly, most of these are now extinct, victims of human exploitation. It was thought the granitic island form had suffered the same fate

PROTECTED AREAS

Literally 1,000 miles (1,600 km) from anywhere – India to the north, Africa to the west, Sri Lanka to the east and Madagascar to the south – the Seychelles islands were uninhabited until the late 18th century. While the natural beauty of other Indian Ocean islands was gradually destroyed, that of the Seychelles has been carefully preserved. There are many protected areas where nature lovers can marvel at unspoilt flora, fauna and marine life: the Morne Seychellois National Park, Mahé; the Vallée de Mai, Praslin; the Veuve Reserve, La Digue; and special reserves on the islands of Cousin, Aride and Aldabra.

LEFT: giant tortoise on Aldabra.
RIGHT: the Seychelles black paradise flycatcher is easily identified by its long black tail.

until the discovery of some unusual tortoises. These were brought to Silhouette by the Nature Protection Trust of Seychelles for captive breeding *(see page 312)*. It is possible that they retain some characteristics of two granite island forms of tortoise, the Seychelles giant tortoise and Arnold's tortoise. However, most scientists believe there was only one species throughout Seychelles, the Aldabra Giant Tortoise, which survives in the granitics (on Curieuse, Frégate, Cousin and Cousine included) in several intro-

CALL OF THE WILD

The call of the male Aldabra tortoise is said to be the loudest noise in the reptile kingdom. It is, in fact, a seduction technique – the actual mating is a silent affair.

to tourists. Thankfully, the authorities recognised that live turtles have a higher value, enhancing the reputation of the country while encouraging ecotourism. The sale of all tortoiseshell products is now banned.

Two species breed here – the hawksbill turtle and the green turtle. Remarkably, the granitic islands are the only place in the world where hawksbill turtles come up to breed in the daytime. Green turtles occasionally nest in the granitic islands but their stronghold is Aldabra where around 4,000

duced wild populations. Many are also kept in pens in hotel gardens, at the Botanical Gardens and elsewhere so there are plenty of opportunities to see this lovable Seychelles symbol.

Once it was traditional to present a baby tortoise to a newborn girl and raise the animal as a family pet until the girl grew up and married. The tortoise would then be slaughtered at the wedding feast. This tradition has died out, though many Seychellois still keep a few lumbering giants as pets.

Likewise, the future of turtles is slowly brightening. In the past they were slaughtered mainly for their "tortoiseshell" which was converted into jewellery and other trinkets for sale

females haul themselves ashore each year to breed. In the past, they were heavily exploited for their meat and, although poaching still poses a threat, they have escaped the near total extermination suffered elsewhere. Aldabra is one of the few places on earth where turtles, classed as among the most endangered of creatures under the Convention on International Trade in Endangered Species (CITES), are increasing in number.

Unique reptiles

For sheer quantity of reptiles, there is nowhere quite like the seabird islands of Seychelles, particularly Cousin, Cousine and Aride, which have a greater concentration of these beasts than anywhere else on earth. It is partly thanks to the seabirds that the lizards survive in such large numbers. They feed on eggs or chicks left unguarded or a catch that has been dropped. Most reptiles found here are unique to Seychelles, including the Seychelles skink, Wright's skink and several species of green gecko.

One of the characteristics of ocean islands is the absence of amphibians. Once again, Seychelles is an exception to the rule. The islands support 13 amphibian species in all, 12 of which are unique to Seychelles; one of these was described for the first time in 2002. Among the

Land and sea birds

The lure of birdwatching in Seychelles is not the number of species. You may see more varieties in a single day in East Africa than in a lifetime in Seychelles. Also, island birds tend to be less colourful than their continental cousins. However, what they lack in variety and spectacular plumage they more than make up for in their rarity value.

Successful programmes have been implemented to restore the fortunes of two of the rarest birds in the world, the Seychelles warbler and Seychelles magpie-robin. Programmes are also underway to study, protect and reverse

frog species is the minuscule pygmy piping frog. Though difficult to spot, its high pitched squeak is often the only sound to be heard in the higher hills. Another species, the croaking carrycot frog, has evolved the surprising habit of carrying its tadpoles on its back. Amazingly, the only other places frogs do this are New Zealand and tropical South America – opposite ends of the former super-continent.

LEFT: Cousin warden counting turtle eggs.
ABOVE: a pygmy piping frog – a candidate for the title of the world's smallest frog.
RIGHT: the Seychelles green gecko is unusually active in the daytime.

the historical decline of other species. This includes probably the most beautiful of the endemic birds of Seychelles, the Seychelles black paradise flycatcher. It is the symbol of La Digue, where a special nature reserve has been established for it. The male is staggeringly beautiful with its shiny black plumage and long tail feathers. Though less spectacular, the female is also an attractive bird, chestnut above, white below, with a black head.

The enigmatic Seychelles scops owl occurs only on Mahé, its population concentrated in the Morne Seychellois National Park, while the white eye survives on five islands. Both are among the rarest birds in the world. Praslin, too, has its own special bird, the Seychelles black parrot. Its piercing whistle is often the only sound echoing around the Vallée de Mai. One of the world's smallest birds of prey, and the only bird of prey in the granitics, is the Seychelles kestrel. It is found mainly on Mahé with smaller numbers on Praslin and elsewhere, often announcing its presence with its far-reaching "ti-ti-ti-ti" cry (its name in Kreol is *katiti*). The Seychelles fody (*toktok* in Kreol) survives on five islands including Aride and Cousin, the easiest places to spot it.

More common, but also unique to the granitic islands, are the Seychelles blue pigeon, Seychelles cave swiftlet, Seychelles bulbul and Seychelles sunbird. Even the laziest of bird-watchers can spot them, possibly in their hotel grounds, but certainly in Victoria's Botanical Gardens in the early morning or late afternoon.

Aldabra Atoll is particularly rich in avifauna *(see page 350)*. This World Heritage Site is home to the last surviving flightless bird of the Indian Ocean, the Aldabra rail. Aldabra is also famous for its seabird colonies, including the world's second largest colony of frigatebirds. Closer to the main islands, there are more spectacular seabird colonies, notably Aride (10 breeding species), Cousin (seven breeding

SAVED FROM EXTINCTION

Conservation success stories are few and far between but Seychelles has more than its fair share. Take the humble Seychelles warbler. By 1960, it stood on the threshold of annihilation. An international appeal was launched and in 1968 Cousin was placed under the protection of the Royal Society for Nature Conservation and BirdLife. The warblers thrived. By the 1980s numbers reached around 350. However, it was too early to take the species off the critical list so long as they remained confined to one island where a local disaster might threaten their survival. In 1988, 29 birds were transferred to Aride. It was hoped they might settle to breed around the usual time in January. The birds

had other ideas. With virtually unlimited space and food supply they bred year-round and by 1999 there were almost 2,000 birds. With smaller colonies also established on Cousine and Denis, the species is now one of the few to be taken off the Red Data list of endangered species.

The Seychelles magpie-robin is now receiving similar treatment. Once widespread in the granitic islands, its tame and trusting behaviour meant it fell victim to man and introduced predators. Down to fewer than 20 birds on Frégate, a BirdLife recovery programme was launched. Cousin, Aride, Cousine and Denis now host breeding populations and numbers have increased to almost 200 birds.

photographers, film-makers and conservationists present a programme of films and lectures to visitors and residents.

Seychelles seascape

Whether you're an experienced or first-time diver, Seychelles has so much to offer. The unique granite rock formation of the northerly island group, known as the Inner Islands, creates submarine conditions that are much more varied than might be expected, supporting a prodigious variety of marine life. The diversity is further broadened by the coral atolls to the south, which include Aldabra, the world's largest raised coral atoll and a designated UNESCO World Heritage Site.

The water temperature, which is somewhere between 26 and 30°C (79–86°F), promotes the prolific growth of sponges, corals and invertebrates, which paint the granite walls and canyons in a kaleidoscope of colours. The underwater terrain of the Inner Islands is a mirror image of the landscape above the surface, characterised by dramatic granite formations. The rocks and boulders form natural gullies and crevices that are prime real estate for many marine creatures. A common inhabitant of these nooks and crannies is the moray eel, a species with an undeserved notoriety. Its reputation stems mainly from the habit of greeting visitors with its toothy jaws gaping in an apparently threatening manner. But appearances are deceptive. These eels live quiet lives, bobbing about harmlessly in their crevices. There is little water flow and so they have to gulp water over their gills in order to breathe, hence the gaping jaws. Morays are successful hunters of fish, crabs and snails, but have little interest in bigger fare.

Another crevice inhabitant occasionally found around the reef during the day is the octopus. This, the most highly developed of all the molluscs, is an extremely active predator, feeding mainly at night on other molluscs, crabs and small fish, catching prey with the muscular suckers lined along its eight arms. The octopus is also a master of disguise, especially the marbled octopus commonly found on the granitic reefs. Its skin has special cells which allow it to change colour and alter its texture.

LEFT: divers admire a hawksbilll turtle.
RIGHT: the moray eel's impressive dentition keeps unwanted visitors at bay.

Distinctive fish

Visitors to Seychelles are always impressed by the sheer volume of fish encountered. The brightly coloured butterfly and angelfish are often the most apparent but with a little practice you can become familiar with the extreme body shapes of some species. The elongated cylindrical forms of the trumpet fish and flutemouths are an easy first step; however, discerning between the two can take patience – the trumpet has a fan-like tail and is generally seen in several colour forms on the coral reef, while the flutemouth is normally seen just below the water's surface and has a whip-like tail.

Another easy to distinguish group are box fish and pufferfish, the former having angular cube-like bodies with apparently undersized fins while the puffers resemble deflated tropical fruit swimming over the reef – they only "puff" up if harrassed or cornered. Both these groups have teeth sharp enough to cut through coral and can deliver a deep and painful bite if tormented.

Lionfish and their cousins the scorpionfish are also fairly easy to identify; lionfish by their dramatic array of long feather- or whip-like spines on their back and side fins; scorpionfish by their camouflaged and bottom-dwelling habit. The problem with scorpionfish is actually finding them to begin with.

Once the odd-shaped fish species have been identified you're still left with a bewildering array of "fish-shaped" fish. Of the reef dwellers, the majority belong to the parrotfish or wrasse families. Parrotfish come in a huge range of sizes and colours but all exhibit the characteristic horny coral-cutting beak, like that of a real parrot. Wrasse, an equally large group, have no such distinguishing characteristics. Keen divers and snorkellers should invest in a fish spotter's guide to identify fish beyond this level.

> ### SEX CHANGE
> Some fish have the ability to change sex: parrotfish, anthias and wrasse start as females and can become males as needed.

along the reef's perimeter. Keen underwater photographers home in on these fans as they support their own array of co-inhabitants, ranging from small cowry shells and spider crabs to their own specialised, if somewhat small, predator. The long-nosed hawkfish uses the fan corals as a look-out point from which to capture the small crustaceans on which it feeds.

Big fish

The other attraction of these remote island spots is the chance to encounter larger fish and pelagic species such as shark, barracuda and tuna. Diving and snorkelling along the vertical walls of some islands almost guarantees the sighting of the dog tooth tuna, a real warrior of the deep. These large powerful fish swim with a slightly open mouth proudly displaying a set of canine-like teeth; their large black eyes seem to follow your every move.

As there is comparatively little fishing here, the marine ecosystems in the outer regions are under less pressure and should have more abundant marine life. The food chain supports a larger number of predators and on many reefs the various species of grouper, such as the rare potato cod, are typically abundant. These large fish can grow to well over 1 metre (3 ft) in length and are characterised by large, black potato-like blotches on their grey bodies. The species has a reputation for being aggressive, which may or may not be deserved; however, any fish of this size should be treated with respect.

Outer island terrain

Visitors to the Outer Islands will notice a distinct difference in the underwater terrain to that of the Inner Islands. These islands and atolls are either large sandbanks, such as Bird Island and African Banks, or coral atolls such as Aldabra. The coralline islands often have dramatic walls which plunge from the surface into deep water and thus have a very different range of inhabitants. The deeper sections of these walls are characterised by intricate gorgonian fan corals which are supported by a springy backbone of horn-like material. They grow at right angles to the current so that they can filter out food particles from the water as it runs

Turtle spotting

Turtles are another common sight on the Outer Islands. While hawksbill turtles are the predominant species of the Inner Islands, as you travel south the green turtle becomes more common. Green turtles are generally larger then their sharp-billed cousins and have a broader head and less pronounced bill. A third species, the loggerhead turtle, is rarely seen; while it seems to have a blend of characteristics from the other two species, it can normally be recognised by its massive head, large eyes and immensely thick and powerful beak, which is much more heavy-duty than that of either of the common species. ❑

LEFT: male stoplight parrotfish.

Top Dive Sites

There are numerous world-class dive sites in Seychelles. The following are the top Inner Island sites as rated by resident divers. Apart from Ave Maria on Praslin, most of these are only suitable for experienced divers. However, the list is by no means comprehensive. The dive centres on Mahé, Praslin and La Digue include many more interesting sites in their programme, suitable for novices and experienced divers alike. *(For more information on diving and dive centres in the Inner Islands, see Travel Tips, Activities.)*

Shark Bank

A granite massif with a depth of between 20 and 35 metres (65–115 ft), this outcrop between northwest Mahé and Silhouette island is a focal point for schooling fish and predators. The rocks are especially renowned for sightings of large marbled stingrays. A deep site which can have strong currents, it is suitable for experienced divers.

L'Îlot

This classic granite island lies off the northwestern tip of Mahé. Thanks to its position at the confluence of the east and west coast currents, its waters support a plethora of marine life. It is one of the few Inner Island sites with good soft coral formations and good schooling fish opportunities. Although the maximum depth is only 23 metres (75 ft), currents and patchy visibility mean that in adverse conditions divers need to have suitable experience.

Brissare Rocks

A granite massif 5 km (3 miles) off the northeast coast of Mahé, this site attracts many schools of fish including a resident school of six-line snappers and a family of Napoleon wrasses. With depths of down to 20 metres (65 ft) this site is suitable for all but novice divers.

The Wreck of the Ennerdale

The remains of this stricken tanker lie 8 km (5 miles) off the northeast coast of Mahé at a depth of 30 metres (98 ft). Due to the distance from shore and its exposed position, the wreck is not often visited and so hosts good marine life. The structures are encrusted with corals and inver-

RIGHT: there are some excellent sites for schooling fish around Seychelles.

tebrates but over the passage of time metal fatigue and corrosion are beginning to compact some sections of the wreck. When conditions are good, this is an excellent dive for experienced divers, with schooling fish, shark and ray prospects.

Marianne

The southern tip of Marianne Island is a rarely visited site. The terrain of jagged granite rocks and giant boulders offers refuge for many large fish and it is the seasonal home for a group of grey reef sharks which, for some unknown reason, are all female. An exciting dive to 27 metres (88 ft), with or without the sharks, for experienced divers.

Ave Maria

Praslin's version of L'Îlot; this granite group is renowned for a broad range of fish species as well as regular shark and stingray sightings. With a maximum depth of 26 metres (85 ft), in good conditions this site is suitable for all divers.

The Outer Islands

Outer Island sites have not been included here as this area would need a whole chapter to do it justice. The Desroches Drop is one of the best-known sites *(see page 345)*, but anyone lucky enough to experience diving off Alphonse, Astove, Cosmoledo and Aldabra will find the richness of marine life incomparable. ❑

FISHING

Fish and fishing are dear to the souls of all Seychellois. That's hardly surprising:
they're surrounded by some of the richest fishing grounds in the world

Fish is the staple diet of all Seychellois and, indeed, quite a few tourists. The bounty of the Indian Ocean includes a tremendous variety of fish, excellent for both sport fishing and the dinner table. There are many game fishing boats to serve the tourist industry, equipped with the finest fishing gear around. Fly-fishing

is a relatively new sport in Seychelles, following the discovery of unexploited grounds, described by specialists as among the best in the world. Indeed, Seychelles holds world records for both fly-fishing and game fishing.

Big game fishing

The majority of game fishing boats operate out of Mahé. However, with the growth of tourism on Praslin and La Digue, these islands also have a number of good boats available. Each of the resorts on Silhouette, Frégate, Bird, Denis (a popular venue for serious big game fishermen), Desroches and Alphonse also have boats. Most charter boats fish exclusively by trolling (draw-

ing bait through the water with rod and line), as this is the best way to catch the finest game fish. Tag and release is favoured by some operators and, if you believe in promoting this technique, it is as well to discuss it in advance.

The quality of fishing will depend partly on weather conditions, but the best fishing grounds are at the drop-off at the edge of the Seychelles Plateau (up to 32 km/20 miles offshore), within easy reach of all the granitic islands: bigeye tuna, dogfish tuna and yellow fin tuna all inhabit the edge of the Seychelles Bank; sailfish are commonly caught in waters between Mahé and Silhouette; dorado can be caught over the Bank in season; and barracuda, jobfish *(zob)*, even sharks are sometimes caught on trolling lures.

Though some fish – tuna and bonito, for example – can be caught all year round, others come and go according to the season. The best time of year for catching sailfish is during the southeast monsoon, from June onwards. Though dorado can be caught all year round it is most commonly seen between January and September. Kingfish, also known as wahoo, are most plentiful from January to March, and trevally *(karang)* from November to December. Huge marlin weighing in at 150 kg (330 lb) or more can be caught year round, including blue, striped and black marlin, but they are encountered far less frequently than sailfish.

Bear in mind that sea conditions can be rough during the southeast monsoon (June to September). Larger boats afford a more stable platform from which to fish but, unless you are sharing the cost with other people, this can be expensive: the bigger the boat the bigger the expense.

For the real enthusiast, live-aboard charters are available and may be customised to take into account the needs both of the fisherman and family members who may have other priorities, such as exploring the islands.

For details on live-aboard charters and game fishing specialists see Travel Tips, Activities.

LEFT: yellow fin tuna fighting a losing battle.
RIGHT: landing "the big one".

CREOLE CUISINE

Seychelles cuisine is a product of its history and geography, rooted firmly in the riches of the sea and the spices of the tropics

With the exception of the family pig, a clutter of chickens kept behind the house and a few cattle, there has never been a tradition of rearing livestock in Seychelles because of the limited land available. Meat was only served on special occasions. The ocean has always been the main food supplier, and little has changed. Today, the Seychellois are among the biggest per capita consumers of fish in the world.

Fish and shellfish

Seychellois love fish; but not just any old fish. They have such a bounty of marine life around their islands that they can afford to be choosy. For example, the meaty tuna known locally as bonito can make a delicious curry, but most Seychellois look down on it as inferior and feed it to their dogs. They love the firm, white, flaky flesh of the *bourzwa* or red snapper, which is left whole but scored with long slits on both sides that are stuffed with ginger, garlic, chilli, onions and other spices. It is then wrapped in banana leaf (for purists) or tin foil and cooked over charcoal. Many Seychellois consider the finest meat from a red snapper is to be found in the head, and make good use of it in fish soup. Mackerel is also grilled in a parcel over hot coals, or on bamboo skewers, and drizzled with freshly squeezed lime to keep the flesh moist. *Zob* (another type of snapper) and *karang* (trevally) are served as steaks.

Parrotfish is put into fish stews, or battered for a Seychelles slant on the British favourite, fish and chips. Steaks of tuna, kingfish and swordfish are marinated in oil and spices then grilled on the barbecue. Shark meat is grated with garlic, ginger, *bilimbi* (a sour fruit), lime, onions and turmeric, then stir fried until it looks like yellow desiccated coconut. This dish is known as shark chutney. Sailfish is cut wafer

thin and smoked, to produce a delicacy every bit as good as smoked salmon, delicious on crusty bread with salad.

Shellfish are also popular in Seychellois cuisine. The favourites are *tektek* and *palourd*. *Tekteks* are winkle-like shells collected fresh from the sandy beaches and put into soup. It is

not uncommon, even on busy Beau Vallon beach, to see a Seychellois woman, often assisted by a couple of her young children, stooped over the sand at the point where the waves lap the shore. As the water recedes it uncovers the *tektek*, which quickly burrow out of sight, pursued by a darting hand.

By contrast, *palourd* are found on muddy shores such as in the estuarine area north of Victoria's Inter-Island Quay. They are similar to cockles and delicious when cooked in herbs and garlic butter. The superb local prawns offered in most restaurants are a relatively new addition to the local diet. Prawns do not occur naturally in sufficient numbers around Sey-

LEFT: food served up at the higher-class hotels is often an eclectic mix of local fish, home-grown produce and imported ingredients.
RIGHT: fish is a menu staple.

chelles to be worth harvesting. However, there is now a farm on Coetivy Island producing both for the local and export markets. The prawns are excellent, particularly the large ones, grilled in garlic butter, in a traditional Seychellois curry or in sweet and sour sauce.

Hot and spicy

Indian and Chinese cuisines have not influenced Seychellois cooking as much as in the Mascarenes. Most restaurants specialise in creole cooking and seafood. However, one Indian dish Seychelles has taken and made very much its own, is curry. A Seychelles curry (usually

fish, but also, commonly, chicken, pork, goat or beef) is simply crammed with flavours, and is hot! An exception to this rule is the *kari koko zourit* a mild octopus curry with creamy coconut milk. How they get the octopus so tender is kept a closely guarded secret by some; others will happily confess the secret is to cook your octopus in a pressure cooker. Whatever the truth, when cooked properly, it comes out more tender than chicken, melting in the mouth.

Spicy local sausages figure in a local speciality, sausage and lentil stew. Although there are *tenrecs* on the islands (small mammals similar to hedgehogs in appearance), originally introduced from Madagascar as food, Seychellois no longer eat them. They occasionally eat fruit bat, caught by hanging nets close to the fruit trees where the animals feed.

As for accompaniments, be warned, Seychellois love their chillies hot. The tiny ones are the hottest. To the average Western palette a single seed can set the mouth on fire, yet Seychellois think nothing of eating them whole or ladling copious amounts of the minced chilli in vinegar that comes separately in a little dish onto their meal.

Vegetables and salads

Rice (plain, white, boiled) is the staple, but you will occasionally be offered breadfruit, a versatile potato-like "fruit" served up as crispy chips, boiled and mashed, or stewed in coconut milk and sugar to make a gooey dessert. Best of all is baked breadfruit, the perfect complement to any beach barbecue. It is put whole among the burning coals until black on the outside and tender on the inside, then cut into piping hot slices and served with melted butter. Local legend has it that if you eat breadfruit, you'll be sure to return to Seychelles.

There is not a great deal of variety in the vegetable department. It is not easy to grow them in Seychelles due to the limited amount of flat land and the relatively poor soil. Exceptions include aubergines (usually served as deep fried fritters), watercress and the tasty spinach-like *bred*. Avocados are abundant in season and salads are more than just the token lettuce leaf. Any true creole spread will come with a range of so-called chutneys – finely grated pawpaw, mango or *fisiter* (golden apple) with onion, lime juice and pepper. They make a refreshing and cooling addition to a spicy meal.

CONSIGNED TO HISTORY

Seabird eggs were once of great importance to the Seychellois, simply because the annual bounty of eggs was a welcome variation in an otherwise monotonous diet. Egg exploitation is now controlled, in an attempt to ensure the survival of the sooty tern colonies, but a seabird egg omelette is still considered a delicacy.

Turtles and tortoises were also eaten on special occasions. Traditionally, a baby tortoise was bought on the birth of a daughter and kept until the girl's wedding day, when it would be eaten at the wedding breakfast. This practice is now illegal. Both the giant tortoise and the turtle are protected species.

Starters on a creole menu usually include octopus salad, raw fish marinated in lime juice, and *palmis* salad. This became known as millionaire's salad, because the whole tree had to be sacrificed to obtain the shoot. Conservation legislation now protects this unique majestic palm and, today, the salad is made with the living shoot of the coconut palm, which grows all over Seychelles, chopped into thin slices.

Banana feast

More often than not the dessert choice is limited to local ice creams or fruit salad. Occasionally the fruit salad will come with coconut

if fresh juice is available. Try passion fruit juice or lime with a pinch of salt and sugar to taste. *Sitronel*, a kind of tea made from lemon grass, is also refreshing.

You are unlikely to be offered any of the local alcoholic brews with your meal but these are a part of local culture. *Kalou* (or toddy) is made from coconut sap, which ferments quickly and naturally, and makes the ideal lazy man's tipple. *Baka* is a rum-like drink made from fermented sugar cane juice (a far cry from Bacardi). The most lethal of the local firewaters is *lapire* made from almost anything that will ferment when mixed with sugar. ❑

nougat (caramelised coconut) or coconut milk. There are 25 species of banana in Seychelles, ranging from the foot-long *sen zak*, used to make crisps, to the stubby *mil*, which is extremely sweet and crops up in the fruit bowl, or comes flambéed or stewed in *ladob*.

Drinks

There are plenty of fruit juices, soft drinks, locally brewed beers and imported (expensive) wines available. At restaurants, it pays to ask

LEFT: grating coconut.
RIGHT: a young girl carries bananas straight from the plantation to market.

CRACKING COCONUTS

Many a tourist works up a sweat trying to crack a coconut found at the roadside by hurling it against a rock or attacking it with a small penknife. Forget it, it doesn't work. To remove the thick fibrous husk that protects the nut, most Seychellois have a sharpened spike stuck in the ground. The husk of the coconut is impaled on this and worked loose. It takes an islander a few seconds, but for the novice a little practice is required.

On some excursions you may be offered *koko tann*, a green coconut with the top lopped off so you can drink the milk (refreshing, but an acquired taste). The thin jelly-like flesh of the unformed nut is also delicious.

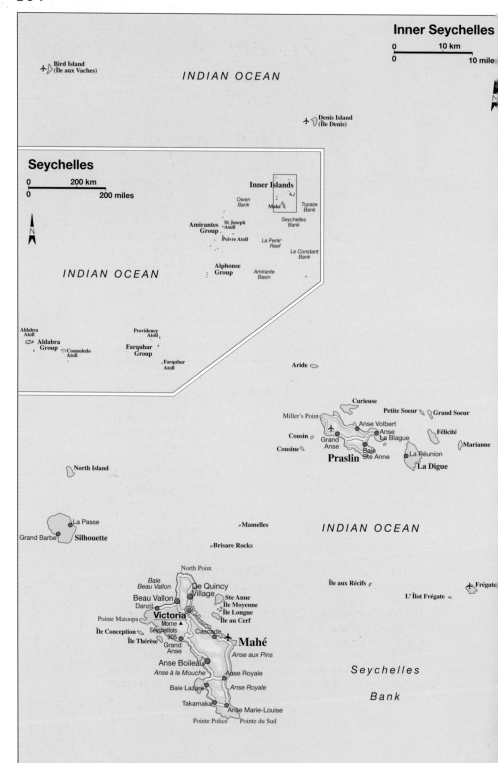

Inner Seychelles

0   10 km
0   10 mile

Bird Island
(Île aux Vaches)

INDIAN OCEAN

Denis Island
(Île Denis)

Seychelles

0   200 km
0   200 miles

N

INDIAN OCEAN

Inner Islands

Owen
Bank

Mahé

Topaze
Bank

Amirantes
Group

St Joseph
Atoll

Poivre Atoll

La Perle
Reef

Seychelles
Bank

Le Constant
Bank

Alphonse
Group

Amirante
Basin

Aldabra
Atoll

Aldabra
Group

Cosmoledo
Atoll

Providence
Atoll

Farquhar
Group

Farquhar
Atoll

Aride

Curieuse

Miller's Point

Petite Soeur

Grand Soeur

Anse Volbert

Cousin

Grand
Anse

Anse
La Blague

Félicité

Marianne

Cousine

Baie
Ste Anne

La Réunion

North Island

Praslin

La Digue

La Passe

Grand Barbe

Silhouette

Mamelles

INDIAN OCEAN

Brisare Rocks

North Point

Baie
Beau Vallon

De Quincy
Village

Île aux Récifs

Frégate

Beau Vallon

Danzil

Ste Anne
Île Moyenne

L' Îlot Frégate

Pointe Matoopa

Victoria

Île Longue

Île Conception

Morne
Seychellois
905

Île au Cerf

Île Thérèse

Grand
Anse

Cascade

Mahé

Anse Boileau

Anse aux Pins

Anse à la Mouche

Anse Royale

Seychelles

Baie Lazare

Anse Royale

Bank

Takamaka

Anse Marie-Louise

Pointe Police

Pointe du Sud

PLACES

A detailed guide to Seychelles, with principal sites clearly cross-referenced by number to the maps

To plan the perfect Seychelles holiday, you have to get three things right: the time of year (make sure you know beforehand when and where the monsoons hit); the quality of hotel (in the past, these have not enjoyed a great reputation, but there have been great improvements in recent years); and, last but not least, the choice of island.

Each of the many Seychelles islands that now welcome overseas tourists has its own special attractions. Most tourists flying into Mahé head straight for their final destination, without taking time to explore the main island. It may be more commercial and developed than its fellow granitic islands, but beyond the tiny capital of Victoria, Mahé has some spectacular beaches and forests of its own to discover, with the added advantage of art and cultural attractions.

However, if you only have time to visit one island, Praslin is the one. Apart from its beaches, bordered with granite boulders, the other main attraction is the Vallée de Mai, a magnificent dense palm forest – home of the unique coco de mer, its notorious love nut – which could well have inspired the set designers of *Jurassic Park*. Praslin also makes a perfect island-hopping base: Cousin, Curieuse, St Pierre, La Digue and Aride are all just a short boat ride away.

Laid-back La Digue can be visited on a day trip from Praslin, but to take in the spectacular coastline – a favourite location for fashion shoots – and explore the inland trails by bike or on an ox-cart, a couple of days here would be well spent.

Even quieter than La Digue, Silhouette and North are the least-known of the Inner Islands. Seemingly stuck in a time warp, Silhouette is a paradise for walkers. There are no roads but plenty of paths – not all well-trodden – that cut through the tangled and mountainous interior. In 2003, a new ecotourism resort opened on North Island, a luxury resort that has begun to draw a new wave of environmentally conscious tourists.

Frégate, the most remote and exclusive granitic island, is privately owned. At five-star prices, for most of us it remains the stuff of dreams.

The coral islands of Bird, Denis, Desroches and Alphonse are perfect for getting away from it all. Each island has its own luxury resort, but has been developed to carefully preserve the environment. With facilities for sailing, diving, snorkelling, deep-sea fishing and birdwatching among other activities, there's plenty on offer for those who want to do more than just dream the days away lounging by crystal waters. ❑

PRECEDING PAGES: traditional creole house on La Digue.

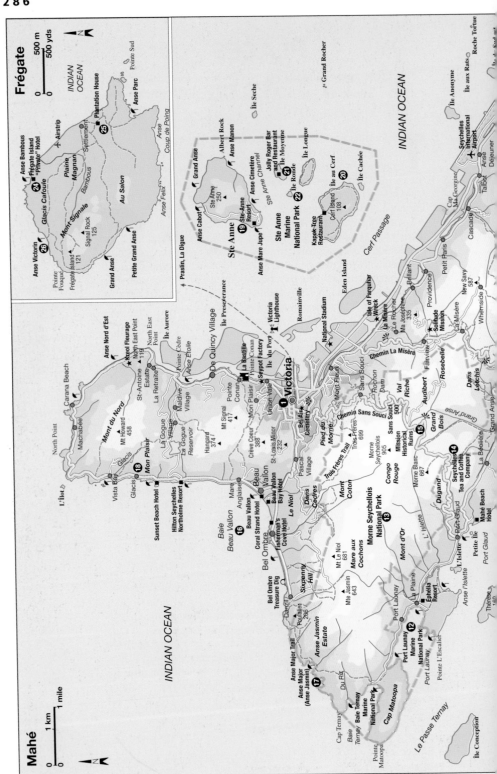

Mahé

0 1 km
0 1 mile

Frégate

0 500 m
0 500 yds

Colonial grandeur

The Roman Catholic **Cathedral of the Immaculate Conception** ⓒ, built in the French colonial style, was completed in 1874, but has had many additions since. On weekdays the church is quiet, but on Sunday mornings the strains of the organ and choir ring out from the open doorways, and the congregation, dressed in their best, spills out onto the steps. Sunday Mass is as much a social occasion as a religious one.

Just down the street from the cathedral is Victoria's most impressive building, **Capuchin House** ⓓ. Built in 1933 with funds from the Swiss Capuchin order, and designed by one of the monks, it is used as a seminary for priests and brothers, some of whom still teach in the schools.

Morning market

Heading back south towards the town centre, you'll pass the pedestrianised Market Street and the **Sir Selwyn Selwyn Clarke Market** ⓔ, also known as Victoria Market. Saturday morning is the best time to come here. The fish stalls are the commercial heart of the market, piled with freshly caught barracuda, parrotfish, cordonnier, bonito and kingfish. Produce stalls are stacked with neat pyramids of exotic fruits and seasonal vegetables. Others are laid out with trays of mixed spices, neatly rolled quills of fresh cinnamon bark, packets of turmeric and old jars crammed with small but deadly red and green chillies.

For a bird's eye view of the goings-on, climb the stairs to the upper floor. There are a few craft shops open here, selling the more usual lines in souvenirs.

Cutting through the market, leaving by the side entrance, you come out into a little alley called Benezet Street. Turning left, past the bakery (which does

Map
on pages
286-7

"Hellfire" chillies – hot favourites among the Seychellois.

BELOW: waiting for a thirsty customer.

SOUVENIR SHOPPING

Codevar is an artisans' association set up by the government to promote local craftsmanship. One of the best places to pick up gifts and souvenirs is the **Codevar Craft Centre** at **Camion Hall** in Albert Street (named after the old open lorries or *camyons*, used as buses, which used to set out on their routes from this spot). There is a shop on the street front selling pottery, woodcarvings, textiles and various objects made from coconuts and shells. In the arcade **Kreolor** has a wide range of jewellery made out of green snail shell, tiger cowrie and coconut shell in combination with gold, and crafts made from local woods, coconut shell, coconut wood and polished palm seeds. Immediately across the road, the **Sooty Tern** boutique specialises in stained-glass work. Round the corner in Revolution Avenue, **Memorabilia** sells a wide range of crafts and books. **Sunstroke Gallery** on Market Street has a range of locally made beachwear, jewellery, hand-printed tablecloths and bed linen. Upstairs there is a gallery of local artwork. **Antigone**, the town's best bookshop, is in Passage des Palmes. **Antik Colony** in the Pirate's Arms building, sells quality souvenirs on colonial themes. On either side of the entrance to the Stadium Car Park are craft kiosks that sell beachwear, T-shirts, coconut crafts and spices.

excellent bread), you'll come back on to Revolution Avenue. If the heat and noise have made you weary, turn right and keep walking until you reach **Kaz Zanana** (Pineapple House), a quiet spot to pause for a bite to eat. The restaurant is on a terrace at the back, overlooking the garden. They serve light meals throughout the day and the best cappuccino and chocolate cake in Seychelles. The rest of the house is made up of small galleries which exhibit paintings and drawings by local artist George Camille.

Strolling south

The shady **Fiennes Esplanade** which runs alongside Francis Rachel Street was laid out by a British governor with the splendid name of Sir Eustace Edward Twisleton-Wykeham Fiennes (1918–21), father of explorer Sir Ranulph Fiennes. At the start of the esplanade is a **bust of Pierre Poivre**, the governor of Mauritius who arranged for the first spice plants to be brought to Seychelles for propagation (*see page 247*).

Towards the end of the Esplanade is a large modern building, the National Library. The **History Museum** (open Mon–Tues, Thur–Fri 8.30am–4.30pm, Sat 9am–1pm; entrance fee) is housed on the ground floor. In the entrance is the Stone of Possession, a stone placed by the French in 1756 to claim the islands. Displays are fairly basic, but they give an excellent introduction to the history of the islands, from pirates and explorers through wars and colonial times to the modern day. The tranquillity of the hall is a pleasant contrast to the hustle and bustle of Victoria, while the cool air-conditioned atmosphere is welcome after a hot walk.

There is a small art gallery on the opposite side of the museum car park to the library, Carrefour des Arts (open Mon–Fri 9am–5pm) with original paintings on

TIP

Parking is restricted in Victoria and police are keen. If you have come to town by car, the best place to park is the Stadium Car Park on Francis Rachel Street, which is free. Otherwise, you have to buy parking coupons (available from many shops).

BELOW:
a not-so-busy day at the market.

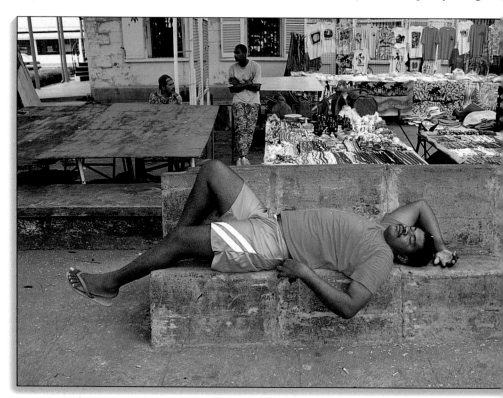

sale. Across the road is Kenwyn House (open Mon–Fri 8am–4pm, Sat 9am–noon). Built in the 1860s and renovated in 2005, it is probably the best preserved 19th-century building in Victoria. It also contains an excellent art gallery featuring a range of local artists.

Map
on pages
286–7

East to the quays

East of the Clock Tower, on Independence Avenue, is the **Natural History Museum** ⊕ (open Mon–Fri 8.30am–4.30pm, Sat 8.30am–noon; entrance fee), with displays of endemic birds, reef life, tortoises, geology and the skulls of estuarine crocodiles that once lived in the mangrove swamps around Mahé's coast and terrorised the colonists.

Opposite the museum is Victoria's best-known rendezvous, the **Pirates Arms** (open Mon–Sat 9am–midnight, Sun 4–11pm), a large, informal café-bar popular with tourists and locals alike. There is a small arcade of shops beside it, several of which sell curios. A little further down the street on the same side is the **tourist office**, a good place for advice and literature on accommodation, excursions and museum opening times. They also have leaflets on walks and trails in Mahé, Praslin and La Digue.

Continuing straight on, past the Trwa Zwazo (Three Birds) roundabout (named after the sculpture erected in 1978 to celebrate 200 years of human occupation), the road swings left. This is Flamboyant Avenue, leading to **Inter-Island Quay** ❶, the departure point for ferries and boats to the islands, and for fast catamarans to Praslin. The traditional island schooners also ply between Mahé, Praslin and La Digue from this point, and the fleets of the largest charter boat operators are based here.

While waiting for your ferry, **Le Marinier** restaurant on the quayside offers a ringside seat to watch the comings and goings and you're left to linger over your drink for as long as you like. The charter boat marina is at the north end of the jetty, where catamarans and schooners line the pontoons. Just south of the Trwa Zwazo roundabout, on 5th June Avenue, is the **Marine Charter Association**, the departure point for glass-bottom boat and subsea viewer trips, and for some charter yachts.

Gardens and graves

The walk from the Clock Tower to the **Botanical Gardens** ❶ (open daily 8am–6pm; entrance fee) at the foot of Mont Fleuri takes about 20 minutes. They were laid out in 1901 by a Frenchman, Rivaltz Dupont, who collected many of the plant specimens on his travels. The site he chose was not ideal – the soil was poor and the land scattered with huge boulders – but it was the only affordable piece of land near town. Wandering through this green oasis today, it is hard to imagine the unprepossessing site Dupont was confronted with. The boulders are now an attractive feature, and the bubbling streams that run down either side of the park create a cool, soothing atmosphere.

At the top of the hill the gardens open out onto broad lawns dotted with specimen trees and shrubs. One of

The "Three Birds" sculpture on Freedom Square represents the African, Asian and European elements of Seychelles' heritage.

BELOW: tuna fishing boats.

The cannonball tree in bloom.

the most noticeable is the elephant apple, with fruits like huge, heavy apples that smell of rubber. There are attractive ponds with water lilies and darting dragonflies. The path leading from the ponds takes you past a mighty banyan tree and several drumstick trees that shed remarkable, long, thin fruits. One tree you can't miss, if it is in flower, is the cannonball tree, which sheds its leaves when flowering to reveal bizarre, fleshy coral pink flowers. A number of Aldabra giant tortoises are kept here in a large pen shaded by a coco de mer palm.

The gardens are shady enough to explore at any time of day, but it's best to avoid the heat of the midday sun. Ask at the entrance kiosk for the leaflet which maps out the gardens and names all the plants. There are no refreshment facilities inside the gardens, so it's a good idea to pick up a drink on the way.

On the outskirts of Victoria, at the beginning of the Sans Souci road, is **Bel Air Cemetery** 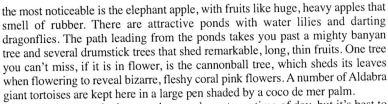, Seychelles' oldest cemetery. Tombstones lie strewn haphazardly, there are no signposts and no guide, but it is an atmospheric place, nonetheless. Settlers and their slaves were buried here from the earliest times. The more splendid tombs bear the names of illustrious Seychelles' families. According to legend, a young giant was killed by local people and buried here in the 1870s. The grave of French corsair, Hodoul, is also rumoured to be here.

THE EAST COAST

There are two roads leading out of Victoria that head south towards the airport. For speed and convenience, the new road (Bois de Rose Avenue) is the one to take. But if you're in no hurry, a journey along the narrow, winding, rather chaotic old Mont Fleuri Road (which becomes East Coast Road further along) will tell you far more about Mahé. The buildings that line it are a fascinating jumble of the modern (such as the Pentecostal Assembly on the junction of Mont Fleuri Road and Liberation Road) and the charmingly dilapidated. You can catch glimpses of elegant old planters' homes peeping over high stone walls, identifiable by their steep-pitched roofs, shuttered windows, wide verandahs and high, stone foundations.

BELOW: the church of St André, in Cascade, has some fine stained glass.

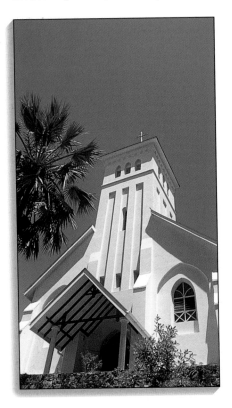

The two coast roads recombine at Providence, leading to **Cascade**, a traditional fishing village now dominated not by the fishing industry, but the nearby airport built on reclaimed land. The blessing of the fishing boats here on the feast of St André (November) used to be an important celebration in Seychelles, attracting spectators from all over Mahé. The number of boats is far fewer nowadays, but about half a dozen pirogues, decorated with flags and flowers, still gather here for the annual blessing.

Old plantations

Another 6 km (4 miles) down the coast road, past Anse aux Pins, on the site of a former plantation, is the **Craft Village** ❷ (Le Village Artisanal) where you can while away a bit of time looking at the workshops and shopping for souvenirs (*see Travel Tips, Activities*). In the middle of the village the old plantation house, dating from 1870, has been furnished in typical colonial style. The cool, dark rooms smell of wax polish and cinnamon, and conjure a picture of the genteel existence once enjoyed by the privileged few. It's easy to imagine a candlelit social gathering, the ladies in their long dresses frantically fanning themselves and the gentlemen in full evening dress savouring the fine wines imported at great expense from France. **Vye Marmit Restaurant** is a good place to sample local specialities such as fruit bat, octopus, crab and fish.

Map on pages 286–7

Deserted coves

Beyond the Pointe au Sel promontory, **Anse Royale** ❸ is the main east coast beach. The sheltered, sandy bay is scattered with giant boulders, dividing the beach into a series of mini-coves, pretty much deserted on most weekdays. The snorkelling is reasonably good around the offshore islet of Île Souris. The currents between the mainland and the island can be strong, but run parallel to the beach, and it is fairly easy for a confident swimmer to cross them.

Kaz Kreol at the southern end of Anse Royale is an informal restaurant right on the sand, where you can turn up in your swimming costume for lunch.

The King's Garden

Continuing south, the next turning off the main road is Les Cannelles. Sweet Escott Road is a left turning off this road. It was around here, in 1772, that Antoine Gillot, under instruction from the French government, planted a Royal Spice Garden *(see pages 247–8)*, but this is long since overgrown. In its memory, the **Jardin du Roi** ❹ (King's Garden; open daily 10am–5.30pm; entrance fee) has been established on the hillside above Sweet Escott Road. This renovated spice plantation, based on the former L'Enfoncement Estate, gives you a chance to see many aromatic plants growing (including nutmeg, pepper, cinnamon, vanilla and cloves). There is a walk laid out which you can follow using the printed guide. The small museum in the plantation house has some interesting exhibits, including old prints, maps and photos of Seychelles, and information on growing and using spices. On Sunday the restaurant serves a popular curry buffet *(see Travel Tips, Restaurants)*.

BELOW: a colonial house.

THE WEST COAST

The east coast road continues to Anse Marie-Louise where it turns sharply inland and cuts across the southern end of Mahé. At Quatre Bornes, a road leads down to a spectacular bay, **Anse Intendance** ❺ where there is a very exclusive hotel, **The Banyan Tree Resort**. The long, pristine beach is pounded by crashing breakers, exhilarating to watch as they sweep in with a tremendous roar and a haze of spray. A strong swimmer might enjoy body surfing in the waves, but it's easy to get caught in the rollers and dumped hard on the beach or rocks. As with many of Seychelles' beaches, conditions vary according to the monsoon season. Seas are at their roughest during the southeast monsoon (May to October) and there can be a strong undertow. During the northwest monsoon (October to April) the waves here are still big, but the water is calm enough to swim in. Intendance is a popular picnic spot for Seychellois at weekends and can get quite busy, but the beach is so long there is room for all.

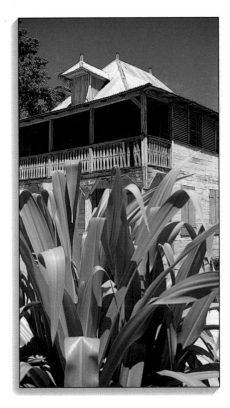

Rejoining the main road at Quatre Bornes and heading west, you'll reach **Anse Takamaka** , the first beach on the west coast road, whose large shady takamaka trees and golden sands entice many tourists and surfers. However currents are strong around here and swimming is dangerous.

Baie Lazare

The road swings northward, staying fairly close to the shore, offering dramatic views at Pointe Maravi of the rocks below before it descends again to **Baie Lazare** ❼. Here, beside the coast, there is a **monument** (an anchor on a stone pedestal) commemorating the 250th anniversary of the first recorded French landing on Mahé by Lazare Picault in 1742 (in fact, Picault landed at Anse Boileau). Baie Lazare has a long expanse of beach, though swimming here during the southeast monsoon is not recommended. The best way to explore it is to park near the monument and stroll along the beach towards **Plantation Club Hotel** (currently closed). To the rear of the hotel is an attractive marsh, an aspect of the Seychelles' landscape not often seen.

Baie Lazare village, on the hill overlooking the beach, is a typical Seychelles hamlet, centred around the neo-Gothic church of St Francis of Assisi. This is the starting point for the **Chemin Dame Le Roi** forest drive. The winding road leads uphill from **Quatre Bornes takeaway**, and passes through scattered houses, forest and plantations of pineapple, cassava and sugar cane (mostly grown to make *baka*, a local spirit). This is old Mahé, still firmly fixed in another age, where chickens peck around the washing laid out on the boulders to dry.

Second best bay in the world

Just north of Quatre Bornes takeaway a road leads on to a western promontory which has three bays. The best of these is **Anse Soleil** ❽, an enchanting small sandy beach, rated the second best "hidden secret" in the world by the German magazine *Reise & Preise*, with good swimming and excellent views. It is rarely busy, except on Sundays, when the simple but very good restaurant is popular with locals. Neighbouring **Petite Anse** is another attractive sandy cove, about 10 minutes' walk along a shaded track. Reaching **Anse Gouvernement** from here requires backtracking to the junction and following the signpost pointing to the right. The narrow concrete track leads downhill, passing on the right Studio Antonio – where unusual wooden sculptures are on display – before emerging at the beach. This sandy bay, dotted with massive granite boulders, is wild and windswept during the southeast monsoon, so not good for swimming at this time of year. Weekends apart, it is very quiet and romantic.

Artists' studios

Continuing northward on the coast road, the next place you come to is **Anse aux Poules Bleues** ❾ where you'll find Michael Adams' Studio (open Mon–Fri 9am–4pm, Sat 9am–noon). The best-known artist in Seychelles, his jungle landscapes are a riot of leaves, stalks and stems, criss-crossing and clashing in

BELOW:
walking the dog
Seychelles style.

very shade. He also takes a wry look at village life. Excellent prints of his work are on sale at the studio, but they are expensive.

The wide vistas of **Anse à la Mouche** open up as the road curves around the bay. The beach has the usual pristine white sand and plenty of shade, and the shallow waters are calm all year round, which makes it ideal for children. It's also a good place for beach parties, and groups of Seychellois often get together here at weekends, although on weekdays it is usually very quiet. The **Anchor Café** serves drinks, snacks and simple meals at reasonable prices.

Les Cannelles Road at the end of Anse à la Mouche leads inland to Santa Maria and the studio of **Tom Bowers** (open Mon–Sat 9.30am–5.30pm), which is signposted on the right as you climb Les Cannelles from the coast. Like so many artists before him, the London-born sculptor visited Seychelles, fell in love with it and settled. He uses resin for his sculptures of local people, which are then cast in bronze.

Coastal views

Back on the west coast, the next right turn is Chemin Montagne Posée, not worth the diversion unless you intend to walk the mountain trail near the summit. For a less strenuous introduction to the lower slopes of Mahé there is an attractive palm forest outside the **Biodiversity Centre Nursery** at Barbarons and at the opposite end of the bay just after the hotel, an excellent well-marked walk, the **Sentier Vacoa Trail ⑩**. The shaded trail leads uphill alongside a clear stream bordered by endemic palms and trees.

The following turn-off, just after the unmistakable giant masts of the BBC World Service Relay Station, is La Misère Pass, which rejoins the east coast

Map
on pages
286–7

Tom Bowers' sculptures of local people are sold in limited editions.

BELOW: watching the waves at Takamaka beach.

Souvenirs made from the coconut palm – a versatile resource for artisans.

BELOW: tea picker.

at Mont Fleuri close to Victoria. Cutting across the west side of the mountains, this pass is quiet, with few houses, and views over the coast. The road falls steeply from here and the views over the east coast and the Inner Islands are spectacular. There is an off-road **viewing point** about 2 km (1 mile) after the summit.

The west coast road continues past Grand Anse Agricultural Station to the bay of **Grand Anse ⓫**. This is a majestic, tree-lined beach with fine white sand and granite rocks, but the treacherous offshore currents make it unsuitable for swimming (a governor of Seychelles drowned here in 1962). Over the brow of the hill, the road descends to Mahé Beach Hotel and tiny picturesque Petite Île.

The last 5-km (3-mile) section of the west coast road is a narrow stretch that comes to a dead end just before **Baie Ternay**. There is no access beyond this point. The drive is spectacular, passing over a causeway and through a mangrove swamp and, as it climbs, giving marvellous views over the **Port Launay Marine National Park ⓬** (formed in 1979 to protect the reef). To reach the beaches of **Port Launay Bay**, pull over in a convenient spot and stroll down to the shore. The snorkelling here is good and reaching the reef is easy over calm waters.

NORTHERN MAHÉ

If you only have a day on Mahé, the first place you should drive to is the Sans Souci road, most of which runs through the Morne Seychellois National Park *(see page 299)*. The circuitous drive from coast to coast takes about an hour and is an ideal way to experience the mood of the mountains; the eerie silence

MISSION RUINS

The area known in colonial times as Venn's Town is now called Mission. The ruins, dating from 1875, are those of a school built by Anglican missionaries for the children of rescued slaves. Following the abolition of slavery in the colonies, the British ran an anti-slavery patrol in the Indian Ocean. Their main purpose was to intercept Arab dhows transporting captive Africans to the Middle East. Those they managed to save from slavery were not taken back to Africa for fear they would be rounded up again, so they were brought to Seychelles and freed. Their children were given a basic education by the missionaries prior to being apprenticed or sent into service.

Marianne North, an intrepid Victorian traveller and botanical artist, made a trip to Venn's Town in 1883 by mule, and later commented in her diary "...the situation...is one of the most magnificent in the world, and the silence of the forest around was only broken by the children's happy voices". Nowadays the only sound here is the rustling of the trees, and perhaps some echoes of the past in the forest – some say the ruins are haunted.

You can see this view for yourself. A short avenue leads to the viewing platform, built for the visit of Queen Elizabeth II in 1972.

Once around Pointe Cèdre, the hillsides to the right and cliffs to the left become more thickly dotted with houses as you approach Victoria's environs. The most notable building before you reach town is **La Bastille**, just after Pointe Conan. This sombre, impressive house was built in the 1930s as a family home. It once housed the Seychelles National Archives (now in the National Library in Victoria). The gardens are open to the public (Mon–Fri 9am–4pm). There is a collection of traditional medicinal plants, a sugar cane press and a dilapidated model of a traditional creole house. Nothing is labelled, but the staff are friendly and willing to help.

Map on pages 286–7

THE SATELLITE ISLANDS

The Portuguese called Seychelles the Seven Sisters on their charts because Mahé stands like a grand elder sister surrounded by her lesser siblings, of which six lie just off the east coast, encircling Victoria's magnificent natural harbour. These islands lie within the **Ste Anne Marine National Park**, created in 1973, the first such park in the Indian Ocean. Unfortunately, the corals are a shadow of their former selves, due in part to siltation from land reclamation around Victoria, with the effects of the El Niño weather system and perhaps global warming also implicated. To protect this fragile environment, motorised sports, fishing and the collection of coral, shells and live shellfish are banned. The marine life is still prolific (with more than 200 species of fish) and the short journey to the marine park, combined with lunch on one of the charming and peaceful islands that have restaurants, is still a very pleasant way to spend a day. Tour operators offer full-day trips by glass-bottom boat or subsea viewer starting from Marine Charter in Victoria *(see page 293)*. The subsea viewer gives a superior view, but is completely enclosed and some people might feel claustrophobic. Either way, you'll have plenty of time to swim or snorkel.

Enjoying the underwater world without getting wet.

Ste Anne ⑲ is the largest of the islands off Victoria. The first Seychelles settlers lived here rather than on Mahé, perhaps because of the crocodiles then inhabiting Mahé's extensive coastal mangrove swamps. Once people began to settle on Mahé, Ste Anne was largely left in peace as a coconut plantation, and since then has been put to various uses. In 1832 a whaling station was established here and in World War II the British had a fuel store here. In the 1980s, Ste Anne was briefly a centre for the National Youth Service, a political experiment that was eventually abandoned. Then it became the headquarters of the Marine Parks Authority (now moved to Baie Ternay on Mahé). Today, it is the site of a five-star hotel, the Sainte Anne Resort *(see Travel Tips, Accommodation)*, which controls access to the island.

BELOW: north coast hideaway haven.

Île au Cerf ⑳ is a small, low-lying island, mostly covered in coconut palms and scrub, and it is easy to find trails up the hill if you want to explore inland. You can either come here as part of an excursion organised by a tour operator, or hire a boat from the Marine Charter Association. Tourist boats land on the sheltered northern coast near **Kapok Tree**

Map on pages 286–7

Restaurant where lunch is provided. After an excellent creole meal, you can take a walk along the shore, past the homes of some of the 80 or so residents, a number of whom commute to Victoria by speedboat. One of Seychelles' most famous residents, South African writer Wilbur Smith, used to have a house here.

To stay on Cerf is a wonderful way to experience the tranquillity of life on an island with no roads or shops and just two small resorts, secure in the knowledge that all the conveniences of modern life are just a 10-minute boat ride away. The beach is always sheltered, good for swimming and snorkelling. Guests often hire pedalos to visit the beaches around Cerf, and even get as far as Moyenne, Ronde or Ste Anne.

Île Cachée is a tiny dot off the southeast coast of Cerf. It's possible to wade over to the islet at low tide.

Île Moyenne ㉑ has been owned since 1962 by an Englishman, Brendon Grimshaw, a former newspaper editor, and is open to day visitors. Visitors to Moyenne usually question the owner closely on two subjects: the pirate treasure said to be buried somewhere on the island and the ghost of Miss Best, an eccentric Englishwoman who lived on the island with a pack of stray dogs, until she died in 1919.

Moyenne covers just 9 hectares (4 acres) and is easy to explore. In 2008 it was declared a National Park, the smallest in the world. Sixteen thousand trees have been planted here, including rare endemics such as coco de mer and Wright's gardenia. A circular trail, which takes no more than an hour at a leisurely pace, goes from the **Jolly Roger Bar and Restaurant** near the landing, past the house Miss Best built for her dogs, along the beach at Coral Cove and back past the graveyard, the chapel, through Coco de Mer Vale, past the museum (with a small array of items relating to the island and its natural history) and back to the bar. Snorkellers should head for the northwest coast and the waters between Moyenne and Ste Anne. The island and its bar-restaurant are open daily.

You can walk around the tiny **Île Ronde** (Round Island) **㉒** in less than 10 minutes. The island is now the exclusive domain of the residents of a small up-market hotel.

Île Ronde is best known for its excellent restaurant, **Chez Gaby**, housed in old buildings, once part of an isolation camp for women suffering from leprosy. The menu features creole cuisine and its barbecued tuna steak is a Seychelles legend. After lunch, most people are happy just to relax in the shade of the flame trees by the restaurant.

Île Longue (Long Island) was once a prison and is now being developed as a five-star resort. Longue was a quarantine station in the days when the dreaded smallpox might arrive aboard a ship and spell disaster for the isolated Seychelles' population.

Île Thérèse ㉓ on the west coast is a beautiful island for a day trip. However, there is no longer a regular boat service to the island. There is a beautiful beach facing Mahé, and the shelter of the mainland makes swimming here easy. ❑

BELOW: a free ride. **RIGHT:** sailboards and catamarans can be hired at most hotels.

FRÉGATE

Map on page 286

Once home to pirates, Frégate is now an exclusive destination with seven beaches and just one resort, where the emphasis is on the "private island experience"

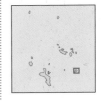

he most isolated of the granitic islands, Frégate lies 55 km (34 miles) east of Mahé. Covering 3 sq km (1 sq mile) and surrounded by coral reefs, this privately owned island is the kind of place most of us can only eam of staying in. Frégate is very exclusive; most of the guests (limited to at a time) are super rich and come here to hide away in one of the resort's luxury villas.

rates' lair

égate was christened by the French explorer, Lazare Picault, during his 1744 pedition. He probably named it "Île aux Frégates" after the frigatebirds once esent on the island. Among the mysterious ruins found on the island were the lls of a large enclosure, thought to be the remains of a pirate settlement, a ad-lined water conduit and three tombs built of coral. Early residents found a ak mast set in a stone platform at Anse Lesange and in 1812 a gold cross-belt d shoulder strap were discovered. In 1838, a visitor from Mauritius reported at golden Spanish coins were frequently found on the beaches. He also scribed the wreck of a large ship lying offshore. There is no direct evidence that ese artefacts were left by pirates; they could just as easily be traces of an Arab ading post. Whatever their origin, these various finds ake Frégate one of the few sites of archaeological terest in Seychelles.

In 1802 Frégate became a place of exile. A shipload Jacobin terrorists, accused of having plotted to sassinate Napoleon, had been sent from France to eychelles. Quincy, the commandant of Seychelles, spected several of these deportees of joining forces ith the slaves and inciting them to rebellion, and so sent the ringleader, Louis Sepholet, together with ree slaves, to Frégate. They were among the first habitants of the island, though they didn't stay long. iter the same year, Sepholet was transported to njouan in the Comoros with 35 of the other depor- es. They all died there; it is said they were poisoned the orders of the sultan.

LEFT: a siesta in the shade.
BELOW: a jacuzzi in the sun.

uxury resort

he only way you can stay on Frégate is as a guest of e hotel **Frégate Island "Private"** ㉔. Opened in 98, this resort is a celebrity haunt. Pierce Brosnan ent three weeks here before the release of *The World Not Enough*. The design of the spacious villas, strung ong the beautiful **Anse Bambous**, was influenced by e architecture of Bali and Thailand. Each one has a ing room, large bedroom and two bathrooms with owers inside and out, all linked by a terrace, plus a ivate garden, secluded outdoor jacuzzi with amazing

*Until recently an
endangered species,
the magpie-robin now
thrives on Frégate.*

BELOW: have a drink
at the bar or have it
brought to your villa.

views, and a sundeck with a king-size sunbed. The resort is centred around Frégate House, where the main dining room, gymnasium and library are located with a freshwater swimming pool and bar nearby. Facilities for every water sport you can think of are available and the German multimillionaire owner has also built a marina here for his own private yacht and other boats, which can be chartered. In short, Frégate is completely kitted out for the ultimate paradise island experience.

Plantation House

As a result of intense farming, most of the island is now covered with introduced vegetation. The higher hills are dominated by indigenous trees, among which coffee, breadfruit, banyan, cashew and ylang ylang all grow. Plantations were laid out on the flat land and have been regenerated to provide fresh food for the new resort, including pawpaw, banana, cabbage, lettuce and sweet potato. Cattle, pigs and chickens are also reared to provision the hotel. The original **Plantation House** ㉕ not far from the airstrip has been restored and now houses a restaurant specialising in creole cuisine.

Wildlife walks

Apart from four other islands, Frégate is the only place where the Seychelles magpie-robin now survives. This pretty black and white bird had become extinct on the other granitic islands where it was once common. It was perilously close to disappearing from Frégate too but was rescued from extinction by the intervention of BirdLife International. It is now thriving again and new populations have been reintroduced to the other islands. Other birds hotel guests can spot here

ood reputation. Diving, windsurfing and jet surfing can be arranged by **Bleu Marine**, based at the small hotel here. There is a pleasant walk from the bay that takes you along the shore, past Petite Anse and up a hill towards Anse La Farine. From the top of the hill you can see Île Ronde and La Digue.

The Côte d'Or

The inland road that links Baie Ste Anne to Anse Volbert and the northeast coast passes through casuarina woodland. **Anse Volbert ❸**, also known as Côte d'Or, is the island's main tourism centre. Its long beach is sheltered by Curieuse Island so that swimming is safe all year and there are no large breakers, making it ideal for children. The beach shelves very gradually so you need to walk out a long way to find water deep enough for swimming. The best snorkelling is around the boulders at the northern end of the beach and out towards **Chauve Souris Island**.

While it is by no means overdeveloped, Anse Volbert is relatively crowded by Seychelles standards. Beside the beach there are several hotels, guesthouses, restaurants and souvenir shops, with more restaurants, boat operators and watersports centres strung along the coast road. Several of these organise snorkelling trips to **St Pierre Islet** as well as trips further afield to the islands of Curieuse, Cousin and Aride.

Next stop on the east coast road is **Anse Possession ❹**, a lovely bay with a view of Curieuse Island. It was around here, in 1768, that the first French explorers erected a plaque, claiming possession of the island. A cairn of stones and a flagstaff marked the spot. However, the location was lost. The French accused the English, who visited the island soon after, of deliberately obliterating the spot. The coast north of here, facing Curieuse island, is picturesque, quiet and good for swimming. The road runs through takamaka and casuarina groves and passes the pretty bays of **Anse Takamaka** and **Anse Boudin**. The short excursion from here to the top of Grand Fond (340 metres/1,115 ft) is worthwhile for the view across Praslin and the surrounding islands.

The best beach in the world

After Anse Boudin the road turns inland over the hill to **Anse Lazio ❺**, hailed as "the best beach in the world". The sand here is as fine and soft as caster sugar and is scattered with granite boulders. The swimming is excellent except when the northwesterly winds are at their strongest, mainly around January and February. Snorkelling is best around the rocks and at the two small coves at the northeastern end of the bay. To enjoy the beach at its finest it is best to come early in the morning before the crowds. There are two restaurants, **Bonbon Plume**, with thatched umbrellas dotted across a lawn by the sea; and at the opposite end of the beach, **Le Chevalier Restaurant**, set back from the shoreline. Both offer mainly seafood and Creole cuisine.

Exploring the west coast

If you are flying in, you will land on the west side of the island, 3 km (nearly 2 miles) from Grand Anse –

Map on page 316

Most of Praslin's hotels, restaurants and souvenir shops are concentrated around Côte d'Or.

BELOW: cooling off after a ride.

the other place to pick up a hire car *(see Travel Tips, Transport)*. The coast road leading north of the airstrip from Amitié goes through a coconut plantation and farmland, past **Anse Kerlan**  to **Petite Anse Kerlan**, both beautiful sand beaches framed by granite rocks. The sea can be wild in rough weather but on calmer days the area is excellent for swimming and snorkelling, though you should always beware of strong currents.

Petite Anse Kerlan is home to the **Lemuria Resort**, an exclusive hotel complex in a spectacular location spread over 36 hectares (90 acres) with three beaches and Seychelles' only 18-hole golf course. Birdwatching in the grounds is excellent but it is necessary to call in advance to arrange access *(see Travel Tips, Activities)*. Further north, lying within the grounds of the golf course, is **Anse Georgette**, a wild and remote beach worth exploring.

Back at Amitié, opposite the airstrip by the sea, is **Black Pearl (Seychelles) Ltd** (open Mon–Fri 10am–4pm, Sat 10am–1pm; entrance fee), where black pearls are cultured in the first and only pearl farm in the Indian Ocean region. A series of open concrete aquarium tanks have also been set up; here you can see giant clams and corals, reef fish and invertebrates. The guide is helpful and informative. Within the same complex is a jewellery boutique.

Around Grand Anse

The first settlement south of the airport is **Grand Anse** ❼. It's the largest village on Praslin, but it is far from commercialised and retains a sleepy character. The beach here is good, though often covered in seaweed. There are several small hotels, as well as shops, banks, takeaways and restaurants. The travel agents all have their Praslin offices here. **Scubamania Dive Centre** is based at

BELOW:
the Pagoda at
Coco de Mer Hotel.

he Hotel Marechiaro which, together with Maison des Palmes Hotel, runs boat rips to the small islands around Praslin.

From Grand Anse the coast road continues southward past a series of picturesque bays. The 5-km (3-mile) walk from Fond de l'Anse to Anse Marie-Louise is pleasant and easy with beautiful views. There are a couple of hotels and restaurants en route. This is the best stretch of coastline for deserted beaches, though not all are good for swimming as the water is shallow except at high tide. The first bay along this road is **Anse Citron**, followed by **Anse Bateau**, which has Les Rochers Restaurant, one of the best on Praslin, at its far end. Sirene Boat Excursions operates from here to islands around Praslin. **Anse Bois de Rose** is noteworthy for the Black Parrot Restaurant and **Coco de Mer Hotel**. Rounding Pointe Cocos, Anse Consolation is less ideal for swimming due to the beach rock barrier, but neighbouring **Anse Marie-Louise ❽** is the best bathing beach of all the above and a particularly quiet and picturesque spot. From this bay, the road winds steeply and passes the exclusive **Château de Feuilles Hotel and Restaurant** before descending to **Baie Ste Anne**.

A journey back in time

One of Seychelles' greatest natural treasures is the **Vallée de Mai ❾** (open daily 8am–5.30pm; entrance fee, free for children under 12), a primeval forest claimed by General Gordon in 1881 to be the Garden of Eden. The valley, designated a UNESCO World Heritage Site, occupies the heart of Praslin, midway between Grand Anse and Baie Ste Anne. Several well-marked nature trails run through it; the brochure maps these out quite clearly. It also lists the plants and

Map on page 316

Seychelles' rich underwater world makes snorkelling a highlight of any trip.

BELOW: running through the streets of a forest village.

Coco de Mer

When he visited the Vallée de Mai in 1881, the British general, Charles Gordon (of Khartoum fame) was so struck by its natural beauty that he truly believed he had discovered the original Garden of Eden. He concluded that the coco de mer tree *(Lodoicea maldivica)* must be the Tree of Knowledge and its nut the forbidden fruit. His reasoning was that "the heart is said by the scriptures to be the seat of desires and ...the fruit [of the coco de mer] externally represents the heart, while the interior represents the thighs and belly... which I consider to be the true seat of carnal desires". While some might demur as to his Biblical conclusions, few people could argue that the coco de mer nut that grows on the female tree does resemble the thighs and belly of a woman, complete with a strategically placed tuft of hair. The enormous catkin of the male tree is equally suggestive.

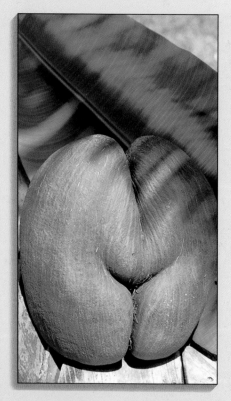

The average male coco de mer grows to 15 metres (50 ft) and the average female to 9 metres (30 ft). Each nut weighs somewhere between 18 and 22 kg (40–49 lb), which makes it the heaviest seed in the world. The male tree, which can reach up to 32 metres (105 ft), grows taller because it lives longer, but its height is also thought to facilitate wind pollination. The female tree, on the other hand, which can be heavily laden with more than a dozen nuts, is more susceptible to being felled by high winds. This may be nature's way of ensuring that the trees spread up the steep slopes as well as down the valley.

The pollination of the coco de mer is still a mystery. The wind probably acts as one agent, but the large white slugs often seen feeding on the male flowers and the green geckos common among the trees, may also act as pollen carriers. Legend has it that on stormy nights the male trees uproot themselves and engage in passionate love-making with the female palms. Some say that witnesses to this orgy are certain to die.

It is estimated that the coco de mer palm can live for between 200 and 400 years. Though now confined to Praslin and Curieuse, coco de mer trees may once have been much more common worldwide. During excavations for a new airport in Brussels in the 1980s, skeletons of large tortoises and fossils of nuts similar to the coco de mer were unearthed and dated to about 50 million years ago.

"Love nuts" have been highly prized since their discovery. They fetched such a high price in Europe that they became like gold dust. Today, they are more plentiful and carefully protected. Nuts gathered by the Ministry of Environment are hollowed out to reduce the weight and polished to be sold as souvenirs. Official collection is controlled and each nut is numbered and stamped, and sold with a permit. The fact that they still fetch a high price (a good one costs around 2,000 rupees, around €92) has encouraged poaching, so if you are offered a nut without a licence you can be sure it has been acquired illegally and is liable to be confiscated at the airport. ❏

LEFT: some people believed the voluptuous coco de mer nut had aphrodisiac properties.

COUSIN, COUSINE AND ARIDE

Map on page 326

*A Special Reserve and a haven for land birds and sea birds,
Cousin has been the centre for recovery programmes for
some of the rarest birds in the world*

These islands belong to the birds. Cousin and Cousine are the breeding ground for hundreds of thousands of sea birds; Aride is home to over a million. All three are a refuge for rare land birds, most notably the Seychelles warbler and Seychelles magpie-robin. Thanks to the efforts of conservationists, particularly the Royal Society for Nature Conservation (RSNC), Government of Seychelles and BirdLife International, both species have been saved from extinction.

COUSIN

In the mid-1960s, **Cousin Island** came on the market. As a coconut plantation of insignificant proportions with no other source of income it was not deemed to be a particularly desirable investment. However, it emerged that Cousin was the final refuge of the Seychelles brush warbler, which was down to the last couple of dozen specimens. An international appeal was launched by conservationists and interest in the island grew, as did the owner's price. It was finally purchased by the RSNC on behalf of BirdLife International for £15,500 ($25,000), a small price for saving one of the rarest birds in the world. Today it is managed locally by Nature Seychelles.

Cousin is now a nature reserve for many other bird and animal species. It is easily visited from Praslin, being just 2 km (1¼ miles) from Amitié on the west coast, and is accessible all year round (Mon–Thur, mornings only), though landing is generally easier during the southeast monsoon (May to October) when Praslin provides shelter from the strong trade winds. This is also the best time to visit to see the greatest numbers of nesting seabirds.

Most Praslin hotels and many independent boat owners arrange trips, which are often combined with afternoon visits to Curieuse and St Pierre islands to make a full-day excursion. There is a resident Nature Seychelles warden and several knowledgeable rangers who provide guided tours that last about 90 minutes. Tours are given in French, English and Kreol. Visitors are not permitted to explore the island unaccompanied and there is no overnight accommodation available.

Bird life

To minimise the risk of rats or other pests getting ashore no boats are allowed to land directly; instead, visitors transfer to the island's own boat to reach the sandy shore. As the noise of the engine is cut, the noise of the sea birds takes over. Seven species thrive on the island: four species of tern (lesser noddy, brown noddy, bridled tern and fairy tern), two shearwaters (Audubon's and wedge-tailed) and the white-tailed tropicbird.

LEFT: the waters around Aride are often choppy and landing is not as easy as it looks.
BELOW: fairy tern.

However, it is the land birds for which Cousin is most famous, the Seychelles warbler in particular. The cessation of plantation activity and the regeneration of the native vegetation led to a rapid recovery in its numbers. The future of this tiny wren-like bird has been deemed secure enough to remove it from the current world Red Data list of critically endangered species. It is a remarkable bird in that the sex of its offspring is determined by food availability. When food is plentiful, 80 percent of chicks are males, which leave soon after fledging to seek territories of their own. When food is scarce, nearly 90 percent will be female, which remain to help parents with future broods.

The Seychelles magpie-robin, a distinctive black and white bird, was once found on most of the granitic islands, but was wiped out by a combination of direct persecution and introduced predators, which had confined the bird to Frégate by the 1930s. Attempts to establish a breeding population on Cousin, begun in 1994, then on Cousine the following year, met with success. Today, this charming, tame endemic is often spotted hopping along the tourist paths. Nevertheless, it remains one of the rarest birds on earth. A third rare endemic, the Seychelles fody, breeds here and on just five other islands (Cousine, Frégate, Aride, Denis and D'Arros)

The dense population of sea birds on Cousin supports a large number of skinks.

Flora and other fauna

Of the 11 reptile varieties on Cousin, skinks are the most common. These bronze-coloured lizards feed on dead chicks and eggs. Hermit crabs are also common in the undergrowth and you'll probably spot one of the few giant tortoises that roam the island. Cousin is also one of the few places a visitor stands a reasonable chance of seeing a hawksbill turtle as Seychelles is the only place on earth where these animals come out by day *(see box page 327).*

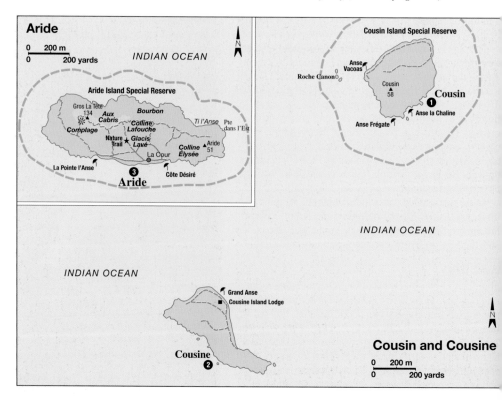

The vegetation is dominated by indigenous species. These include the *bwa torti* (tortoise tree), so called because its fruits look like the carapace of a tortoise. They are also eaten by Cousin's resident tortoises, not put off by their unpleasant smell. Also common here is the remarkable pisonia that flowers to coincide with the peaks of activity in the lesser noddy nesting colony; its sticky seeds attach themselves to the birds' feathers, the soft, malleable leaves make good nesting material and the horizontal branches are ideal nest sites.

Map on page 326

COUSINE

Cousin's sister island is a more exclusive destination. It is a privately owned nature reserve with four colonial-style chalets that can accommodate up to 10 guests at a time. It is a rare opportunity to experience living on an island teeming with wildlife. Attractions on **Cousine** ❷ include hawksbill turtles that come ashore to lay their eggs, mainly between September and January, along the sandy beach that fringes the eastern coast. Endemic birds include the Seychelles magpie-robin and Seychelles warbler, while many thousands of seabirds also breed here including the largest population of wedge-tailed shearwaters in Seychelles. Day-trippers are allowed by special arrangement made in advance (tel: 321107).

These islands belong to the birds.

ARIDE

Lying about 10 km (6 miles) north of Praslin, **Aride** ❸ is the most northerly of the granitic isles and arguably the most unspoilt island in the Indian Ocean. The name Aride (so called because there are no streams or other sources of fresh water) first appeared on French charts drawn up after exploratory voyages

BELOW: newly hatched turtle – if it survives, it will be up to 40 years before it returns to nest.

HAWKSBILL TURTLES

Though famous for birds, Cousin is also one of the most important breeding sites for hawksbill turtles, with possibly the longest-running monitoring programme (more than 35 years) anywhere in the world. Elsewhere, the hawksbill turtle population has been greatly reduced following years of exploitation – not for the flesh, which is sometimes poisonous, but for the shell which, until the early 1990s, was made into trinkets to be sold to tourists. It will take decades for populations to recover as hawksbills do not breed until 25–40 years of age.

In Seychelles, the turtles nest in daylight hours from August to April. A single female may emerge up to six times per season to lay her eggs at intervals of 14 days. Each nest may contain up to 180 eggs. Older turtles lay even more eggs, more frequently. They hatch after about 60 days. The young turtles that emerge scurry straight to the sea, but not all of them make it. On the way, some fall victim to crabs, others to seabirds. Those that reach the sea are still not safe, as many will be eaten by large fish. As a result, very few survive to adulthood. Recent research includes attaching transmitters to adult turtles linked to satellites in order to discover the mystery of where they spend their time outside the breeding season.

BELOW: helicopter and schooner off Cousin island.

in 1770 and 1771, but the island had no settlers until 1861. Thereafter, it was run as a plantation until 1973 when it was purchased by Christopher Cadbury of chocolate fame (1908–95), a keen conservationist and at the forefront of campaigns to set up nature reserves on Cousin, La Digue and Aride. But it was his purchase of Aride island, given to the Royal Society for Nature Conservation and its establishment as a nature reserve in 1979 for which he is most remembered. An engraved granite plaque on La Pointe l'Anse is dedicated to his memory. Today, Aride is owned by Island Conservation Society.

The island is covered in a rich flora and fauna and all species can be seen from the set nature trail. This begins at the settlement of **La Cour**, crosses the flat coastal plateau and winds uphill to a **viewing point** at the peak of Gros La Tête, 134 metres (435 ft), where the cliffs drop dramatically to the sea. From here you can see hundreds of frigatebirds, noted for their huge wingspan, which can stretch to 2 metres (6½ ft), soaring over the sea. On clear days, the coral island of Denis is just visible on the horizon, but where the waves crash against the foot of Aride's cliffs are the last granite rocks before India and Sri Lanka. Once on the hill, visitors are not allowed to deviate from the path as the ground either side is riddled with the burrows of nesting shearwaters, which are easily inadvertently destroyed. You return to the Visitors' Shelter at the beach in time for lunch, with the afternoon free to swim, snorkel or explore the plateau.

The reserve is open three days a week, usually Sunday, Monday and Wednesday, 10am–3pm, but days and times vary according to weather conditions. The island warden and local rangers, the only inhabitants, give guided tours lasting about two hours. Most of the larger hotels organise day trips (the crossing from Praslin takes about 45 minutes), and lunch and the entrance fee to the reserve are included in the price.

A million sea birds

Like Cousin and Cousine, Aride is a rat-free zone and consequently has remained a haven for vast numbers of sea birds. Ten species breed on Aride; more than the rest of the granitic islands combined. Chief among these is the sooty tern, numbering 300,000 birds. Aride has the world's largest colony of the lesser noddy, sheltering almost 200,000 pairs, as well as the largest surviving colony of the rare roseate tern in the Indian Ocean. The breeding season of terns and noddies coincides with the southeast monsoon, which lasts from March to October. All in all, there are over a million breeding birds milling about the island, making Aride an extremely noisy place at this time of year.

The elegant fairy tern, symbol of Air Seychelles, nests throughout the year, as does the white-tailed tropicbird, one of the most beautiful of all sea birds. They can be seen all over the island but you need to walk to the top of the hill to find the few pairs of red-tailed tropicbirds breeding in the only site outside the Aldabra group. Completing the seabird scene are the wedge-tailed shearwater and Audubon's shearwater. Shearwaters leave their burrows before dawn, returning after nightfall and are more likely to be encountered at sea en route to Aride.

helles paradise flycatcher, the symbol of La Digue, the reserve was set up to preserve some of the last remaining takamaka and Indian almond *(badanmyen)* trees in which it feeds and nests. This habitat is under tremendous pressure from the island's growing population and boat-building industry. *Veuve (Vev* in Kreol) means "widow", a reference to the magnificent, long black tail feathers of the male, reminiscent of a widow's black veil. The female, by contrast, lacks the elongated tail feathers and is chestnut and white with a black hood. Once widespread in the Praslin group, the paradise flycatcher has survived as a breeding bird only on La Digue, though a few sightings have been reported on neighbouring Félicité. They can be seen almost anywhere on the coastal plateau in the early morning, but chances of a sighting in the reserve are more or less guaranteed in the early morning and late afternoon. A Visitors' Centre at the reserve entrance provides information on the birds and the warden gives useful pointers on where they can be spotted. Entry is free and the path that begins at the roadside Visitors' Centre is navigable both on foot and by bike.

Sorting and cleaning vanilla pods.

Continuing inland from the reserve, the road bends northwards to run parallel with the coast road leading to **Château St Cloud ❸**, a grand and enchanting building that now houses a small hotel *(see Travel Tips, Accommodation)*. It was built at the height of the Napoleonic wars as the plantation house of a vanilla farm. Vanilla was introduced to La Digue in 1866 and quickly overtook coconuts as the most lucrative commodity. The further development of synthetic vanillin in the early 20th century caused the industry to crash, bringing hardship to the islanders. Ruins of the slaves' quarters and remnants of the vanilla factory can still be seen.

A road near the chateau heads up the steep hillside to **Belle Vue**, just below the summit of Nid d'Aigles. It is too steep to ride a bicycle and a tough walk except in the cool of early morning or late afternoon. The easiest way to tackle this road is by taxi. It is worth the fare for the fabulous view over the coastal plateau and out towards Praslin.

South of the Flycatcher Reserve the road leads back to the coast and turns southward once more past two art galleries, and the pretty Catholic church of **Notre Dame de l'Assomption**. Beyond these, the track leads to **L'Union Estate ❹** (open daily 8am–6.30pm; entrance fee), an old plantation. Here, there is a working *kalorifer* where copra (dried coconut) is heated and dried, and a coconut oil press pulled by an ox. Other features include **La Digue Rock**, a towering granite boulder appearing like a natural sculpture, giant tortoises, horse riding (strictly within the plantation grounds) and a picturesque **plantation house**. The old colonial **cemetery** nearby, where the early settlers are buried, is also worth a look.

The best beach

On the far side of the plantation reserve is one of Seychelles' most beautiful beaches, **Anse Source d'Argent ❺** (Bay of the Silver Spring). It is reached by following the palm-shaded trail that runs past La Digue Rock and the plantation house. There are no facilities here at all, but that is part of its beauty. The silver white sands are framed by giant granite boulders and perfectly positioned palms – the ultimate in exotic back-

BELOW: La Digue Island Lodge restaurant.

drops and a popular spot for fashion shoots. A coastal path, easy to follow on foot, continues southward past a series of equally beautiful coves.

Bicycles are an efficient form of transport on La Digue.

East to Grand and Petite Anse

Near the entrance to L'Union Estate, the road turns inland and cuts through an area of marshland known as **La Mare Soupape** (*soupap* is the Kreol name for the terrapins, or mud turtles, that inhabit the area). Beyond the marsh, the road climbs steeply and it is quite an effort to cycle or walk to the crest of the hill. Perseverance is rewarded with stunning views as the road descends through thick vegetation to the velvety sands, granite outcrops and turquoise waters of **Grand Anse ❻**, the island's largest beach. It's a perfect place to relax and picnic, but the sea can be wild and dangerous, particularly between June and September, when the waves create a powerful undertow.

A footpath leads northeast of Grand Anse towards two more magical bays. Often deserted, the white sands of **Petite Anse ❼** and **Anse Cocos ❽** are also surrounded by spectacular rock formations. Like Grand Anse, however, currents are strong and swimming can be dangerous. Unless you are particularly adventurous it is not worth exploring further than Anse Cocos where the track turns inland crossing **Pointe Ma Flore** – which offers a lovely view over Anse Cocos and the northeast coast – to Anse Caiman, then peters out before you reach the road at Anse Fourmis.

La Passe to Anse Fourmis

BELOW: Anse Source d'Argent.

The easiest way to reach Anse Fourmis is by cycling the 4 km (2½ miles) around the northern coast from La Passe. Though walking is also easy, the route has not

much in the way of shelter from the hot sun. The wild, unspoilt scenery is the main attraction. The beaches en route are all beautiful, though not all of them are good for swimming. The first of these is **Anse Sévère** ➒ which lies beyond the promontory of Pointe Cap Barbi, followed a little further on by the rockier bay of **Anse Patates** ➓. Both beaches are good for swimming and snorkelling (snorkelling can be difficult at low tide due to the swell over the shallow reef but is relatively easy a couple of hours either side of high tide). The corals are not fantastic but fish life is prolific, particularly around the rocks where the waters teem with butterflyfish, angelfish, parrotfish, squirrel fish, Moorish idols, batfish and hawkfish.

Continuing south, you'll pass a succession of small, rocky bays, washed by rougher seas – **Anse Gaulettes, Anse Grosse Roche** and **Anse Banane**. The road comes to a dead end at **Anse Fourmis**. Here, in calm weather, snorkelling is good around the rocks.

Islands north of La Digue

The waters around the neighbouring islands of Félicité, Marianne, Petite Soeur, Grande Soeur, Île Cocos, Île La Fouche and Île Zavé are rich in bird and marine life. All are within close proximity to La Digue and make ideal day-trip destinations, offering a choice of activities: swimming, diving, snorkelling, birdwatching, fishing, or just relaxing and eating. (All the islands, except Félicité, can also be reached by boat from Praslin.) Excursions to these largely uninhabited islands can be arranged through your hotel, the tourist information office at La Passe jetty or at one of the roadside stalls offering trips. Itineraries can be flexible if you discuss priorities in advance with the

Map on page 332

TIP

The restaurant at Grand Anse, Loutier Coco (daily 9am– 5.30pm), serves creole cuisine, sandwiches and omelettes at reasonable prices.

BELOW: hard day at the bar, Grand Anse.

Map on page 332

boat owner, and lunch and soft drinks are usually included. Most operator require a minimum of four people per trip.

For snorkelling, the best site is the tiny **Île Cocos** ⓫. Access to the water around this Marine National Park was forbidden to visitors during the 1980 because of the damage to its coral reefs caused by tourists. The corals are no\ slowly recovering and it is still a beautiful site. Sea birds are the main attrac tion on **Île La Fouche** ⓬ a rocky islet off the north coast of Île Cocos, an **Île Zavé**; the latter, lying south of Île La Fouche, is little more than a jumbl of rocks but holds five breeding species of sea bird: the wedge-tailed shear water, bridled tern, lesser noddy, brown noddy and fairy tern. This is also a excellent snorkelling site, weather permitting. There are large numbers o parrotfish, sweetlips and groupers. Whale sharks are commonly seen aroun November.

Just north of Cocos, **Marianne** ⓭ could have been Robinson Crusoe's ver island. Uninhabited and blanketed with coconut palms, it has a single beac\ on the western coast where small boats can land. **Grande Sœur** and **Petit Sœur** (known collectively as The Sisters; entrance fee) are owned by the Prasli hotel Château de Feuilles, which reserves them exclusively for guests at week ends. During the week, other boat owners are allowed to offer trips.

There are no day trips to **Félicité Island**, 3 km (1½ miles) northeast of L. Digue. It is owned and managed by Per AQUUM whose Zil Pasyon (Isle of Pas sion) development, due to open in late 2010, will comprise 28 residences linke to a 5-star resort. The residences, whose angled walls have been designed t merge into their rocky setting, will be available for private ownership, amon the first in Seychelles to be opened up to foreign buyers.

BELOW: sorting a bumper haul.
RIGHT: L'Union Estate.

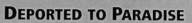

DEPORTED TO PARADISE

In 1798 there was a rebellion in the French colony c Réunion. The insurrection, led by a former sergeant Etienne Belleville, and a priest, Jean Lafosse, marched o the capital, St-Denis, protesting against taxation levels an rumours that the island was to be given to the English The revolt was easily quashed, and the decision taken t exile the dozen or so ringleaders to a suitable locatio somewhere on the coast of India. They were put aboar the *Laurette* under the command of Captain Loiseau, bu were never to reach India. Loiseau later claimed that the had to seek shelter from bad weather at Mahé. Holdin the crew at knifepoint, the deportees mutinied and force them to sail the ship to La Digue, where they went ashore letting the *Laurette* sail on to Praslin.

This story is probably a cover-up. As the deportee told it, they thought La Digue made as good a place c exile as any, and Loiseau did little to dissuade them. I fact, more than half of the newcomers did settle peace fully on La Digue, their families joining them later. Amon those who stayed was Célestin Payet, and to this da the Payets are one of the leading families of the island Belleville and Lafosse, the rebellion leaders, bot returned to Réunion in the early 1800s.

iday at this exclusive island lodge nestling under the palms of an old coconut plantation. The chalets skirting the beach provide accommodation for no more than 40 guests.

Map on page 344

Most of the 50 or so inhabitants of Desroches are contract workers, mainly from Mahé, engaged in agriculture. They live at **Settlement**, 2 km (1 mile) northeast of the resort. Hotel guests and visitors on charter boats are free to visit this area, which is a good place to get a feel for island life in colonial times. Look out for the old copra drier and the circle where an oil press once stood. The little lock up, with its barred doors, was the destination for anyone falling foul of island justice. Not surprisingly, the most common offence on these remote islands was drunkenness. The old hospital, if you can call it that, was little more than a room with a bed and a few basic medicines. In the early days, these would simply be medicinal plants that could be grown around the village, such as castor oil and datura.

Diving off Desroches is excellent, especially between November and April, and the island is famous among the diving fraternity for the amazing **Desroches Drop** – the edge of a coral plateau that forms the southern rim of the island, pitted with gulleys and deep caves (these can only be explored under the supervision of a qualified divemaster). The dive centre here runs courses for beginners and caters for other water sports (canoeing, windsurfing, sailing, snorkelling). A boat can also be chartered for game fishing trips or visits to nearby islands. The big game fishing is sensational, the waters rich in tuna, bonito, kingfish and sailfish. The hotel also has its own floodlit tennis court and hires out bicycles, perfect for exploring this flat island. A map with basically two routes – coastal and inland – is produced by the lodge.

Louis Poiret, the mystery man who claimed he was Louis XVII, the lost king of France (see page 248) came to Poivre in 1804 and was apprenticed at the cotton gin.

BELOW: a close encounter.

Southern islands and atolls

Only a day's sail from Desroches, **Poivre Atoll** is the largest atoll in the Amirantes group. It is made up of three islands – Poivre, South Island (joined together at low tide by a man-made causeway) and Florentin – all with first-class beaches. Although it was a coconut plantation before it was abandoned, in its early days its major production was cotton. Plans for the building of an island resort are in the pipeline, but at present, there is nothing here except a small settlement on Poivre. One of the most beautiful of the Amirantes islands, Poivre is named after the former governor of Mauritius (1763–72), Pierre Poivre, who was responsible for introducing spices to Seychelles *(see page 247)*. It is famous for its deep sea fishing and diving and, although it is privately owned, a limited number of visitors are allowed access, provided they have been given permission in advance; permission from IDC (Islands Development Company), New Port, Victoria; tel: 224640.

Cruising on a charter yacht is one of the best ways to explore the Outer Islands.

Etoile and **Boudeuse** are tiny uninhabited islands with nothing but breeding terns, notably the sooty tern and roseate tern, and Boudeuse has a huge colony of masked booby. The islands have the same uncanny beauty, enhanced by a sense of real isolation, as African Banks *(see below)*. You can only visit by charter boat, and landing is only possible in very calm conditions.

Marie Louise ❷ is in some ways the prettiest of the Amirantes, a coral island version of the granitic islands of Aride and Cousin, with large populations of seabirds. It has an airstrip to serve the small settlement, but there are no regular flights and no facilities for visitors. It is simply a beautiful place to include on your charter itinerary.

BELOW: sooty terns on African Banks.

The southernmost island of the Amirantes group is **Desnoeufs**, famous in Seychelles for the vast numbers of sooty terns that breed here, the eggs of which are considered a delicacy in the granitics. Egg-collecting is limited to half the island. It is hoped that this restriction will ensure that a sufficient number of birds are left to breed successfully. Outside the egg-collecting season, the island is abandoned. Again, visiting is only possible on a charter boat; even then it's difficult to get ashore. Landing should not be attempted by any but an experienced boatman or strong swimmer.

Northern islands and atolls

African Banks is a tiny island with nothing but a lighthouse. The landscape of sweeping white sand hovers like a mirage on the brightest turquoise and ultramarine waters you have ever seen. Seabirds breed here in considerable numbers. The sands are crisscrossed by turtle tracks as if a safari rally had been held during the night. The urge to go ashore and explore makes landing irresistible.

Rémire was originally named Eagle Island, named after a ship sent here in 1771 by the British in Bombay to find out what the French were up to in Seychelles. Today it is a holiday retreat for the president and other top government officials, and visitors must have special permission to land here by boat or plane. It is an island of gentle beauty, with shaded paths through the woodland and attractive beaches all around.

D'Arros and neighbouring **St Joseph Atoll** (the property of the same private owner) were important coconut-producing islands during the early years of the 20th century, often yielding over 40,000 nuts a month. D'Arros is an oval-shaped platform reef. It has an airstrip and a guesthouse offering an exclusive retreat which has been a haven for heads of state, wealthy Arabs and film stars. **St Joseph Atoll**, separated from D'Arros by a deep channel, is made up of 13 small islets, which together make up less than 1 sq km of land. They are all deserted, but some have old colonial ruins which are interesting to visit and speculate upon. Diving here is excellent.

Map on page 344

THE ALPHONSE GROUP

The Alphonse Group consists of two neighbouring atolls, **Alphonse Atoll** and **St François Atoll**.

Alphonse Atoll

Alphonse was a productive plantation in its heyday, generating 100,000 coconuts a month on a regular basis during the 1930s. The plantation was abandoned in recent times, and the island is now leased to **Alphonse Island Resort ❸**, whose chalets and villas skirt the tranquil lagoon. There is an **airstrip** for transfers from Mahé, an hour's flight away. (Visitors on charter boats need advance permission from IDC on Mahé, *see page 346*.)

The resort's Dive Centre offers facilities for diving the wall of Alphonse where forests of gorgonian fan corals, sharks, rays and huge schools of predatory fish such as barracuda, as well as a host of colourful reef fish, may be seen. The best snorkelling is at the pass into the lagoon, but this is a long way out and can only be reached by boat. Island Conservation Society runs conservation

Just south of St Joseph Atoll is a tiny deserted tuft of land called Sand Cay. It has no vegetation and is often submerged by high spring tides, but it is a popular destination for roosting terns. It is often seen covered with up to seven different species.

BELOW: the D'Arros guesthouse.

programmes on the island and arranges guided walks for visitors. The Alphonse Island Resort arranges day trips to nearby Bijoutier and St François, the uninhabited islands of St François Atoll.

Alphonse is shaped like an arrowhead. Two of its three points are named after ships: Pointe Doille is named after a guano vessel that used to call here and Pointe Tamatave is named after a British steamship that ran aground in 1903.

St François Atoll

To reach the other islands from Alphonse you must cross the **Canal la Mort** – Death Channel! The water here is deep, cold and treacherous with powerful currents. The 5-km (3-mile) journey is worth it, however, to reach the near-perfection of **Bijoutier**. The name means "little jewel" and that is just what this island is. Perfectly round, capped with bright green vegetation, fringed with the whitest of coral beaches and encircled by purple reefs and turquoise sea, this is the closest any island comes to the paradise ideal.

St François is surrounded by a fearsome reef, girdled by shipwrecks. At least six are still visible on the horizon, a grim reminder that the waters in these parts should be treated with respect. It is possible to enter the huge lagoon of St François in safety through **La Passe Traversé**. Over the coral crest, the tranquil lagoon waters are fairly shallow and a world away from the ferocity of the waters beyond the reef. The enormous plain of sand, left dry at low tide, is a feeding ground for hundreds of wading birds. Apart from its beauty and birdlife, the biggest attraction of St François is fly-fishing in the lagoon.

THE FARQUHAR GROUP

BELOW: Bijoutier, a jewel in Seychelles' crown.

The Farquhar group, which comprises Providence Atoll, St Pierre island and Farquhar Atoll, is about 700 km (435 miles) from Mahé. The islands are only accessible by sea, but with the growth of habitable cruising they are no longer

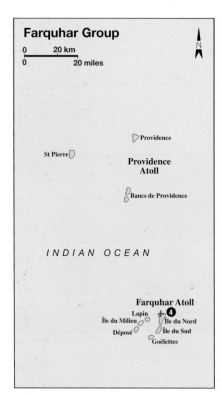

Farquhar Group

0   20 km
0   20 miles

N

◁Providence

St Pierre ◯

Providence
Atoll

◦ Bancs de Providence

INDIAN OCEAN

Farquhar Atoll
Lapin ◦ ➍
Île du Milieu ◦◦   Île du Nord
Déposé ◦   ◦ Île du Sud
◦ Goëlettes

entirely out of reach. There are also plans to build a hotel on Farquhar and it is already possible to charter a plane from Islands Development Company (IDC) and use an eight-room facility in an existing building.

Providence Atoll

This is a long, thin atoll oriented roughly north–south. **Providence**, the main island, lies at its northern tip, while across 40 km (25 miles) of shallow water **Bancs de Providence** lies at its southern extreme. Most of the reef is out of sight of land and, consequently, many a ship has foundered here. The huge shallow lagoon attracts hundreds of grey herons and this is the only place in Seychelles where herons outnumber all other bird species. Providence has a small transient human population employed by IDC in copra production, but Bancs de Providence is strictly for the birds and turtles.

St Pierre

Due west of Providence is the extremely strange raised coral platform of **St Pierre**, rising to about 10 metres (33 ft) above sea level. There is no beach at high tide and landing is only safe when the tide recedes to reveal a tiny sandy corner in the northeast. This island, now abandoned, was once mined for guano and you can still see the walls of the rotting stores and the twisted metal of what was once a quay.

Farquhar Atoll

South of Providence are the 10 islands of **Farquhar Atoll ❹**. The lagoon is a popular anchorage for yachts and schooners. On the main island, Île du Nord, there is a small settlement where a little copra is still produced. The island

Maps on pages 344 & 348

TIP

When tides are low, a good pair of plastic shoes or similar footwear is essential for wading ashore across reef flats with sharp coral fragments and possibly poisonous cone shells.

BELOW: burning coconut husks on Farquhar.

also has an airstrip. Many of the trees on neighbouring Île du Sud have been turned white by the droppings of hundreds of red-footed boobies that nest here. The southern tip of the atoll, Goëlettes, is also the most southerly island of Seychelles. It is swept almost bare of vegetation by the strong southeasterly winds, but is a haven for sea birds, with 260,000 pairs of sooty terns and a healthy number of black-naped terns, a species that breeds only on coral atolls.

The name Aldabra may originate from the Arabic al-khadra, "the green", due to the reflection cast by the shallow lagoon waters on clouds above the atoll, a sight probably familiar to Arab traders between Comoros and the Middle East.

THE ALDABRA GROUP

Aldabra is the most remote and most interesting of all the Outer Island groups. Geographically a part of Seychelles, these islands lie closer to Madagascar than they do to Mahé, more than 1,000 km (625 miles) away. The archipelago is made up of **Astove** and **Cosmoledo Atoll**, lying due west of Farquhar Atoll, and **Assumption** and the **Aldabra Atoll** beyond. There are no hotels on the Aldabra group which, apart from visiting scientists and the occasional small cruise ship or charter boat from Mahé, sees few visitors. For the most part the only foot-prints in the sand belong to the birds and turtles.

Aldabra Atoll

Aldabra **5** is the world's largest raised coral atoll; the exposed coral cap of a volcanic seamount rising more than 4 km (2 miles) from the ocean floor. Geologically, it is part of a chain that includes the Comoros. It is made up of four main islands – Picard, Polymnie, Malabar and Grand Terre – and a number of other small islets, stretching 32 km (20 miles) from east to west. This ring of coral islands encloses a vast lagoon which is fed by several channels that carry in new life with each tide.

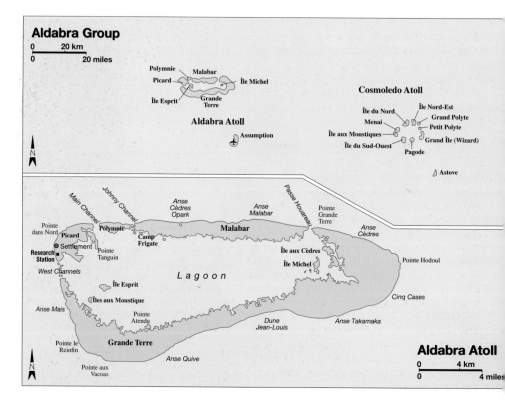

TRAVEL TIPS

T RANSPORT

GETTING THERE AND GETTING AROUND

GETTING THERE

By Air

Air Mauritius (airline code MK), the national carrier, flies from destinations in Europe (London, Paris, Frankfurt, Munich, Geneva, Milan), Africa (Johannesburg, Durban, Cape Town, Nairobi, Antananarivo), Asia (Hong Kong, Singapore, Kuala Lumpur, Mumbai, Delhi) and Australia (Melbourne), and with frequent daily flights from Réunion. Flights to Rodrigues are only available from Mauritius.

Other international carriers are: Air Austral (UU), British Airways (BA), Air France (AF), Condor, Corsairfly, South African Airways (SA), Air Seychelles and Virgin Atlantic. Emirates fly to Mauritius from Dubai.

Air Austral (tel: 0825 013012; fax: 0141 920137; email: paris@air-austral.com), based in France, offers routings to Mayotte, South Africa (Jo'burg), the Comores, Madagascar, Seychelles, Réunion and Mauritius.

No charter airlines serve Mauritius directly but you can fly from Paris to Réunion on a charter flight *(see page 380)* booked through a French travel agency such as Nouvelles Frontières (www.new frontiers.com) and fly on to Mauritius from there. Several planes a day fly between Réunion and Mauritius with Air Mauritius and Air Austral. It is important you have a recognised address to go to on arrival in Mauritius, or you will be denied entry to the country.

Airport tax is included in the price of all major airline tickets and many package deals.

Airline Contacts

Air Mauritius: tel: 207 7070; fax: 211 0366 (reservations); tel: 207 7171; fax: 211 4014 (sales)
Air Mauritius (Rodrigues): tel: 832 7321; fax: 832 7301
Air Austral: tel: 202 6677
Air France: tel: 202 6747
Air Seychelles: tel: 202 6727
Austrian Airlines: tel: 202 6703
British Airways: tel: 202 8000; fax: 212 8886
Corsairfly: tel: 210 2020
Emirates: tel: 213 9100
Ireland Blyth Ltd: tel: 202 7711; fax: 202 7339. Also general sales agents for Air Madagascar and Cathay Pacific
Virgin Atlantic: 7 Duke of Edinburgh Avenue, Port Louis; tel: 206 0900

Package Tour Operators

The following UK-based operators specialise in Mauritius:
Beachcomber Tours: tel: 01483 445621; www.beachcombertours.co.uk
Carrier Indian Ocean: tel: 0161 491 7610; www.carrier.co.uk
Elegant Resorts: tel: 01244 897505; www.elegantresorts.co.uk
Elite Vacations: tel: 01707 371000; www.elitevacations.com
Expressions: tel: 020 7433 2636; www.expressionsholidays.co.uk
ITC Classics: tel: 01244 355400; www.itcclassics.co.uk
Sunset Faraway Holidays: tel: 020 8774 7100; www.sunset.co.uk
Virgin Holidays: tel: 0871 222 5825; www.virginholidays.co.uk

From the Airport

Sir Seewoosagur Ramgoolam International Airport, abbreviated to SSR, occupies the area of Plaisance, 48 km (30 miles) south of Port Louis, and is often referred to simply as Plaisance. The international code

for the airport is MRU, tel: 603 3030; fax: 637 3266; http://aml.mru.aero
Bus service: An hourly express bus service, often crowded with locals, links with Mahébourg and Port Louis 6.30am–6.30pm but is only convenient if you have no luggage.
Taxis: If a taxi is not equipped with a meter, which they should be, agree a price before starting any journey. A metered taxi ride to Rose Hill, for example, with two items of luggage, should work out at around R750. An unmetered ride for the same journey, depending on your bargaining skills, may work out slightly less.
Sir Gaëtan Duval Airport, Rodrigues: tel: 832 7888; fax: 832 7078. Tour operators usually collect their own visitors from Rodrigues' airport, a modern building south of the island. Independent travellers can take the Supercopter bus to Port Mathurin for R150. To return to the airport, call Ibrahim Nalla on 831 1859 for pick ups from any guesthouse or hotel location in and around Port Mathurin.

By Sea

There are no international passenger shipping services to Mauritius although cruise ships occasionally call at Port Louis, either as part of a round-the-world trip or on a cruise from South Africa. Nor can you travel by sea between the Mascarenes and Seychelles, unless, of course, you are chartering a yacht.

Passenger/cargo vessels MS *Mauritius Pride* and MS *Mauritius Trochetia* operate between Mauritius and Réunion. The journey takes about 12 hours and children travel half price. The ships also operate a service to Rodrigues two or three times per month *(see page 358)*.

If you are considering planning a long-distance sea trip, make sure you choose the right season. Long-haul ocean trips are not generally made during the cyclone season.

GETTING AROUND

Driving

The British legacy of Mauritius and the Seychelles is most evident on the roads where driving is on the left and the roundabouts operate as in Britain with priority on the right. Not every local driver seems to be aware of this rule, however, and in practice he who hesitates least goes first. Beware of poultry, goats and dogs on the roads, hawkers and foragers with heavily overloaded bicycles. Scooters carrying entire families need to be given a wide berth! Public buses often drive dangerously fast on small, winding roads – make plenty of room as they will often cross the central line on sharp bends. If driving through the sugar cane areas, watch out for deep gulleys on either side of the road, especially at night.

Mauritians tend to sound their horns when attending or approaching a junction. It is meant as a friendly warning, not as a reprimand. **Rules of the road:** 80 kmph (50 mph) on "motorways" and 50 kmph (30 mph) elsewhere. The wearing of seatbelts, and rear seatbelts where fitted, is compulsory. Always carry your driving licence.

The police should attend any accidents resulting in personal injury. Where damage only is involved, exchange names and addresses on the prescribed form supplied by the car hire agency and notify them. In cases of doubt or difficulty call the police.

There is a strong presence of traffic police, particularly on the Mahébourg–Grand Baie road, where speeding is common and driving habits verge on the dangerous.

Main Routes

Mauritians refer to the road linking Mahébourg and Grand Baie as the "motorway" but it is really only a well-surfaced trunk road which crosses the island from south to north linking the plateau towns. Most of the 1,600 km (995 miles) of roads are surfaced, but many of the highways and minor roads are badly potholed. The best roads are the "motorway" and the road through Black River Gorges National Park; the worst are in towns and villages.

Names of towns and villages may appear in French and/or English and can be poorly positioned or concealed by sugar cane. Roads are adequately signed (with UK-style signposts) but navigating through towns can be a challenge. Make sure you have a good map *(see page 374)*. Distances and speed limits are shown in kilometres and, more rarely, miles.

Parking

Parking can be a nightmare at all times in Port Louis so head for the car park behind Caudan Waterfront. Short-term parking up to two hours is also available at the Port Louis Waterfront.

Parking restrictions apply in towns and to avoid being fined, display a parking coupon on your windscreen. These can be bought in booklets at petrol stations.

Driving Times

● Airport–Belle Mare	1¼ hours
● Belle Mare–Pamplemousses	55 mins
● Belle Mare–Trou d'Eau Douce	30 mins
● Belle Mare–Grand Baie (via the coast)	1 hour
● Port Louis–Curepipe (without holdups)	40 mins
● Le Morne–east coast (via interior)	2 hours

Car Hire

To hire a car you must be aged over 23 and have a full valid driving licence, which must be carried with you when driving. Car hire rates usually include comprehensive insurance and collision damage waiver but always check first. Tyre punctures can be repaired cheaply at any garage. If you hire a motor cycle you should be provided with a crash helmet. If you only want a car for a short while to see round the island, consider hiring one with a driver-guide, who will know the best places to go and will save you the bother of driving.

Major credit cards and cheques are increasingly becoming accepted by smaller companies.

Car Hire Companies

Avis: Al-Madina Street, Port Louis; tel: 208 1624; fax: 211 1420; www.avismauritius.com
Budget Rent a Car: S. Venkatesananda Street, BP 125, Rose Hill; tel: 467 9700; fax: 454 1682; www.mauritours.net
Europcar: Pailles; tel: 286 0140; fax: 286 4705; www.europcar.com
Hertz Mautourco: Gustave Collin Street, Forest Side; tel: 674 4301; fax: 670 5910; www.mautourco.com
Société J.H.A. Arnulfy and Co: Labourdonnais Street, Mahébourg; tel: 631 9806; fax: 631 9991; www.henri-vacances.com

By Bus

Buses are plentiful, inexpensive and generally reliable although the service is less frequent in the evening. There are two bus stations in Port Louis, one linking it with the north and the other with the plateau towns in the south. Fares range from R12 up to R70 for travel by express service.

Some of the older buses do not inspire confidence; they chug along belching out heavy black exhaust, but get to their destination eventually. If you're in a hurry take one of the

BELOW: Flamboyants, with their deep red blooms, flank many a roadside.

On Your Bike

Many visitors hire bicycles in Grand Baie. Several villages and resorts are only a few miles away and can easily be reached by bike. Most good hotels and tour operators such as White Sand Tours (tel: 212 3712) and Mauritours (tel: 467 9700) organise bike rental.

express buses but always check the destination with the conductor. Queues are orderly and tickets are bought on board. Stop bells are located at each seat. Avoid travelling between 8am and 9am and 4pm and 5pm during the week when buses are very crowded; carry small change for the fare.

Buses operate in urban regions from 5.30am to 8pm and in rural regions from 6.30am to 6.30pm. In the country buses will normally stop on request. Night owls should note that the last bus from Port Louis to Curepipe via Rose Hill, Quatre Bornes and Vacoas leaves at 11pm. The tourist office should provide a comprehensive list of bus services operating throughout the island although in practice you'll find that they are so frequent during the day a timetable is not really necessary.

In Rodrigues bus services grind to a halt at around 4pm.

By Taxi

Taxis are equipped with meters but they are rarely switched on so always agree a price before starting a journey. Try to use them only for short journeys as the fare depends on the whims of the driver and includes the taxi's return fare to base. The official tariff should be displayed inside the vehicle, with waiting time chargeable for the first 15 minutes and every additional 15 minutes. Drivers do not expect to be tipped.

In practice drivers do not adhere to these rates and any complaints should be made to the Mauritius Tourist Promotion Authority or the National Transport Authority, Victoria Square, quoting the number plate, driver's name and details of the journey.

For longer journeys it may be cheaper to hire a taxi for the day and fix a price, which should be less than a day's car hire. If you find a knowledgeable taxi driver who can act as a guide, try to keep his custom by using him regularly.

Licensed "taxi trains" or shared taxis operate near bus stops in some

towns and villages. They cover a prescribed route and the fare is divided between the number of passengers. The taxis are dilapidated and overloaded but travelling this way can be cheap, fun and fast with rates working out at not much more than the official bus fare.

Taxis are recognisable by black registration numbers on white plates. Unlicensed taxis or *taxis marrons* are instantly recognisable because they are nothing more than private cars, i.e. they have white numbers on black plates and lurk near taxi stands, bus stations and the airport. They often incur the wrath of their licensed competitors; their rates are low because they're uninsured to carry passengers.

Taxis can be hired from licensed taxi stands. Some hotels have a special arrangement with taxi drivers who are expected to charge reasonable fares. However, if you feel you are about to be ripped off, warn the driver that you will report him to the hotel. It usually works.

In Rodrigues there are only 11 taxis servicing the island. There is a taxi stand beside Port Mathurin bus station.

By Helicopter

Air Mauritius helicopters undertake transfers and regular sightseeing tours with prices depending on flying time and route. Current tariffs start at R18,700 per helicopter which can accommodate up to four people. Transfers from the airport to any hotel, for four people, is R25,000 per helicopter.

Reservations can be made in your home country through Air Mauritius (tel: 603 3754; fax: 637 4104), travel agents or email: helicopter@airmauritius.com

Sightseeing Tours

There are numerous tour operators but the following provide a wide range of sightseeing tours and other services and have hospitality desks at major hotels:

On Mauritius

Grand Baie Travel and Tours: Coast Road, Trou aux Biches; tel: 265 5261
Mauritours: 5 Venkatasananda Street, Rose Hill; tel: 467 9700; fax: 454 1682; www.mauritours.net
MTTB/Mautourco: 84 Gustav Colin Street, Forest Side; tel: 670 4301; fax: 674 3720; www.mautourco.com
Summertimes: 5 Avenue Bernadin de St Pierre, Quatre Bornes; tel: 427

1111; fax: 427 1010; www.summer-times.com
White Sand Tours: DML Building, PO Box 738, M1 Motorway, Port Louis; tel: 212 3712; fax: 208 8524; www.whitesandtours.com

On Rodrigues

Ecotourisme Rodrigues: Complex La Citronelle, Rue Max Lucchesi, Port Mathurin; tel: 831 2801; fax 831 2800; email: ecotours@intnet.mu
Rodtours: Camp du Roi, Port Mathurin, tel: 831 2249; fax 831 2267; email rodtours@intnet.mu; www.mauritours.net
Rotourco: Place François Leguat, Port Mathurin, tel: 831 0747; fax: 832 0747; mobile 875 6777; www.rotourco.com

Island Hopping

Tour operators organise excursions to both Rodrigues and Réunion depending on sailings. To travel on the MS *Mauritius Pride*, it is advisable to book directly, as soon as you arrive in Mauritius, through Mauritours, which has desks in major hotels. Better still, make arrangements through your own travel agent before you leave your home country, as you are unlikely to get a cabin in first class at short notice and the airline-style seats in economy class sell fast. Sailings between Mauritius and Rodrigues are between two and three times a month and it goes six times a month to Réunion.

Another alternative is the *Mauritius Trochetia*, which cruises regularly between Mauritius, Réunion, Rodrigues and Madagascar. It takes up to 112 passengers and there are 54 cabins, a bar, a shop and a children's corner. In Mauritius, details of sailings can be obtained from **MSC Coraline Ship Agency**, Nova Building, I Military Road, Port Louis (tel: 217 2285; fax 242 5245; email: msc@coraline.intnet.mu; www.mauritiusshipping.intnet.mu) or through your travel agent.

In Réunion contact **SCOAM**, 4 Avenue du 14 juillet 1789, 97420, Le Port (tel: 0262 42 19 45; fax: 0262 43 25 47; email: pax@scoam.fr).

Boat trips from Rodrigues to the nature islands of Ile aux Cocos and Ile aux Chats can be organised through your hotel or local tour companies such as **Rodtours** in Port Mathurin *(see listings above)*. Bookings must be made in advance as there are restrictions on the number of visitors at a time.

Lai Min
56–8 Royal Road
Tel: 242 0042
Chinese dishes that are out of this world, served in exotic surroundings. Open daily 11.30am–2.30pm and 6.30pm–9.30pm. €€€

Cap Malheureux

Coin de Mire Restaurant
Coast Road
Tel: 262 8070
Smugglers' cove-style eatery with authentic creole atmosphere and views of Coin de Mire island. The grilled pork makes a superb sizzling starter before a choice from the extensive menu. €€

Grand Baie

Café de la Plage
Sunset Boulevard
Tel: 263 7041
Fashionable hang-out for Grand Baie groupies and a good venue for relaxing over a snack and a drink. You can also dine in the thatch-roofed restaurant on the beach. €€
Don Camillo
Coast Road
Tel: 263 8540
Located near the fuel station in Grand Baie. Welcoming owner offers tasty pizzas and pastas and delicious garlic bread in a convivial atmosphere. Try the gratin de fruits de mers followed by scrumptious fish skewers. €€

Happy Rajah
Royal Road
Tel: 263 2241
A hot favourite if you're after authentic Indian food with a good range of vegetarian and meat dishes. Smoking and non-smoking areas. Open daily. €€€
La Pagode
Coast Road
Tel: 263 8733
People-watch and gorge on various Chinese dishes on the verandah of this restaurant overlooking the main road. Popular with Mauritians, excellent value for money and child-friendly. Try the saucisses chinoises (spring rolls) and fantastic crab. €€
Sakura
Royal Road
Tel: 263 5700
Elegant Japanese restaurant specialising in teppan yaki, tempura, sushi and sukiyaki. Advance notice required for some dishes and reservations recommended. Closed Sunday. €€€

Pereybère

Caféteria Péreybère
Coast Road
Tel: 263 8539
For snacks, drinks and lunch this popular beach side café/restaurant offers real value for money. The poisson gingembre is well worth trying. €
Sea Lover
Coast Road
Tel: 263 6299

Sophisticated ambiance, sea-facing views and excellent seafood and fish. €€€
Wang Thai
Coast Road
Tel: 263 4050
Delicious Thai cuisine served in spacious air-conditioned restaurant with a terrace. Try the steamed crab and noodles or fill up on tiny appetisers. Closed Monday. €€

Trou aux Biches

Coco de Mer
Royal Road
Tel: 265 7316
Slow service but worth the wait for its selection of unusual Seychelles specialities, which include fish curry in coconut milk. Try the "eat as much as you like" buffet on

Saturday. Reservations recommended. €€
Florensuc Pâtisserie
Trou aux Biches Road
Tel: 265 5349
Real espresso and cappuccino, melt-in-the-mouth pastries and take-away snacks for those on a budget. Closed evenings. €
Le Pescatore
Coast Road
Tel: 265 6337
Fine dining and wines in elegant surroundings with an Italian-Mauritian touch. Unmissable for succulent seafood – the seafood lasagne is worth a try. €€€
Souvenir Snack
Tel: 265 7047
Just across the road from Trou aux Biches police station, gargantuan portions of mine frite (fried noodles) and tasty rice dishes served in an authentic creole atmosphere. €

BELOW: Spicy samousas make a filling snack.

EAST COAST

Anse Jonchée

Paranamour Restaurant
Domaine d'Anse Jonchée
Tel: 634 5011
Offers panoramic views of Grand Port Sud Est. Watch Mauritian curries being cooked by Indo-Mauritian women and then walk off the excesses along wooded paths bounded by indigenous species of flora. Only open for lunch. Reservations recommended

unless you go as part of a tour group. €€€

Belle Mare

Chez Manuel
Royal Road, St Julien Village
Tel: 418 3599
Fax: 418 3888
The taxi ride to this inland village is well worth it to sample the superb Chinese and local dishes. Open daily except Sunday. Reservations highly recommended. €€€

Symon's Restaurant
Pointe de Flacq
Tel: 415 1135
Restaurant specialising in seafood, creole and Chinese cuisine. Popular with guests staying at hotels along the east coast. €€

Trou d'Eau Douce

Chez Tino
Tel: 480 2769
Lunch or dine in the

upstairs restaurant. Excellent creole specialities in a very informal atmosphere. Open daily for lunch and dinner. €

PRICE CATEGORIES

Price categories are for two people including soft drinks or beer:
€ = less than R400
€€ = R400–600
€€€ = R600–1,000
€€€€ = more than R1,000

SOUTH COAST

Riambel

Cap Sud
Coastal Road
Tel: 625 5413
Authentic creole dishes and seafood in simple surroundings. €

Souillac

Le Batelage
Tel: 625 6083
Souillac's only restaurant in the warehouse of the "Tourist Village" overlooking the river.

Good for European and creole specialities. €

The Hungry Crocodile
La Vanille Réserve des Mascareignes, Rivière des Anguilles
Tel: 626 2503/2843

Try the crocodile croquettes! Or play safe with *croque monsieur* and some interesting local goodies, such as *samousas*, washed down with wine from the extensive list. €€

WEST COAST

Black River

La Bonne Chute
On the forecourt of the Caltex Petrol Station, Tamarin
Tel: 483 6552
Don't be put off by the strange address. This long established restaurant, often used for wedding receptions, serves excellent creole and European cuisine. €€
Le Kiosk
Ruisseau Créole
Tel: 483 7004
Trendy hang-out for snacks, drinks and hefty salads

after a day in the adjacent shopping complex. €
Pavillon de Chine
Black River Village
Tel: 483 5787
Serves tasty creole food and excellent South African wines. There is a good family atmosphere and high chairs for toddlers. Watch the world go by from the verandah. Closed Thursday. €€
Pavillon de Jade
Royal Road, Trois Bras
Tel: 483 6151
Colourful Chinese restaurant serving excellent food to hungry walkers

visiting Black River Gorges. Car parking facilities. €€

Chamarel

L'Alchimiste
Rhumerie de Chamarel, Route Royale
Tel: 483 7980
www.rhumeriedechamarel.com
Enjoy mountain views and à la carte lunch in the grounds of a magnificent rum distillery. The menu features venison, wild boar, duck and organic produce grown on the estate. Open Mon–Sat 11.30am–3pm. €€€€

Flic en Flac

Domaine Anna
Morcellement Anna
Tel: 453 9650
Blow the budget on mountains of Chinese fare in this huge, circular restaurant built from local stone. Specialities include seafood with heart of palm salad and fish with ginger sauce. €€€€
Ocean
Tel: 453 8549
Great Chinese treats in this friendly restaurant. Excellent value. €€

PLATEAU TOWNS

Curepipe

La Potinière
Hillcrest Building,
Sir Winston Churchill Street
Tel: 676 2648
Excellent French restaurant with a long-standing reputation. €€

Floréal

La Clef des Champs
Queen Mary Avenue
Tel: 686 3458

Gourmet French cuisine with creole touch in sophisticated colonial-style setting. Reservations recommended. €€€

Quatre Bornes

Happy Rajah
St Jean Road
Tel: 257 3877
www.happyrajah.com
Under the same ownership as its namesake in Grand Baie, this 90-seater restaur-

ant set in a beautifully restored colonial-style house specialises in authentic Indian food prepared by chefs from Delhi. Dine indoors or on the verandah. Open for lunch and dinner. Closed Sunday. €€€

Trianon (near Quatre Bornes)

Mokafé
Trianon Shopping Park
Tel: 464 4996

Busy little French-style café; great for baguettes or a salad and good coffee. Popular pit-stop after shopping at Trianon or Quatre Bornes. €

Mon Repos
Tel: 467 6437
Fax: 467 6419
Email: jamrosa@intnet.mu
Lunch on the veranda or in the garden of this old colonial house, which is conveniently close to Trianon shopping centre. €€

RODRIGUES

Port Mathurin

Le Capitaine
Johnston Street
Tel: 831 1581
Doubles up as a disco and restaurant. Try seafood, chicken croquettes or go for the popular *menu du jour*. €€

Chez les Italiens
Rue François Leguat
Tel: 831 0541
First-floor eatery overlooking the street and run by Italian couple; specialises in pastas and local cuisine. Closed Monday. €
Paille en Queue
Duncan Street
Tel: 832 0084

Serves excellent Rodriguan curries and Chinese food. €€

La Mangue

John's Resto
Tel: 831 6306
This restaurant is noted for fresh seafood and Chinese specialities but if you're after something a cut

above, order in advance. €€

PRICE CATEGORIES

Price categories are for two people including soft drinks or beer:
€ = less than R400
€€ = R400–600
€€€ = R600–1,000
€€€€ = more than R1,000

ACTIVITIES

MAURITIUS

NIGHTLIFE, SPORT AND SHOPPING

NIGHTLIFE

There is usually something going on somewhere in Mauritius, whether it be a hotel dinner show, a sega performance, a Hindu, Chinese, Muslim or Christian festival *(see page 375)* or some kind of play or theatrical show. Most tourist hotels offer Las Vegas-style cabarets, sanitised sega shows, live music and themed cultural programmes, and some have casinos. For up-to-date information on cultural events and evening entertainment consult the local tourist office or your hotel receptionist. The Mauritius Tourism Promotion Authority produce a range of free guides containing basic information, but the main bars, nightclubs and casinos are listed below.

Nightclubs

Mauritius is not hot on nightlife, though the Caudan Waterfront in **Port Louis** has brought new life to the capital, which, for the most part, goes quiet after dark. Pubs and bars rather than nightclubs can be found here. Party animals can find a clutch of discos, with names like N-Gyone, Buddha Club and Les Enfants Terribles, around **Grand Baie** – although some are the haunts of prostitutes and sailors. Discos and nightclubs usually open only on Friday and Saturday nights.

In **Rodrigues** look out for hand-written bills advertising the **Grande Soirée Dansante**, dance nights organised in the town's three discotheques, when everyone from babes in arms to robust Rodriguan grannies bop to reggae and the fusion that is seggae. For clean family fun make for the alfresco disco **Les Cocotiers** next to Residence Tamaris, but for rum, rhythm and red-blooded recreation, try **Le Récif**.

Cinema

Most films shown in Mauritius are in French and a few cinemas also show Hindi and Tamil films. The cinema at the **Caudan Waterfront** shows the latest films from Hollywood, Bollywood and France, but don't expect to watch anything in English. The Mahatma Ghandi Institute at **Moka** sometimes screens English-language films. Consult the local newspaper for times and programmes. **Rose Hill** also has a cinema.

Casinos

If you're feeling lucky, head for the **Caudan Waterfront** casino or the Casino de Maurice in **Curepipe** and try your luck at roulette and blackjack, or pump your money into one of the many slot machines. Many of the top hotels also have their own casinos, including **La Pirogue** in Wolmar and **St Géran** in Poste de Flacq. There are casinos at Domaine Les Pailles near Port Louis and in Flic en Flac, and slot machines at Ti Vegas at Grand Baie. Visit www.casinosofmauritius.com. None of the casinos require you to show your passport and entry is free, but you are expected to dress smartly. Casinos are open every day from 10am to 4am.

Theatres

Productions by the Réunion-based theatre company, **Centre Dramatique de l'Océan Indien**, are sometimes staged at one of the island's two theatres:
Plaza Theatre, Rose Hill.
Théatre de Port Louis, Intendance Street, Port Louis.
Regular jazz, choral performances and other musical events are promoted by **Otayo** (www.otayo.com).

SPORT

Throughout the year football and athletics attract huge crowds and for details of these and other sporting events consult the tourist office, local newspapers or the general secretary of the **Mauritius Amateur Athletics Association** at Le Réduit, tel: 464 2256.

The Mascarene Islands regularly take part in the **Indian Ocean Island Games**, a sort of mini-olympics event involving Mauritius, Réunion, Madagascar, Seychelles and the Comores Islands, held every four years and hosted in turns by a member nation.

Outdoor Activities

Mauritius is ideal for water sports. The coral reefs provide a fascinating and magnificent underwater landscape and many establishments offer snorkelling and diving expeditions. Undersea walks, submarine excursions and glass-bottom boat trips may appeal to the less adventurous.

Offshore breezes provide ideal conditions for windsurfing and sailing on the west coast, and the glassy lagoons and sheltered bays are perfect for water-skiing, paragliding, pedalo trips and

RÉUNION

SEYCHELLES

kayaking. Big game fishing is popular out in the Indian Ocean and you are unlikely to return from a trip empty handed.

On dry land, the many nature reserves offer a network of hiking trails and the possibility of spotting indigenous wildlife rescued from extinction. Horse riding and mountain biking are also available. **Mauritours** (tel: 467 9700; fax: 454 1682) has a desk at many hotels and can organise a wide range of sporting activities for you.

For a fun family day out, try the **Belle Mare Water Park** (Coastal Road, Belle Mare; tel: 415 2626; fax: 415 2929; open daily in summer 10am–5.30pm and winter 10am–5pm; entrance fee). The complex includes food kiosks, fast food outlets, children's and adult pools, giant water slides, jacuzzi and wave pool.

Watersports

Diving and Snorkelling

Nearly 30 dive centres are attached to hotels and offer excursions to shipwrecks and dive sites. The following cater for all levels, from beginners to experienced divers, and some provide night dives. Check out www.mauritius-info.com/sports/index.htm or contact the **Mauritian Scuba Diving Association**, tel: 454 0011; email: msda@intnet.mu; www.msda-cmas.org
Beachcomber Fishing Club, Le Morne, Black River; tel: 450 5142. Also specialists in big game fishing.
Blue Water Diving Centre, Le Corsaire, Trou aux Biches; tel: 265 7186.

Exploration Sous Marine, c/o Villas Caroline, Flic en Flac; tel: 453 8450; www.pierre-szalay.com.
Paradise Diving Centre, Coastal Road, Mon Choisy; tel: 265 6070.
La Pirogue Diving Centre, Wolmar; tel: 453 8441. Good for learners.

Old hands will find plenty of specialist diving, including night diving. Owned and managed by Pierre Szalay, former president of the Mauritius Scuba Diving Association.

Trou aux Biches has several good dive centres. Hughes Vitry, based at the Blue Water Diving Centre next door to the popular fish restaurant Le Pescatore (see page 365), is a well-known undersea photographer and may take you on a "shark dive".

Rodrigues
Bouba Dive Centre, Mourouk Ebony Hotel, Pate Reynieux; tel: 832 3063; email: boubadiving@intnet.mu
Club Osmosis (for kite-surfing), Mourouk Ebony Hotel; tel: 832 3051; www.osmosis-rodrigues.com
Cotton Dive Centre, Cotton Bay Hotel; tel: 831 8028; email: diverod@intnet.mu
Rodrigues Diving Centre, Pointe Venus Hotel; tel: 832 0104
Rodrigues Underwater Group, Pointe Monier-Rodrigues; tel: 831 2032

Big Game Fishing

The best time for game fishing is from October to April when marlin, espadon, tuna and the big wahoo are plentiful. The Marlin World Cup competition is held at the Centre de Pêche in November. Fishing trips last for a minimum of six hours and take five rods at a time. Book through your hotel or tour operator or directly through the following companies:

JP Henry Charters, Black River; tel: 483 5038; email: info@blackriver.com
Killer Fishing, Coastal Road, Trou aux Biches; tel: 265 6595
Le Morne Anglers' Club, Black River; tel: 483 5801; email: lmacclub@intnet.mu
Organisation de Pêche du Nord, Corsaire Club, Royal Road, Trou aux Biches; tel: 265 5209
La Pirogue Big Game Fishing, Flic en Flac; tel: 453 8054
Sportfisher, Grand Baie; tel: 263 8358; email: karen@intnet.mu

Rodrigues
BDPM Fishing Co Ltd, Port Mathurin; tel: 831 2790
Le Boss Fishing, Anse aux Anglais; tel: 875 9076
Rod Fishing Club, Port Mathurin; tel: 875 0616

Sailing and Cruising

Hobie Cats (small catamarans) can be booked on the beach at most hotels. The following yacht charter companies offer half or full day excursions in large sail boats. Reservations can be made through hotels or direct with:
Centre Sport Nautique, Sunset Boulevard, Royal Road, Grand Baie; tel: 263 8017; tel/fax: 263 7479. Also organises Hobie Cat sailing, kayaking and pedalo trips.
Croisières Australes, La Cuvette Road, Grand Baie; tel: 263 1669.
Croisières Turquoises, Mahébourg; tel: 631 1648. Day-long cruises on a catamaran.
Exotic Cruise, Pointe aux Piments; tel/fax: 261 1724. Sunset and all-day catamaran trips with lunch along north coast to Gabriel Island.
Océane Croisières, Trou d'Eau Douce; tel: 480 2767; fax: 480 1615. Cruise along the southeast coast, stopping off for a snorkel and a visit to the Île aux Cerfs.

Windsurfing and Surfing

Surfing is best on the west coast, around Tamarin and also Le Morne. Most beach hotels supply windsurfing boards or you can book directly through **Centre Sport Nautique**, Grand Baie; tel: 263 8017; tel/fax: 263 7479.

Hiking, Trekking and Adventure

For general information on hiking trails around the island, contact The Director of the National Parks and Conservation Service at the Ministry of Agriculture and Natural Resources, Le Réduit; tel: 464 4016; fax: 464 2993.

Equipped for Snorkelling

Many hotels and dive centres provide snorkelling equipment, but if you plan on doing a lot of underwater exploration, it is always better to invest in your own. Snorkels and masks are widely available, but before parting with your money, make sure the snorkel mouthpiece is soft and comfortable and check the mask fits properly. You can do this by holding it in place without putting the strap over your head, then breathing in through your nose. If the mask stays on with the suction when you let go, it should be fine; if air escapes then try another one.
Identifying fish: a host of different species of tropical fish make their home in the coral reefs and there

are a number of excellent books to assist with the identification of the common species. For snorkellers it would be well worth getting hold of a "fish watchers' slate" – a plastic card printed with colour drawings of the 40 most common species, as this can be taken into the sea.
Sun protection and safety: remember to cover yourself with plenty of waterproof, high-factor sun cream and it's also a good idea to wear a T-shirt while snorkelling to avoid sunburn on your back. If there are jet skis or other motorised craft in the area, it is sensible to mark your location by tying a brightly coloured float to your waist or foot.

In the Dry

If you don't like getting your face wet but don't want to miss out on the beauties of a coral reef, try a solar-powered undersea walk. Wearing a specially designed helmet which supplies you with fresh air from the surface, you can even wear your spectacles or contact lenses. And it is suitable for children as young as seven.
Captain Nemo's Undersea Walk Kiosk next to Caltex petrol station, Grand Baie; tel: 263 7819. Or book through your hotel or tour operator. Open daily from 9am.
Aquaventure, c/o Coco Beach Hotel, Belle Mare; tel: 415 1010 or 256 7953. More undersea walking.
Blue Safari Submarine, Royal Road, Grand Baie; tel: 263 3333; fax: 263 3334; www.blue-safari.com. An air-conditioned hour-long trip under the sea in a submarine. Open daily, 9am–9pm.
Le Nessee. A one-hour trip in a semi-submersible. Departs four times a day from 9.30am and once at night at 7pm. Book through any travel agent or your hotel.

Yanature, tel: 785 6177; www.yanature.com. Organises guided walking tours to Black River Gorges and mountains. Good physical condition is required.
Saint Felix Sugar Estate, tel: 697 7941; fax: 697 2160; www.incentive partnersltd.com. Offers "green tourism" activities in this private sugar estate in the deep south. Play Tarzan for the day attached to a speed zip line over the Rivière des Galets, splash around in waterfalls and finish off with a typical Mauritian lunch at a rustic lodge where you can cook your own chapatis. Also archery and trekking.
Le Pétrin Information Centre near Grand Bassin (open daily 9am–4pm) can provide up-to-date information on walks and conditions of trails in the Black River Gorges National Park, such as the 7-km (4-mile) round walk from Le Pétrin through the Macchabé Forest (spectacular views). Another walk from Le Pétrin is to the Tamarin Falls near Curepipe. Or go to the **Black River Visitor Centre** (open daily 9am–4pm) near the gorges.
Espace Aventure, tel: 670 4301; fax: 674 3720. Adventurous inland nature trails for off-road enthusiasts in Land Rovers, with guide.

Some tours include lunch in local homes.
Vertical World Ltd, tel: 697 5430 or 251 1107. Specialists in hiking, rock climbing and exploring canyons.
Yemaya Adventures, tel: 752 0046. Hiking, mountain biking and sea kayaking.
Quad Biking, Domaine du Chasseur, Nouvelle France; tel: 631 3336; fax: 631 3198; www.leclubdesgrandsbois.com. Discover the interior with a guide by quad biking through countryside, fields and forests.
Wild Things Adventure, Mon Choisy; tel: 933 2835; www.wildthingadventure.com. Quad biking (at R500 for 30 minutes) for speed fanatics, on a track in an isolated area behind Mont Choisy. This company also hires out touring motorcycles.

Abseiling and Canyoning

If you want to try your hand at abseiling head for the Tamarind Falls. For information on excursions, contact Yamaya Adventures, tel: 752 0046 or Vertical World, tel: 251 1107 or 697 5430.

Ecotourism

The **Île aux Aigrettes Nature Reserve**, opposite Mahébourg on the east coast, is home to a large population of pink pigeons and an assortment of reptiles. It is in the process of gradually being restored to its natural original state. Visits are possible through **Mauritius Wildlife Foundation** (MWF; tel: 631 2396).

Golf

18-hole Courses

Anahita, tel: 402 2200.
Belle Mare Plage Golf Hotel and Resort; tel: 402 2600. Championship 18-hole course – the best on the island.
Golf au Chateau, Bel Ombre; tel: 623 5600.
Île aux Cerfs, Le Touessrok Hotel; tel: 402 7000. Splendid 18-hole course with spectacular views.
Le Paradis, Le Morne; tel: 401 5050; fax: 450 5140; email: paradis@bchot.com. An 18-hole course on which the odd helicopter lands from time to time.
Tamarina, Tamarina Bay; tel: 727 6493.

Nine-hole Courses

Coco Beach, Poste de Flacq; Maritim Hotel, Balaclava; St Géran Hotel, Pointe de Flacq; Shandrani Hotel, Blue Bay; Sofitel Imperial, Flic en Flac.

Horse-riding

Horse riding can be arranged through your hotel or tour operator or through **Mauritours**, tel: 467 9700; fax: 454 1682/3.
Try also **Horse Riding Delights** at Mont Choisy (tel: 265 6159); **Les Ecuries de la Vieille Cheminée** (tel: 686 5027).

SHOPPING

What to Buy

You could be spoilt for choice in your wanderings round the new shopping malls in Mauritius, where local products and handicrafts stand alongside luxury imported goods. Haggling in markets is perfectly acceptable. Shops tend to have fixed prices but may offer you a small discount for bulk or major purchases.
Model ships (see box page 370) and **wooden hand-carvings** make good buys. Replicas of wooden creole houses and hand-carved salad bowls, miniature tropical fruits and the inevitable dodo can be bought everywhere. Raw materials such as straw, wood and fabrics turn up as appealing patchwork creole dolls representing people from the various ethnic groups.
Textiles and **clothing** are good quality but not necessarily cheap – good buys to look for are woollens, T-shirts, saris, silk and cotton shirts and casual wear. In up-market shops you'll find rich tapestries, murals, rugs and cushions, embroidered tablecloths and napkins, quilted wall hangings and pottery depicting scenes from Mauritian life.
Markets sell *tentes* or baskets made from the vacoas or pandanus leaf, coconut leaf, raffia, aloe, bamboo and banana fibre which serve as useful shopping bags as they are very strong and hardwearing.
Jewellery Unusual buys include pieces made from mother-of-pearl, coconut or local dried seeds; also gold jewellery, mounted with precious stones.
Flowers Long-lasting cut andreanums and anthuriums, in small, medium or large blooms, travel well and can be bought at the airport in convenient pre-packaged boxes, just prior to your flight. Alternatively, you can visit the plantations and order flowers from there.
Glass-blowing demonstrations from recycled glass can be seen at the Glass Gallery, next to the Mauritius Breweries at Phoenix, between 9am

Model Ships

Making intricate model boats and ships – including replicas of famous galleys – is an art in Mauritius and can be bought from workshops dotted around the island, ranging from the affordable to the very expensive. The **Historic Marine**'s factory, at Zone Industrielle de St Antoine, Goodlands, where nautical furniture in teak and mahogany is made, also gives tours of the workshop.

First Fleet Reproductions at Phoenix has two showrooms at Phoenix and Black River (tel: 698 0161; fax: 698 5424; www.firstfleet reproductions.com).

and 11am and 1pm and 3pm. Slender vases and ornaments can be bought from the adjacent shop (open Mon–Sat 8am–5pm; tel: 696 3360). **Chinese goods** such as kimonos, silks and *objets* made from brass, jade and porcelain can be found in specialised shops, particularly in Curepipe.

Objets d'art can be bought at Diane, Royal Road, Trou aux Biches, tel: 265 5156.

Mauritian food specialities such as spices, sugar, tea and smoked marlin don't cost the earth and make nice gifts.

There are **art galleries** dotted all over the island where you can pick up paintings and handicrafts by local artists and artisans.

Shopping Centres

Caudan Waterfront, Port Louis. Some of the best shops on the island. Several clothes shops and duty free.

Currimjee Arcades, Royal Road, Curepipe. Small centre with a few clothes and duty-free shops.

Galerie des Îles, 1st floor Arcades Currimjee, Royal Road, Curepipe. Large shopping mall where you can buy oriental carpets, objets d'art and furnishings duty free.

Jumbo, Phoenix. Large American-style shopping centre with an enormous supermarket and street of other shops, but not many clothes outlets.

Jumbo, Riche Terre, modern complex with attractive boutiques stocking clothes and handicrafts, fast food court and pleasant supermarket shopping in air-conditioned comfort.

Orchard Centre, Quatre Bornes. More glitzy inside than out. Lots of clothes stores.

Port Louis Waterfront, Port Louis. Boutiques selling everything from bonsai to arts and crafts.

Ruisseau Créole, Black River. Trendy shops selling everything from designer wear to health foods.

Sunset Boulevard, Grand Baie. A mixture of shops with some good clothes stores.

Super U, Grand Baie combines Internet facilities with European-style shopping in a supermarket that stocks just about everything.

Trianon Shopping Complex, popular complex comprising supermarkets, fast food, shops and boutiques. Huge parking area.

Duty Free

Remember to take your passport and airline ticket when shopping for duty-free goods outside the airport and that they must be paid for in foreign currency or by credit card. Duty-free shops will arrange for your purchases to be delivered to the airport before your departure, but you must allow at least one day for the formalities to be completed.

Mauritius Shopping Paradise has duty-free outlets in Port Louis, Grand Baie and the airport, but other names to look for are Sashena Trading, Etoile d'Argent, Linea Azzura Shop, Parure and Bijouterie Bienvenue for perfumes, photographic equipment, cosmetics, sportswear, shoes and jewellery.

Some Duty-Free Shops

Adamas Diamond Duty Free Boutique, Mangalkhan, Floréal; tel: 686 5783; fax: 686 6243

ATVA Gems Factory Showroom, 32 Mon Desir, Bonne Terre, Vacoas; tel: 425 7815/7585; fax: 425 7594

Caudan Waterfront, Port Louis; tel: 211 9500

Cledor, Mangalkhan, Floréal; tel: 686 7140; fax: 698 8961. For duty-free diamonds.

Mauritius Shopping Paradise, Paille en Queue Shopping Centre, John Kennedy Street, Port Louis; tel: 211 6835; fax: 211 6696

Poncini Duty Free Boutique, 2 Jules Koenig Street, tel: 211 6551; fax: 208 8850

Shiv Duty Free Jewellery, Le Pavillon Cinema Complex Shop C14, tel: 211 7294

Tara Cashmere, Espace Ocean, Grand Baie, tel: 263 6688

Bookshops

Publications in both French and English are widely available in the island's bookshops.

Bookcourt Ltd, Caudan Waterfront, Port Louis; tel: 211 9262

Le Cygne, Magic Lantern Complex, 307 Royal Road, Rose Hill; tel 464 2444

Browse all day in this well-stocked bookshop tucked in the arcades at Rose Hill. Choose your books over a cup of tea or coffee at the back of the shop.

Librairie Allot, Currimjee Arcade, Royal Road, Curepipe; tel: 676 1253; Sir William Newton Street, Port Louis; tel: 212 7132

Papyrus, Richmond Hill Complex, Grand Baie; tel 263 7070

Trèfles, Currimjee Arcade, Royal Road, Curepipe; tel: 676 3025

Textiles and Clothes

Floreal Square shopping complex (tel: 698 8016) sells quality garments made from raw imported materials such as cashmere, cotton and silk.

Men fare rather better than women in **made-to-measure outfits** and you can select from a wide range of imported or local cloth to make top-quality trousers and shirts. A wool worsted three-piece suit can be made for less than £200. **House of Caustat** (Rue Chasteauneuf, Curepipe; tel: 676 1195; fax: 686 5441) is considered to be the best men's tailor in Mauritius, with a client list that includes guests of the Royal Palm Hotel. Suits can be made up in 24–48 hours at **Karl Kaiser** (Europe's Hugo Boss) but your tailor will expect you to have one or two fittings before the final stitches are put in place. They will keep measurements on file, if asked, so that new or repeat orders can be made in advance.

Bargain Designer Clothing

Mauritians make up the clothes for many European designers and often have stock left over that is sold at a third of the normal price, such as Bonair, Floreal Knitwear, Shibani and Tara.

Rodrigues

In **Rodrigues**, a **Saturday market** selling everything under the sun, from souvenirs to home-made chutneys and fresh produce, operates in Fishermen Lane, Port Mathurin from 6–10am. You can buy baskets made from vacoas leaves at the **Women's Handicraft Centre** in Mont Lubin, and other handicrafts at **Careco** in Port Mathurin and at **Sir Gaetan Duval airport** at Plaine Corail.

A – Z

MAURITIUS

A HANDY SUMMARY OF PRACTICAL INFORMATION, ARRANGED ALPHABETICALLY

RÉUNION

A dmission Charges

Government-run museums are free but always check to make sure they are open before setting out. There is an entrance fee for all private museums and tourist attractions. Discos and nightclubs may charge admission for men but women often get in for nothing. Sometimes free cultural and dance shows take place

Animal Welfare

The sight of many stray cats and dogs, often in appalling conditions, may be upsetting for some visitors. If you want to do something about it contact PAWS (tel: 631 2304; fax: 631 2296; www.pawsmauritius. org), a local animal welfare charity affiliated to WSPA, at Mahébourg. Their activities include mass sterilisation campaigns, an adoption scheme and a humane animal welfare philosophy. The local MSPCA is not affiliated to the RSPCA International Section.

at the Caudan Waterfront, so ask around for what's happening.

B udgeting for Your Trip

Allow at least R1,000 per day per person to cover meals and snacks, soft drinks and entrance fees. Avoid your hotel room's minibar if you're on a budget. Bottled water, wines, spirits, cigarettes and food are much cheaper at the local supermarket. Eating and drinking outside your hotel is also much cheaper but remember when ordering food that not all menu prices include 15 percent VAT. Portions tend to be generous so unless you're famished it can be quite hard getting through a full three-course meal.

Business Travellers

Business dress in Port Louis is fairly formal; women will feel more at ease in cotton dresses and men should wear lightweight suits or at least a shirt and a tie. It's considered good form to present your business card at the first meeting and shake hands.

All business is conducted in English. Local business people do not object to being phoned at home before the working day but they do expect you to be punctual for appointments.

A useful publication for the business traveller is the annual *International Mauritius Directory* published in Mauritius and available from bookshops. Travellers from the UK will find that their laptop computer plugs are compatible with the square three-pin plug sockets in Mauritius.

C hildren

Kids are welcome at restaurants, festivals and all places of worship throughout the Mascarene Islands. Luxury hotels in Mauritius cater specially for youngsters and offer supervised activities, special meals, babysitting services, family rooms and child discounts on excursions.

If you're travelling with very young children avoid December and January which may be too hot for them. Supermarkets stock a wide range of

SEYCHELLES

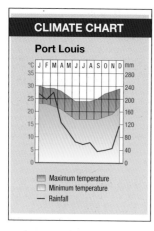

CLIMATE CHART
Port Louis

☐ Maximum temperature
☐ Minimum temperature
— Rainfall

baby food and nappies but you should bring your own from home if you have a favourite brand.

Climate

Mauritius and Rodrigues enjoy a tropical climate with two seasons: summer and winter. The hot and humid summer months from November to May produce prolonged sunshine with temperatures of up to 35°C (95°F) on the coasts, broken by short heavy bursts of rainfall. Humidity is high even at night.

From May to October, temperatures can climb up to 25°C (77°F) with little rain, cooler nights and less humidity. The southeast trade winds blow all year keeping the south and east coasts fresher during the summer but it can get uncomfortably windy during the rest of the year.

Cyclone Warnings

In the southwestern region of the Indian Ocean the following terms describe the intensity of different cyclonic disturbances:
● **Tropical depression:** speed of gusts is less than 90 km (56 miles) per hour.
● **Moderate tropical depression:** speed of gusts is 90–134 km (56–83 miles) per hour.
● **Strong tropical depression:** speed of gusts is 135–79 km (84–111 miles) per hour.
● **Tropical cyclone:** speed of gusts is 180–250 km (112–55 miles) per hour.
● **Tropical cyclone of strong intensity:** speed of gusts is 251–335 km (156–208 miles) per hour.
● **Tropical cyclone of very strong intensity:** speed of gusts is more than 335 km (208 miles) per hour.

For visitors who like to walk, tour and explore, the best time to go is October and November. These are the driest months, which provide less humidity than high summer and are outside the cyclone season. The differences in Mauritius' altitude, topography and wind direction produce varied microclimates; the towns on the central plateau can be cloud-capped, damp and cooler while the coast is clear and sunny.

Cyclones can occur between November and April. They are born hundreds of miles to the northeast of Mauritius and take days to meander westwards. Various weather stations track their route and warnings that a cyclone may develop are broadcast days in advance. Most pass by harmlessly bringing only heavy rain and winds which clear the air after a spell of very hot humid weather. Others may have more devastating effects and you should listen to all cyclone warnings and comply with any directions or advice.

Crime and Safety

Generally, Mauritians are a law-abiding people. However, you should take basic precautions as you would at home. Don't flaunt jewellery and money in public; never leave property on view in your car; always lock doors and windows when you go out, particularly in self-catering accommodation; and after dark don't give a lift to a stranger or go out walking alone.

English is spoken at all police stations in Mauritius and specially

When a cyclone approaches the islands, the Meteorological Office regularly broadcasts cyclone bulletins and red flags are raised on public buildings to denote their intensity:
● **One red flag:** Warning Class I – low risk of gust up to 120 km (75 miles) per hour.
● **Two red flags:** Warning Class II – increased risk of gusts to 120 km (75 miles) per hour.
● **Three red flags:** Warning Class III – great danger of gusts to 120 km (75 miles) per hour.
● **Four red flags:** Warning Class IV – gusts of 120 km (75 miles) per hour have been registered.

Weather information:
tel: 302 6071
Cyclone information: tel: 96

trained Tourist Police are based at Grand Baie (tel: 213 1740 or 210 3894). If you are a victim of crime, try to get names and addresses of witnesses and report the matter to the police. In cases of theft ensure you have documentation for insurance purposes.

Be extra wary of over-friendly characters hanging around isolated locations during the day. Instances have been reported at Rochester Falls and Black River Gorges where tourists have been forced to part with money and valuables.

Customs Regulations

Travellers are allowed to bring in the following duty-free items:
● 250 grams of tobacco (including cigars and cigarettes)
● 1 litre of spirits
● 2 litres of wine, ale or beer
● 250 ml of eau de toilette
● a reasonable amount of perfume
There are stiff penalties for the importation of illegal drugs.

D isabled Travellers

Top-class hotels provide good facilities for disabled travellers but check with your travel agent before leaving home. Beyond the hotels, facilities are generally dire but disabled people joining an organised tour will find that islanders are willing to lend a helping hand.

E mbassies and Consulates

If you are arrested or need legal representation contact your embassy or consulate. However, it should be stressed that officials can't advise on legal matters but may help you find an interpreter or arrange to contact friends or relatives. The main addresses are:
Australia High Commission: 2nd floor, Rogers House, John Kennedy Street, Port Louis; tel: 202 0160; fax: 208 8878
British Honorary Consul: Careco Centre, Camp du Roi, Port Mathurin; tel/fax: 832 0120; email: brhonconrod@intnet.mu
Canada High Commission: c/o Blanche Birger Company Ltd, Jules Koenig Street, Port Louis; tel: 212 5500; fax: 208 3391
UK High Commission: 7th floor, Les Cascades Building, Edith Cavell Street, Port Louis; tel: 202 9400; fax: 202 9407
US Embassy: 4th floor, Rogers House, John Kennedy Street, Port Louis; tel: 202 4400; fax: 208 9534

FURTHER READING

Mascarene Islands

General

The Age of Kali: Indian Travels and Encounters by William Dalrymple. HarperCollins (1998). Contains an interesting chapter on Réunion and creole beliefs in black magic.

Bourbon Journal by Walter Besant. London (1933). Short and amusing diary of a British schoolteacher who holidayed in Réunion and climbed Piton de Neiges.

Culture Shock! Mauritius by Roseline NgCheong-Lum. Kuperard (1997). Cultural insights into Mauritius – good reading for anyone intending to work or stay long term.

The Dive Sites of Mauritius by Alan Mountain. New Holland (1995). A well-illustrated comprehensive guide to diving and snorkelling in Mauritius.

Golden Bats & Pink Pigeons by Gerald Durrell. William Collins (1977). A hilarious account of Durrell's travels to Mauritius and Rodrigues in search of specimens for his Jersey Zoo.

History of the Indian Ocean by August Toussaint. Routledge (1996). A general background history of countries in and around the Indian Ocean with a good reference to pirates, the Anglo–French conflict and British supremacy of the Mascarenes and Seychelles.

The Island of Rodrigues by Alfred North-Coombes. Mauritius (1971).

A most readable history and background to Rodrigues by the Mauritian-born author whose interest goes back to 1937 when he was posted there as a civil servant.

Islands in a Forgotten Sea by T.V. Bulpin. Books of Africa, Cape Town (1969). One of the finest books you'll come across for an overview of pirates and corsairs in the western Indian Ocean, including history and development of the Mascarenes and Seychelles to the 1960s.

The Mauritian Shekel by Genevieve Pitot. Rowman & Littlefield Publishers, Inc. (2000). The full story of Jewish detainees in Mauritius, 1940–45.

Six months in Réunion by P. Beaton. London (1860). Life in Réunion as seen by a British clergyman.

Studies of Mascarene Island Birds edited by A.W. Diamond. Cambridge University Press (1987). Academic study of the dodo, solitaire and other extinct birds of Mauritius and Rodrigues.

Sub Tropical Rambles in the Land of the Aphanapteryx by Nicholas Pike. London (1873). Highly readable and often amusing account of experiences in Mauritius by the US Consul to Mauritius.

Underwater Mauritius by A.J. Venter. Ashanti Publishing (1989). The author describes some amazing dive sites in Mauritius, Rodrigues and the Seychelles.

Voyages and Adventures by François Leguat. London (1707). Written by Rodrigues' first settler and acknowledged as Rodrigues' first guide book this book is a must for anyone going there. Ask your public library to order it for you.

Fiction

The Book of Colour by Julia Blackburn. Jonathan Cape (1995). Set largely in Mauritius this is the story of the author's meditation on the lives of her father and grandfather, which unfolds with surreal precision.

The Mauritius Command by Patrick O'Brian. Collins (1977). Naval adventures around Mauritius during the Napoleonic Wars.

Paul et Virginie by Bernadin de St Pierre (translated by Raymond Hein). Editions l'Ocean Indien. This romantic novel tells the story of the ill-fated St Géran which sank off the coast of Mauritius in August 1744.

The Prospector by J.M.G. Le Clézio (translated by Carol Marks). David R. Godine Publisher (1993). The Mauritian narrator, Alexis, of Nobel laureate J.M.G. Le Clézio's tale embarks on a search for pirate gold in order to restore his family's fortunes. His quest is interrupted by World War I and service in the trenches of Ypres and the Somme.

MAURITIUS

RÉUNION

SEYCHELLES

T RANSPORT

GETTING THERE
AND GETTING AROUND

GETTING THERE

By Air

There are two airports in Réunion; **Roland Garros Airport** (tel: 0262 48 80 68), 10 km (6 miles) from St-Denis; and **Pierrefonds** (tel: 0262 96 80 00) on the west coast, 5 km (3 miles) from St-Pierre. The national carrier is Air France (AF).

Regular daily flights operate between Mauritius and Réunion with Air Mauritius (MK) and Air Austral (UU), which also operates flights to Réunion from Africa and the African islands (Johannesburg, Moroni, Mayotte, Seychelles and several destinations in Madagascar). Based in France *(see details below)*, Air Austral offers routings to the Comores, South Africa, Madagascar, Seychelles, Réunion and Mauritius.

Air Austral: 2 rue de l'Eglise, 92200 Neuilly sur Seine; tel: 08 25 01 30 12; fax: 01 41 92 01 37; www.air-austral.com

Airline Charter Companies

Corsairfly: 2 Avenue Charles Lindbergh, 94528 Rungis; tel: 01 49 79 75 04; fax: 01 49 79 75 04; www.corsairfly.com

Airline Offices in Réunion

Air Austral: 4 rue de Nice BP 611, 97473 St-Denis, and at Roland Garros and Pierrefonds airports; tel: 0825 01 30 12; fax: 0262 90 90 91

Air France: 7 Avenue de la Victoire BP 845, 97477 St-Denis; tel: 0820

82 08 20; fax: 0262 40 38 40; Roland Garros Airport, tel: 0262 40 38 38; www.airfrance.com/re

Air Madagascar: 31 rue Jules Auber, 97461 St-Denis; tel: 0262 21 05 21; fax: 0262 21 10 08

Air Mauritius: 7 rue F-de Mahy, St-Pierre, tel: 0262 96 06 00, fax: 0262 96 27 47; Roland Garros Airport, tel: 0262 48 80 18; Pierrefonds Airport, tel: 0262 96 80 18, fax: 0262 96 80 17; www.airmauritius.com

Corsairfly (Nouvelles Frontières): 2 rue Maréchal Leclerc, 97400 St-Denis, tel: 0820 04 20 42; Roland Garros Airport, tel: 0262 48 17 51, fax: 0262 48 80 13.

From the Airport

You can hire a car *(see below)* or take a taxi from the airport; expect to pay €18–25 and €4.20 or more if travelling after 8pm or on public holidays. Cheaper at €4 is the *car jaune* (yellow bus) to St-Denis, with regular departures 7.30am–8.30pm.

GETTING AROUND

By Car

Whether travelling by hire car or public bus getting around Réunion is easy thanks to an excellent, well-signposted road system. Driving is on the right, as in France. The speed limit is 110 kmph (68 mph) dropping to 50 kmph (30 mph) in towns and built-up areas. Avoid driving during the rush hours, particularly the main coastal route which can become a four-lane traffic jam, and the winding roads in the

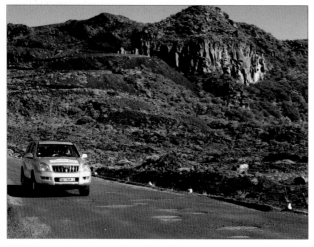

BELOW: Driving through Réunion's dramatic interior.

E ATING OUT

MAURITIUS

RECOMMENDED RESTAURANTS, CAFES AND BARS

Where to Eat

Some of Réunion's best restaurants form part of the **Saveurs et Senteurs de la Réunion** (Flavours and Fragrances) group which is affiliated to the Guild of French Provinces Restaurateurs. These restaurants are often attached to hotels and mainly specialise in both French cuisine and local creole specialities, such as *cari* (curry), *chou chou* (christophene), *brèdes* (a spinach-like vegetable), and pork, chicken and seafood dishes. But don't overlook the many crêperies, bars and cafés and markets for mouthwatering morsels of freshly cooked snacks such as samosas and *boulettes* (fried spiced meat or fish balls). Most restaurants keep to standard lunch times from noon to 2.30pm and offer a fixed-price *menu du jour*. Buying a meal in restaurants outside these times is virtually impossible and you will have to wait till the evening. Many

restaurants are closed on Monday *(see pages 176–7 for more about Réunion's cuisine).*

Country Cooking

Many of the island's farmers and country dwellers offer lunches at good value for hungry trekkers at their homes. Usually the food is traditional creole and in some establishments eaten with the hosts. Contact **Maison de la Montagne et de la Mer** *(see page 389)* or the local tourist office for details. It's advisable to book in advance especially for Sunday lunch.
● **Fermes auberges:** farm-inns where a traditional creole meal is cooked with local produce. Contact **Relais Agriculture et Tourisme**, 24 rue de la Source, 97464, St-Denis; tel: 0262 94 25 94; fax: 0262 21 31 50; www.reunion-chambagri.fr or www.bienvenue-a-la-ferme.com for a list of the island's 14 *fermes auberges.*

Pint of "dodo"

The name of the local beer is Bourbon which has an emblem of the dodo, hence a bottle of beer is referred to as *un dodo.* For draught beer, ask for *une pression.* Wine is popular and as well as being produced in Cilaos, it is also imported from France. But rum in an assortment of concoctions is a speciality of Réunion – as *rhum arrangée*, rum flavoured with spices and fruit, or punch creole, rum blended wth fruit, cane syrup and juice.

● **Table d'hôte:** traditional creole meals are served at the large family table of the host seating up to 20 people. Popular on Sundays.
● **Auberge de campagne:** a country inn at which the farmer can cater for up to 80 people with traditionally cooked home-grown produce.

RÉUNION

BELOW: Mouth-watering creole cooking.

SEYCHELLES

THE NORTH

St-Denis

Chez Piat
60 rue Pasteur
Tel: 0262 21 45 76
Wild duck is just one of
the chef's culinary
creations served in this
charming little restaurant,
which used to be a typical
creole house in a quiet
part of town. Open for
lunch and dinner. Closed
Saturday lunchtime,
Sunday and Monday. €€
Cyclone Café
24 rue St Jean Chatel
Tel: 0262 20 00 23
Fax: 0262 20 14 98
Young and trendy watering
hole open from noon till
late serving salads, meats,
desserts and wines,
sometimes with live music.

Closed Saturday evening
and Sunday. €
Le Karail du Moufia
92a Avenue Marcel Hoarau,
Ste-Clothilde
Tel: 0692 16 55 71
Pleasant cosy restaurant
to the east of St-Denis
with just 10 tables,
specialising in Chinese,
creole and great steak
and chips. Takeaway menu
from €5. €
La Nouvelle-Orléans
12 rue de la Compagnie
Tel: 0262 20 27 74
Gourmet restaurant
specialising in French and
creole cuisine in a sophisticated atmosphere,
popular with lunchtime
business travellers and
tourists. Booking
recommended. €€€

Restaurant La Bourdonnais
14 rue Amiral Lacaze
Tel: 0262 21 44 26
Email:
lelabourdonnais@ilereunion.com
Fresh oysters, fois gras,
lobster and seafood
feature on the menu of
this atmospheric
restaurant housed in a
beautifully renovated East
India Company building.
Open Monday to Friday for
lunch and dinner, Saturday
for dinner. €€€
Restaurant Sur Le Pouce
21 rue Alexis de Villeneuve
Tel: 0262 21 42 13
Popular self-service
eaterie. Eat as much as
you like but do try the
pork in caramel or the
tuna curry. Closed
Monday. €

Roland Garros
2 Place du 20 Décembre,
Barachois
Tel: 0262 41 44 37
For fine wining and dining
in a sophisticated air-
conditioned restaurant
head for the Roland
Garros. Try the menu du
jour or sip drinks on the
outdoor terrace. €€€
La Terrasse
39 rue Félix-Guyon
Tel: 0262 20 07 85
Fax: 0262 21 93 45
Superb French and creole
food, including salads,
pizzas, grills and even
Corsican specialities, all
served up within this
typical creole building. You
can enjoy theme nights
and karaoke evenings
here too. €€

THE EAST

St-André

Beau Rivage
Vieille Eglise, Champ-Borne
Tel: 0262 46 08 66
Reasonably priced restau-
rant specialising in Indian,
Chinese, French and creole
cuisine. Closed Sunday
evening and Monday. €€

Le Cantonnais
620 rue de la Gare
Tel: 0262 58 39 13
www.lecantonnais.fr
Close to La Maison de la
Vanille, this popular
restaurant offers a
good range of creole
and Chinese food.
€€

St-Benoit

L'Hostellerie de la Confiance
60 Chemin de la Confiance
Tel: 0262 50 90 50
Romantic inland hotel
restaurant popular with
honeymooners. Noted for its
creole cuisine
gastronomique. €€

Piton-Ste-Rose

Anse des Cascades
Tel: 0262 47 20 42
Informal easy-going
atmosphere in this
restaurant specialising in
French and creole
cuisine. Closed evenings.
€€

THE SOUTH

St-Pierre

Le Cabanon
28 Boulevard Hubert-Delisle
Tel: 0262 25 71 46
Pleasant restaurant with a
lunchtime buzz set around a
tiny courtyard, serving tasty
French and creole food.
Menu du jour for around
€10. Closed Monday. €€
Le Cap Méchant
Boulevard Hubert Delisle
Tel: 0262 91 71 99
Fax: 0262 91 71 92
On the banks of the river
and overlooking the port
this restaurant is popular
with tourists and locals

alike for the heart of palm
salad and hot curries.
Reservations
recommended particularly
at weekends. €€
Le Latina Bar
17 Boulevard Hubert-Delisle
Tel: 0292 70 38 07
On the seafront, this trendy
watering-hole used to be
the old railway station.
Ideal for people-watching
from the open-air terrace.
€€
Le Retro
34 Boulevard Hubert-Delisle
Tel: 0262 25 33 06
Expensive but worth trying
for its first-class service

and creole and French
cuisine. €€€
Vacoas
Grande Anse
Tel: 0262 56 95 17
Panoramic ocean views
from this simple restaurant
to the south of St-Pierre,
run by a local chef who
serves excellent octopus
curry and smoked papaya
cari légumes. Open daily for
lunch and dinner. Closed
Monday. €

Basse Vallée

Etoile de Mer
Basse Vallée

Tel: 0262 37 04 60
Typical creole menu and
seafood, including grilled
lobster, against an ocean
backdrop. Closed Sunday
night and Monday.
€€€

St-Philippe

Chez Laurent
26 Route Nationale 2, Le Baril,
near St-Philippe
Tel: 0262 37 07 03
Small and welcoming
restaurant ideal for a
creole or Indian lunch or
just take-away baguettes.
€

TRANSPORT

GETTING THERE
AND GETTING AROUND

GETTING THERE

By Air

Air Seychelles flies non-stop from London to Seychelles as well as from Mauritius, Paris, Singapore and Johannesburg. Kenya Airways fly from Nairobi. Emirates (via Dubai) and Qatar Airways (via Doha) operate flights several times a week with good connections from London, Manchester and elsewhere. All international flights arrive at **Seychelles International Airport**, Mahé. The **Domestic Terminal** north of the international departure terminal serves Air Seychelles' and IDC flights *(see box below)*.

It is essential to reconfirm your return flight at least 72 hours prior to departure. **Airport tax** is included in the cost of air tickets.

Airline Contacts

Air Austral: tel: 323262; fax: 323129
Air Seychelles: tel: 381000; fax: 224305
Emirates: tel: 292700; fax: 292705
Kenya Airways: tel: 322536; fax: 324162
Qatar Airways: tel: 224518; fax: 224525

Package tour operators

Many tour operators offer package and specialist holidays to Seychelles, such as diving, birdwatching or weddings *(see Mauritius – Weddings on page 376)*.

The following UK-based operators specialise in Seychelles:
Aardvark Safaris Ltd: (island hopping combined with an African Safari); tel: 01980 849160
Abercrombie & Kent Ltd: (tailor-made luxury travel) tel: 0845 618 2200
Aquatours Ltd: (diving holidays) tel: 020 8398 0505
Cox & Kings Ltd: (up-market travel) tel: 020 7873 5000
Cresta Holidays: (sailing holidays) tel: 0871 664 7963
Elite Vacations Ltd: tel: 01707 371000
Frontiers International Ltd: (fly-fishing) tel: 01285 741 340
Hayes & Jarvis Ltd: tel: 0871 200 4422
Jarvis Seychelles: (tailor-made travel) tel: 01492 680444
Just Seychelles Ltd: tel: 020 8840 0969
Kuoni Travel: tel: 01306 747002
Naturetrek: (wildlife) tel: 01962 733051
Ornitholidays: (birdwatching) tel: 01794 519445
Planit World Travel: tel: 0800 634 3548

Inter-island Flights

The small Air Seychelles planes make regular trips throughout the day from the Domestic Terminal on Mahé to Praslin, and operate a single flight daily to Bird and Denis (chartered by the hotels on these islands, through which bookings must be made). IDC operate scheduled flights most days to Alphonse and Desroches plus charter flights to other outer islands:

● Mahé – Praslin	15 mins
● Mahé – Bird	25 mins
● Mahé – Denis	25 mins
● Mahé – Frégate	15 mins
● Mahé – Alphonse	1 hour
● Mahé – Desroches	50 mins

Seychelles Connections: tel: 0870 741 9967
Seychelles Experience: tel: 01202 419219
Seychelles Travel: tel: 01202 877330
Sunset Faraway Holidays: tel: 020 8774 7100
Tropical Locations: tel: 0845 277 3310
Tropical Places: (weddings) tel: 0870 160 5025
Worldwide Journeys and Expeditions: (tailor-made and special interest) tel: 020 7828 4856

GETTING AROUND

Most of the granitic islands may be visited from bases on either Mahé or Praslin. Mahé is the base for trips to the islands of Ste Anne Marine National Park, Silhouette, North and Thérèse. Praslin is the base for trips to Aride, Cousin, St Pierre and Curieuse. Either Praslin or La Digue may be used as a base for visits to Grand Soeur, Marianne and Cocos. La Digue may be visited on a day trip from Praslin but a longer stay is preferable, to enjoy the atmosphere of the island. To visit Bird, Denis and any of the Outer Islands requires overnight accommodation.

By Air

Air Seychelles (tel: 381000) offers internal flights to Praslin throughout the day. The same planes are chartered to the resorts of Frégate Island, Bird Island and Denis Island for guests and staff (no day trips by air are possible). **Islands Development Company** (IDC; tel: 224640; fax: 224467) also operates

MAURITIUS

REUNION

SEYCHELLES

planes to Desroches and Alphonse resorts. IDC planes may be chartered to other islands where airstrips exist. There are no facilities on planes and no in-flight services.

By Helicopter

Helicopter Seychelles (tel: 385858; fax: 373055) offers shuttle services between Mahé, La Digue and Praslin Thur–Tues 10am–midnight. A minimum of 2 passengers is required to confirm a flight. Scenic flights are also offered. Chartered flights are available and may be tailored to meet specific needs. Charter destinations with helipads are Aride, Bird, Cousine, Denis, Félicité, Frégate, North, Ste Anne and Silhouette. Specialised services include search and rescue, aerial surveys and filming/photography. In an emergency, Medivac services can be arranged. Helicopters accommodate a pilot and four passengers. Children over the age of two require their own seat by law. Passengers should avoid taking more than 10 kg (22 lb) of baggage without prior consultation.

By Sea

Ferries operate between Mahé, from **Inter-Island Quay**, Victoria, Praslin (Baie Ste Anne) and La Digue (La Passe jetty). Two fast **catamarans**, **Cat Cocos** (Mahé, tel: 324843; Praslin, tel: 233340) and **Praslin Express** (Mahé, tel: 225046; Praslin, tel: 236065) take one hour to cross between Mahé and Praslin. Praslin Express also runs to and from La Digue via Praslin on Mon, Wed and Sun and direct to La Digue on Fri and Sat. It is advisable to book, particularly at weekends when there is considerable local traffic.

    Ferries are the main form of transport between Praslin and La Digue and they operate daily. It is essential to book seats in advance (tel: 232329/232394). Arrive 15 minutes before departure for all ferries.

    Schooners operate throughout the day with seven daily return journeys departing Praslin Mon–Thur 7am–5.15pm and La Digue 7.30am–5.45pm. On Fri and Sun the last sailing in each direction is 30 minutes later. On Sat the last sailing from Praslin is 6.15pm.

By Yacht or Motorboat

Day trips or trips of several days on a yacht or motorboat can be arranged to most islands. Contact **Marine Charter Association** (tel: 322126) or a local tour operator (see page 416) for a tailor-made excursion.

By Bus

Buses are cheap and reasonably good but times and routes are geared to local requirements, not tourists. On Mahé, if travelling at peak periods you may have to stand and at other times, particularly weekends and public holidays, you may have a long wait at bus stops. Buses are less frequent on Praslin. On La Digue buses take the form of open-sided covered lorries (camions) that roam the island with no fixed timetable. Elsewhere there are no buses. Buses on Mahé operate mainly between 5.30am and 8pm and on Praslin between 6am and 6.30pm.

By Taxi

There are plenty of metered taxis available on Mahé but not so many in Praslin. It is often necessary to ask the driver to turn on the meter to avoid any argument over the fare at your destination. If the meter is broken (often the case) a fare should be agreed in advance. On Mahé taxis can be found at the airport, Victoria taxi rank in Albert Street (next to Camion Hall) and by the clock tower in Independence Avenue. Your hotel will also organise one for you.

    Taxi drivers can often make very good, amusing and informative guides to the islands and can be hired by the hour or day for negotiable rates, which you must agree on before setting off. On La Digue most people get around on bicycles (available at La Passe); there are only a few unmetered motorised taxis, and several more ox-carts, which pass for taxis. They may be encountered driving up and down at La Passe or at the jetty when a ferry arrives from Praslin. None of the other islands has taxis.

Driving

Cars are driven on the left in Seychelles. Standards of driving are not high. Drivers tend to roam onto the wrong side of the road with alarming frequency, veering to the left only when absolutely essential. Tourists unfamiliar with driving on the left sometimes forget which country they are in and create added confusion.

    The absence of pavements and the narrowness of roads mean that pedestrians are often added obstacles, particularly at weekends and public holidays when the drink

has flowed a little too freely. The rush hour around Victoria should be avoided if possible (either side of 8am and 4pm). None of this should deter you from taking to the road, however – certainly the best way to explore both Mahé and Praslin.

    Roads on Mahé are very good. Praslin roads are good between Grand Anse, Baie Ste Anne and Anse Volbert, but deteriorate en route to Anse La Blague and Anse Lazio.

    Speed limits are 40 kmph (25 mph) in towns and villages and 65 kmph (40 mph) elsewhere, except for Mahé's east coast road where the limit is 80 kmph (50 mph).

Car Hire

Cars may be hired only on Mahé and Praslin; several car hire companies are represented at Seychelles International Airport and at the larger hotels. You can arrange to hire a car before you leave home through your tour operator. A national or international licence is required. Vehicle standards are variable and it is useful to inspect prior to making a commitment. Vehicles can be delivered or re-delivered to any point, mutually agreed with the hire company. Jeeps and saloon cars are widely available from most car hire firms.

Service Stations

Victoria Service Station, Mahé: open daily 5.30am–11pm
Airport Service Station, Mahé: open daily 6am–9pm
Anse Royale Filling Station, Mahé: open daily 7am–6.30pm
Baie Lazare Petrol Station, Mahé: open Mon–Sat 7am–7pm, Sun and public holidays 7am–noon
Beau Vallon Service Station, Mahé: open daily 6am–9pm
Baie Ste Anne Filling Station, Praslin: open daily 7am–6pm
Grand Anse Service Station, Praslin: open Mon–Sat 7.30am–6pm, Sun and public holidays 7.30am–noon

Parking

Parking is free in Seychelles except in the centre of Victoria. Even here, there is a free car park on Francis Rachel Street next to the sports stadium, convenient for most requirements. To park on other Victoria streets and car parks requires advance purchase of parking coupons, available through many retail outlets. Traffic police have little to do in Victoria and failure to observe the rules where payment is required will almost invariably lead to a fine.

A CCOMMODATION

HOTELS, YOUTH HOSTELS, BED AND BREAKFAST

Choosing a Hotel

Hotels are generally small and exclusive in Seychelles, so prices are usually high and you get a better deal with a package. But the hotels are in beautiful spots and often provide bungalow accommodation. Some establishments offer self-catering accommodation with a restaurant as an option and there are a growing number of guesthouses. Contact the **Seychelles Tourist Board** (tel: 671300; fax: 620620; email: info@seychelles.net) for a list. Supplements may be applied during the peak seasons at Easter, Christmas and New Year and August. A General Sales Tax (currently 7 percent) is levied on all hotel bills. Visitors are required to pay their hotel accounts in some form of foreign currency, usually by credit card, but cash and traveller's cheques are also acceptable. No camping is permitted in Seychelles.

Self-catering

Mahé

Anse Soleil Resort
Anse Soleil; tel: 361090; fax: 361435; email: soleil@seychelles.net
A secluded six-room resort on a hillside with spectacular views and just a short stroll to two of Seychelles' finest beaches. €

Beau Vallon Bungalows
Tel: 247382; fax: 247955; email: bvbung@seychelles.net; www.beauvallonbungalows.com.
Excellently located opposite Beau Vallon beach and close to several restaurants, shops and water sports centres. €

Blue Lagoon Chalets
Tel: 371197; fax: 371565; email: blagoon@seychelles.net; www.seychelles.net/bluelagoon
A very small attractive development with four well-equipped self-catering villas overlooking the tranquil waters of Anse à la Mouche. Two rooms have air-conditioning; all have ceiling fans. €€

Eden's Holiday Resort
Port Glaud; tel: 378333; fax: 378160; email: eden@seychelles.net; www.seychelles.net/eden.
Excellent, well-equipped chalets in a quiet and beautiful location on the west coast. €€

Sun Resort and Properties
Beau Vallon; tel: 285555; fax: 247224; email: sun@seychelles.net; www.sunresort.sc/en/home.htm
Though geared up for self-catering, a restaurant offers breakfast and dinner should you change your mind. The complex is built around a good swimming pool and is just a two-minute stroll from Beau Vallon beach. €€

Praslin

Les Villas d'Or
Côte d'Or; tel: 232777; fax: 232505 email: villador@seychelles.net; www.seychelles.net/villador
Two two-bedroom and eight one-bedroom luxury villas within close proximity to restaurants and shops. Breakfast and dinner can be provided on request. €€

ACCOMMODATION LISTINGS

MAHÉ

Beau Vallon

Le Méridien Fisherman's Cove
Tel: 677000
Fax: 620901
www.lemeridien.com/fishcove
A beautiful Le Meridien hotel right on Beau Vallon beach; 62 rooms; facilities include tennis courts and water sports. €€€€

Beau Vallon Bay Beach Resort
Tel: 287287
Fax: 247943
www.berjayahotels-resorts.com/beauvallon.htm
One of the larger hotels with good facilities including dive centre, water sports, tennis court and casino. Separate restaurants offer pizzas

and snacks, plus Chinese, Japanese and international cuisine. €€

Coral Strand Hotel
Tel: 621000
Fax: 247517
www.coralstrand.com
A dependable, friendly hotel on Beau Vallon beach. Well located for various activities including water sports, glass-bottom

boat, game fishing and diving. €€

MAURITIUS

RÉUNION

SEYCHELLES

ABOVE: Le Méridien Barbarons.

www.lemeridien.com/barbarons
A large 124-room hotel on the west coast with good amenities, including a big swimming pool with a children's pool and a free shuttle service to a nearby casino. €€

Anse Intendance

Banyan Tree Resort
Tel: 383500
Fax: 383600
www.banyantree.com
A modern five-star hotel. There are 60 villas and one presidential villa, all set in lush tropical surroundings on a hillside overlooking a beautiful beach. In a quiet corner of the main island. €€€€

Anse Soleil

Anse Soleil Beachcomber
Tel: 361461
Fax: 361460
www.beachcomber.sc
Good value for money in a superb setting. Off the beaten track, so what you save on accommodation might have to go towards car hire. €€

East Coast

Wharf Hotel and Marina
Tel: 670700
Fax: 601700
www.wharfseychelles.com
A luxury hotel halfway between Victoria and the airport. This is ideal for visitors on a short stay and for those on business or with connecting flights. €€€

Anse Forbans

Allamanda Resort
Tel: 388800
Fax: 388801
www.allamandatclubseychelles.com
Thirty well equipped rooms all with ocean views. Mediterranean cuisine is offered at the Palms Restaurant throughout the day. €€

Anse Louis

Maia Luxury Hotel and Spa
Tel: 390000
Fax: 390010
www.maia.com.sc
Thirty exclusive villas with everything from private butler service to private swimming pool. This is the ultimate in luxury – and price.
€€€€

Glacis

Hilton Seychelles Northolme Resort
Tel: 299000
Fax: 299006
www.hiltonworldresorts.com
Forty luxurious villas on a hillside overlooking Silhouette and North Island, with a small private cove. Infinity pools blend with the view of the Indian Ocean. Complimentary services include transport to nearby water sports and dive centres.
€€€€
Sunset Beach Hotel
Tel: 261111
Fax: 261221
www.sunset-beach-resort.com
A small, quiet, exclusive hotel featuring Spanish-style rooms and one luxury villa on a beautiful secluded bay. Shady terrace. €€€

Bel Air

Bel Air Hotel
Tel: 224416
Fax: 224923
www.seychelles.net/belair
More of a guesthouse than a hotel, this is situated on the edge of Victoria and is ideal for those visiting Seychelles on business. €

Barbarons

Château d'Eau
Tel: 378177
Fax: 378388
A quiet but beautiful small hotel on an excellent beach in a peaceful location. €€€
Le Méridien Barbarons
Tel: 673000
Fax: 673380

PRASLIN

Anse Bois de Rose

Coco de Mer Hotel and Black Parrot Suites
Tel: 290555
Fax: 290440
www.cocodemer.com
Situated on the beautiful, peaceful southwest coast; 52 spacious rooms and suites, all with private verandahs, face the sea and the setting sun. Facilities include water sports, mini golf and an excellent nature trail.

Bicycles and snorkelling equipment are both available for a nominal charge. Deep sea fishing and excursions to nearby islands can be arranged. €€€ (suites: €€€€)

Pointe Cabris

Château de Feuilles
Tel: 290000
Fax: 290029
www.chateau.com.sc
A small, luxurious hotel with a variety of accommodation from rooms to individual chalets. The restaurant has a fixed menu featuring fish dishes.
€€€€

Anse La Farine

New Emerald Cove Hotel
Tel: 232323
Fax: 232300
www.emerald.sc
Overlooking Round Island, Praslin and Baie Ste Anne on a beautiful beach only accessible by sea. Twenty-eight standard and 14 superior rooms, all air-conditioned. Amenities include dive centre and volleyball. €€

Anse Kerlan

Lemuria Resort
Tel: 281281
Fax: 281001
www.lemuriaresort.com
A five-star facility in a spectacular location spread over 36 hectares (90 acres) and with three beaches. Eighty-eight junior suites, eight senior suites, eight luxury villas and a spectacular presidential villa. A choice of restaurants and bars plus excellent amenities including an 18-hole golf course, tennis, birdwatching, dive centre, water sports and fitness centre. €€€€

Anse Gouvernement

L'Archipel
Tel: 284700
Fax: 232072
www.larchipel.com
An excellent small hotel

with magnificent architecture, set on a secluded sheltered beach. A variety of water sports facilities are offered and the restaurant is good, too. €€€

Anse Petit Cour

La Réserve Hotel
Tel: 298000
Fax: 232166
www.lareserve.sc
A beautiful hotel on a secluded private beach, ideal for swimming and snorkelling year-round. Facilities include sports fishing and island excursions. €€€

Anse St Saveur

Villa Flamboyant
Tel: 233036
Fax: 233036
www.villaflamboyanthotel.com
Colonial-style guesthouse set in 2 hectares (5 acres)

of beautiful gardens and trees by the beach. Home cooking with home-grown organic produce. The sea can be seaweedy between June and October. €

Anse Volbert

Acajou Hotel
Tel: 232400
Fax: 232401
www.acajouhotel.com
A small hotel with 28 spacious rooms in two blocks constructed from mahogany (from South African plantations). Rooms have balconies facing the sea, air-conditioning and the usual amenities. €€€

Paradise Sun Hotel
Tel: 293293
Fax: 232019
www.paradisesun.com
A medium-sized hotel with good water sports facilities and an excellent dive centre. €€€

Berjaya Praslin Beach Hotel
Tel: 286286
Fax: 232244
www.berjayahotels-resorts.com/praslin.htm
A large Berjaya hotel with good facilities next to an excellent beach. One of the few on Praslin offering live entertainment.
€€

Côte d'Or Lodge
Tel: 232200
Fax: 232130
www.igrandiviaggi.it
Attractive bungalows overlooking a beautiful beach. A private boat offers excursions to nearby islands.
€€

Grand Anse

Hotel Marechiaro
Tel: 283888
Fax: 233993
www.seychelles.net/marechiaro
Pleasant granite and timber chalets in a tranquil setting. Facilities include a dive centre, tennis court and water sports.
€€€

Indian Ocean Lodge
Tel: 233324
Fax: 233911
www.indianoceanlodge.com
Just a few steps from the beach. There is a free shuttle service to Côte d'Or and daily excursions to Aride, Cousin or Curieuse.
€€

BELOW: Champagne welcome at the Lemuria.

LA DIGUE

Anse La Réunion

La Digue Island Lodge
Tel: 292525
Fax: 234132
www.ladigue.sc
A charming hotel by the beach, with A-frame chalets, rondavels and a restored colonial house painted bright yellow. €€€€
Château St Cloud
Tel: 234346
Fax: 234545
Email: stcloud@seychelles.net
An old château plantation house which once produced vanilla, near the foot of the

hills. A tourist attraction in its own right *(see page 333)*. €€

Anse Patates

Hôtel Océan
Tel: 234180
Fax: 234308
www.hotelocean.info
A small eight-room hotel with a commanding view on a headland, a short way from a sandy cove. Good facilities including air-conditioning. €€
Patatran Village
Tel: 294300

Fax: 294390
www.patatranseychelles.com
Eighteen chalets on a rocky headland overlooking the wild northeast coast of the island. Simple but comfortable rooms. Creole restaurant. €€€

La Passe

Villa Authentique
Tel: 234413
Fax: 234413
Six air-conditioned rooms, two of which are self-catering, two minutes from

the beach. Very friendly family atmosphere. €

L'Union

Paradise Flycatcher's Lodge
Tel: 234423
Fax: 234422
www.paradise-flycatcher.com
Chalets, each comprising two units, with common dining area, living area and verandah. Quiet location, a few minutes from the beach. You can choose between self-catering or restaurant facilities. €€€

MAURITIUS

REUNION

SEYCHELLES

OTHER ISLANDS

ABOVE: Privacy guaranteed on Frégate Island.

There is only one hotel on each of the islands listed here:

Aldabra Research Station
For information contact Seychelles Islands Foundation, La Ciota Building, Mont Fleuri
Tel: 321735
Fax: 324884
www.sif.sc
With no vessels visiting on a regular basis and no trips organised by tour operators as yet, visits require careful planning. Accommodation is in simple rooms each with en-suite shower and toilet (though water may be rationed). €€€

Alphonse Island Resort
Tel: 229030
Fax: 229034
www.alphonse-resort.com
A luxury hotel in a remote island setting. There are 25 spacious thatched chalets, and five executive villas. All have air-conditioning, verandah and en-suites with jacuzzi. Excellent for game fishing, fly-fishing, snorkelling, diving and birdwatching. €€€

Bird Island Lodge
Tel: 224925
Fax: 225074 (Mahé)
Tel: 323322 (Bird)
www.birdislandseychelles.com
Pleasant individual chalets with ceiling fans and basic facilities. The restaurant is excellent. €€€

Cerf Island Resort
Tel: 294500
Fax: 294511
www.cerf-resort.com
Twelve villas of different grades, situated in peaceful beachfront surroundings off the main island of Mahé and at the gateway to the Ste Anne Marine National Park. There are excellent opportunities for water sports. €€€

Cousine Island
Tel: 321107
Fax: 323805
www.cousineisland.com
Peace and quiet come first, together with the promotion of conservation on this island of sea birds and rare land birds. The four chalets, all with sea views, are old French-colonial style, equipped with everything from a refrigerator to a jacuzzi. €€€€

Denis Island Resort
Tel: 288963
Fax: 321010
www.denisisland.com
Comfortable individual chalets with all the usual facilities. Good water sports facilities and diving available. €€€€

Desroches Island Lodge
Tel: 229009 (Mahé Head Office)
Tel: 229003
Fax: 229002
Email: desroches.res@seychelles.net
www.naiade.mu
Twenty spacious, air-conditioned chalets. Good dive centre and non-motorised water sports. €€€€

Frégate Island Private
Tel: 670100
Fax: 670900
www.fregate.com
The only place to stay on this private island is exclusive in every respect (see pages 307–9). Accommodation is limited to 16 luxury villas, each with sun terrace, and designed with integrated glass walls for views of the ocean. Furnished with rare antiques and Asian artworks. Access to seven beaches and all water sports facilities. Maximum 40 guests. €€€€

Labriz Silhouette Resort
Tel: 293949
Fax: 226273
www.labriz-seychelles.com
The only hotel on the third largest island, situated on a beautiful beach. A first class spa, water sports and nature walks are all available. €€€€

North Island
Tel: 293100
Fax: 293150
www.north-island.com
Eleven large private villas on an island with a heavy emphasis on conservation – there are several nature trails. The surrounding waters are excellent for game fishing, snorkelling and diving (equipment for all these activities is provided). €€€€

Round Island
Tel: 671600
Fax: 671625
www.round-island.net
Just 10 minutes from Praslin by boat, there are just three luxurious two-bedroom villas and a spacious three-bedroom "mansion". The ultimate private island. €€€€

Sainte Anne Resort
Tel: 292000
Fax: 292002
www.sainteanne-resort.com
This five-star resort is the only hotel on the island, with a regular ferry to Victoria. There are 82 one-bedroom villas, four two-bedroom and one three-bedroom. Facilities include tennis, mountain bikes, diving, deep-sea fishing and various water sports. €€€€

PRICE CATEGORIES

Price categories are for two sharing a double room for one night with breakfast:
€ = less than €400
€€ = €400–800
€€€ = €800–1,200
€€€€ = more than €1,200

E ATING OUT

MAURITIUS

RECOMMENDED RESTAURANTS, CAFES AND BARS

Where to Eat

One of the most attractive attributes of Seychelles is its cuisine. However, you need to know where to look to find it. There are no beach stalls as in so many other countries, fewer restaurants and if fast food is what you are looking for then you have come to the wrong place. There is no McDonald's – indeed nothing whatsoever very fast in Seychelles, though there are a few takeways (notably in Victoria).

Hotels offer a wide choice of meals to keep their clients from straying, often including a barbecue or a Seychellois buffet on certain evenings. However, to sample the finest local cuisine, a new twist on international flavours and to enjoy informal local surroundings, a trip to a restaurant outside your hotel is an excellent alternative.

Dress is very casual and the atmosphere generally very relaxed.

Booking is unnecessary for lunch but advisable for evenings, indeed essential at some restaurants. Most will open around 6.30pm and by 10.30pm the shutters are beginning to come down. Fish dishes dominate though meat dishes, mainly chicken and beef, are almost always available. Authentic Seychelles curries are hot, but restaurants will offer chilli sauce on a separate dish to allow the customer to control the temperature.

REUNION

RESTAURANT LISTINGS

MAHÉ

Victoria

Doubleclick Café
Maison La Rosiere
Tel: 610590
Near to main bus station in Victoria (and one of the few town locations with free parking), this is a great place for a coffee and snack to top up your energy levels. €
Le Marinier
Inter-Island Quay
Tel: 224 937
Not the place to linger when the air is filled with smells wafting across from the tuna cannery. However, it is quite the best place to sit, relax and enjoy a light meal, snack or just a drink while waiting for a ferry or yacht at the Victoria quayside. €
News Café
Trinity House
Tel: 322999

On the first floor of one of the main office buildings of Victoria, this is another good place to grab an inexpensive bite and an excellent cappuccino. €
Pirates Arms
Independence Avenue
Tel: 225001
Close to the clock tower, this is a popular meeting place to gossip and watch the world go by. Meals are fairly simple but good and there are usually one or two special dishes of the day on offer. €€
Rendezvous
Francis Rachel Street
Tel: 323556
On the first floor of Victoria House, overlooking the clock tower, this is the place for a meal more substantial than the light dishes offered elsewhere in town. Very popular at lunchtime

with the local business community but quieter in the evening.
€€€
Sam's Pizzeria
Maison Suleman,
Francis Rachel Street
Tel: 322499
A very good medium-priced restaurant with relaxed atmosphere and a varied menu. On the first floor overlooking the busy main street €€

Anse aux Pins

Vye Marmit Restaurant
Craft Village
Tel: 376155
In a lovely setting, serving excellent creole cuisine on the verandah overlooking craft shops and an old plantation house. Mainly fish and seafood but some meat dishes too.
€€€

Anse Royale

Le Jardin du Roi
Tel: 371313
Set among spice plants, fruit and ornamental trees, this restaurant is well worth a visit in its own right. The food is excellent, and reasonably priced. Save room for the amazing ice creams: flavours include cinnamon and lemon grass. Curry buffet on Sunday. Advance booking advisable, open lunchtime only.
€€

PRICE CATEGORIES

Price categories are for two people including soft drinks or beer:
€ = less than €50
€€ = €50–75
€€€ = €75–100
€€€€ = more than €100

SEYCHELLES

ABOVE: It might be informal, but you should book ahead at the popular Boat House.

Kaz Kreol
Tel: 371680
A wide variety of inexpensive dishes, such as pasta, curries, salads and fish and chips, in a casual setting by the beach. Chinese cuisine and pizzas are also available. Tues–Sun, lunch and dinner. €€

Anse Boileau

Chez Plume
Tel: 355050
Excellent seafood restaurant. Good desserts, unlike many restaurants, including a superb passion fruit soufflé. €€€

Bel Ombre

Le Corsaire
Tel: 247171
Housed in a romantic steep-roofed stone and thatch building overlooking the ocean, this restaurant offers Italian, international and creole cuisine. Open evenings only from 7.30pm, closed Monday. €€€€

La Scala
Tel: 247535
This family-run restaurant is a popular choice among the local business community, so it is essential to book. Specialises in seafood and Italian, international and creole dishes at moderate prices. Evenings only, closed Sunday. €€€

St Louis

Marie Antoinette Restaurant
Tel: 266222
This restaurant at the foot of Signal Hill is the best place to go for a creole feast in the perfect setting of an old planter's house. The food is consistently good, though the two-course set menu never varies. The first course alone involves five dishes: tuna steak, parrotfish in batter, grilled bourgeois, fish stew, and chicken curry with salad and rice. Dessert consists of fruit salad and ice cream followed by coffee. €€

Anse à la Mouche

Anchor Café and Islander Restaurant
Tel: 371289
The nearest thing in South Mahé to a fast food outlet, this is an informal restaurant, opposite the beach, offering both snacks and more substantial meals. Open 11am–9pm, closed Sunday and public holidays. €€

Beau Vallon

Baobab Pizzeria
Tel: 247167
At the northern end of the bay, this beach-side pizzeria with its stone benches and sandy floor, is a Seychelles institution. As well as dishing up good pizzas, it serves pasta dishes or fish and chips. It's difficult to get a table after 7pm and weekends can get crowded too. Open lunchtime and evening. €

The Boat House
Tel: 247898
Excellent evening fish barbecue in informal surroundings, which commences at 7.30pm. Very popular and booking is essential. €€

Coco d'Or
Tel: 247331
Nor sure what you fancy, maybe Chinese, a pizza or something more substantial? Coco d'Or has three excellent restaurants: Uncle Wills Pizzeria, The Wok Chinese and La Palma Restaurant offering creole and international cuisine. Just a short stroll inland from Beau Vallon beach. €€

La Perle Noire
Tel: 620220
A stone's throw from Coral Strand Hotel, an excellent restaurant serving Italian, international and creole dishes. Evenings only. €€€

Mahek Restaurant
Tel: 621000
Within Coral Strand Hotel, this is the best Indian restaurant in Seychelles. All dishes can be prepared mild, medium or hot. €€

Anse Soleil

Anse Soleil Cafeteria
Tel: 361700
This picturesque feet-in-the-sand restaurant is located directly on one of the best beaches of Mahé. Unless you're staying in the area, you will need a hire car to get here but it makes a great stop on an island tour. No reservations accepted, it's first come first served, so arrive early as this place is popular – especially at weekends. Open daily noon–9pm. €

Pointe au Sel

Fairyland Restaurant
Tel: 371700
An informal, reasonably priced restaurant in a superb beach-side location. Booking is essential especially at weekends when the Seychelles buffet is very popular with locals. €€

Takamaka

Chez Batista
Tel: 366300
A charismatic rustic restaurant next to beautiful Takamaka beach, offering barbecue and seafood specialities. €€€

PRASLIN

Amitié

Touchdown Restaurant
Tel: 233655
The airport is not an obvious choice for a dining destination, but it is well worth booking in early for your flight so as to enjoy good, simple food at reasonable prices with tables overlooking the airstrip. The cakes are excellent. **€**

Anse à La Blague

La Vanille Beach Bar
tel: 232178
Good basic food served at tables on a terrace overlooking the sea. The menu is predominantly fish-based, but meat dishes are also featured. **€€**

Anse Lazio

Bonbon Plume
Tel: 232136
Cuisine with a strong French influence mixed with local flavours, mainly fish and seafood, served at wooden tables shaded by palm-thatched umbrellas. Bonbon Plume is located next to this exceptionally beautiful beach.
€€€€
Le Chevalier Bay
Tel: 232322
Breakfast, lunch and dinner comprised of creole cuisine and curries as well as snacks, sandwiches, salads, chips, and a few other choices besides. Open daily.
€€

Grand Anse

Britannia Restaurant
Tel: 233215
If a walk to see black parrots sounds too much like hard work, relax at a table in the garden of this restaurant, order a drink and a meal and with luck the birds will come to you. Good value creole cuisine. **€€**

Côte d'Or

La Goulue Café
Tel: 232223
A rustic, relaxed outdoor setting near the beach serving good quality, mainly local, dishes and snacks. Open noon–9pm. Closed Sunday.
€€

Les Lauriers Restaurant
Tel: 232241
The best restaurant on Praslin for a creole barbecue with fish and meat specialities, a buffet of local salads, a variety of curries and local desserts to top it off. **€€**
Tante Mimi
Casino des Isles
Tel: 232500
A fabulous restaurant in a beautiful colonial-style building with interesting interior decor. Mainly international cuisine, possibly the best in Seychelles. In the evening, will arrange collection and return to any Praslin hotel. Creole menu Wednesday evening, Sunday lunch on the terrace. **€€€€**

LA DIGUE

Anse la Réunion

Château St Cloud
Tel: 234346
Creole cuisine in a quiet setting at a former colonial plantation house, from the days when vanilla was the mainstay of the local economy. **€€**

Zerof Restaurant and Takeaway
Tel: 234439
Situated opposite the Vev Nature Reserve, serves a wide range of excellent creole dishes with takeaways also available. Closes at 9.30pm.
€€

Grand Anse

Loutier Bar and Restaurant
If you plan to eat out on this side of the island, then the Loutier is definitely the place to come for good value creole cuisine,

sandwiches and omelettes. Closed evenings. **€€**

La Passe

Tarosa Restaurant
Tel: 234407
Located at La Passe jetty, Tarosa has seven separate dining areas, each one with an ocean view that takes in the comings and goings at La Digue's only harbour. Creole specialities are on the menu. Open for breakfast, lunch and dinner.
€
Villa Authentique
Tel: 234413
Excellent creole cuisine at an old plantation-style house, right opposite the beach.
€€

BELOW: Don't miss out on the catch of the day.

PRICE CATEGORIES

Price categories are for two people including soft drinks or beer:
€ = less than €50
€€ = €50–75
€€€ = €75–100
€€€€ = more than €100

A CTIVITIES

NIGHTLIFE, OUTDOOR ACTIVITIES AND SHOPPING

NIGHTLIFE

Seychelles is not the place to come to for the nightlife. The little there is revolves around the hotels. On Mahé there are two tourist-friendly discos and two casinos. On Praslin there are two discos and one casino.

Katiolo Club: Anse Faure, to the south of the airport; tel: 375453. Creole-style nightclub. Ladies' Night on Wednesday (free entry). Buffet on Saturday sometimes followed by an open-air disco, weather permitting, until 3am.

Jungle Disco: Grand Anse, Praslin; tel: 512683. Features a variety of music, both local and international. There are three bars and a pool room. Snacks are available. Open Fri and Sat, 10pm–4am.

Casino des Seychelles: Beau Vallon Bay Hotel, Mahé; tel: 247272.

Casino des Isles: Côte d'Or, Praslin; tel: 232500.

OUTDOOR ACTIVITIES

Birdwatching

Birdwatchers are drawn to Seychelles for three reasons: the rarity value of the endemic land birds, the spectacular sea bird colonies, such as on Bird Island and Aride, and the chance of seeing unusual migrants. The land birds are, of course, present year-round, as indeed are many species of sea bird. However, the huge tern colonies are at their best from May to September. October to December is the best time for migrants from Europe and Asia, when many unusual vagrants have been

recorded including some not known anywhere else in the western Indian Ocean or Madagascar regions.

Top sites on the itinerary of any visiting birdwatcher should include the nature reserve islands of **Cousin** and **Aride**. On **Mahé**, the mudflats adjacent to the Seychelles Breweries is the best site for migrant waders such as **crab plover**, a northwest Indian Ocean speciality. The Plantation Club marsh on Mahé, and the pools of Lemuria Golf Course on Praslin and the wetlands of La Passe on La Digue are the best places to see **yellow bittern**, found nowhere else in the region.

On **Praslin**, **black parrots** may be seen early morning or late afternoon around the entrance to **Vallée de Mai** and in lowland fruit trees such as those around Villa Flamboyant. Birdwatching tours can be booked through local tour companies (*see*

BELOW: Spectacular bird life.

page 416). Several travel companies worldwide organise package birdwatching holidays in Seychelles, such as **Ornitholidays** and **Naturetrek**.

Fishing

Fishing is a way of life in Seychelles (*see* Fishing *on pages 276–7*). Day charters for big game fishing may be organised from Mahé, Praslin, La Digue and on all the islands with single resorts. Customised safaris for up to six people lasting three or more days may be booked with some companies.

Many power boats and yachts are available for charter by the day or longer. Reservations may be made at local travel agents, through hotels, direct with boat owners or through **The Marine Charter Association**, Victoria, Mahé (tel: 224679). Operators include:

Bedier & Son, Côte d'Or, Praslin; tel: 232192/513840; fax: 232356

The Boat House, Beau Vallon, Mahé; tel: 247464; mobile: 510269; fax: 247955

Island Boat Charter, Victoria; tel: 515678; www.reeltime.sc

Le Superbe Hirecraft, Victoria; tel: 322288/764029; fax: 225717

R Savy Charters, Anse aux Pins; tel: 376476/576797; fax: 376476; email: rsavycharter@seychelles.sc

Striker, Coral Strand Hotel Beau Vallon; tel: 247848/511958; fax: 247797; email: striker@seychelles.net.

Water World (Pty) Ltd, Wharf Hotel & Marina, Mahé; tel: 514735/247453; fax: 247607; www.seychelles.net/wworld

Zico 1Boat Charter, Anse Reunion, La Digue; tel: 515557/344615

Fly-fishing is superb, especially at St François and St Joseph Atolls from

Scuba Safety

The Association of Professional Divers, Seychelles (APDS) has set guidelines for the safe and professional operation of diving centres. Many of its members are rated by the Professional Association of Diving Instructors (PADI) as five-star dive centres or resorts. All boats used for diving activities are properly licensed by the local authorities and, in addition to normal safety equipment, carry oxygen and additional emergency equipment. There is a two-man, twin-lock re-compression chamber at Victoria Hospital with a team of hyperbaric doctors and technicians available in the unlikely event of a diving accident.

mid-Sept–mid-May (staying at **Alphonse Island Resort**, *see page 404*). Fly-fishing charters to the more remote atolls of Farquhar, Astove and Cosmoledo can also be arranged on the calmer seas of Oct–Apr. Operators include:
Illusions Liveaboards (Pty) Ltd, Victoria; tel: 760346; www.mvillusions.com
Silhouette Cruises Ltd, Victoria; tel: 324026; fax: 324365; www.seychelles-cruises.com
   An event in which visitors may participate is the **National Fishing Competition** hosted by the Rotary Club of Victoria and held every April.

Diving and Snorkelling

The marine world is easily accessible in Seychelles with many APDS diving centres offering snorkelling *(see Equipped for Snorkelling page 368)* and scuba diving facilities. If you are healthy and can swim, learning to snorkel or dive is easy and most dive centres offer introductory and certification courses.
   Seychelles is one of the best places in the world to learn to dive and has several excellent dive centres. If you are not sure diving is for you, a one-day course is the best way to test the waters. These are offered by several excellent PADI (Professional Association of Diving Instructors) dive centres. You begin at 9am with a session in the hotel swimming pool to familiarise yourself with the equipment and learn basic techniques.
   After lunch, you take a sea dive on a shallow reef accompanied at all times by an instructor. No certificate is issued, but if you decide to

progress, this one-day experience counts as the first step towards obtaining further knowledge and skill on a second day. Successful completion of this stage leads to the PADI Scuba Diver Certificate, which allows you to dive to a limited depth under basic supervision. Two additional days completes your basic diving skills to give you a PADI Open Water Diver Licence. *(See Underwater World on pages 271–5).*
Underwater Centre Seychelles: PO Box 384, Victoria; tel: 345445 (office), 247165 (shop), 542877 (mobile); fax: 344223; www.diveseychelles.com.sc
Beau Vallon Bay Beach Resort has four custom-built dive boats, including a dedicated boat for snorkelling and coastal sightseeing three times a week. They offer the full range of PADI courses from introductory to instructor.
   On Praslin **Octopus Divers** (tel: 232350) is the longest established dive centre and operates dives to sites off the surrounding islands of La Digue, Curieuse, Aride and Marianne.
   Live-aboard diving packages including to the more remote outer islands can be arranged through Indian Ocean Explorer and **Silhouette Cruises Ltd** *(see Chartering page 410).*

Windows on the Reef

To see the wonders of the coral reef without getting wet there are two options. The first is a **glass-bottom boat** which permits a vertical view of the reef from an open-sided flat-bottomed boat fitted with perspex panels along the central floor. Wooden benches run along each side of the vessel facing these viewing panels. The second option is a **subsea viewer,** a semi-submersible vessel from which a horizontal view of the reef may be obtained. Glass-bottom boats can enter extremely shallow water, though the passage of the vessel overhead scares away many fish, particularly the larger ones. Subsea viewers create less disturbance but cannot cross very shallow patches where reef life may proliferate. Some visitors find the subsea viewer claustrophobic.
   Trips from Mahé to **Ste Anne Marine National Park** can be arranged through a local tour operator *(see page 416)*, either for half a day or for a full day with lunch at one of the islands: Moyenne, Round or Cerf. The National Park is the headquarters of the Marine Parks Authority. However, the park has suffered greatly from the combined

effects of El Niño in 1998, which killed more than 90 percent of corals, and the extensive land reclamation along Mahé's east coast that produced some siltation resulting in reef damage.
   Teddy's Glass Bottom Boat: Coral Strand Hotel, Beau Vallon, Mahé; tel: 261125; mobile: 511125. Can also be booked through most tour operators.

Live-aboard Cruising

It can reasonably be claimed that the best way to explore an island nation is by sea. A cruise on a live-aboard vessel is an ideal way to see a number of islands without having to move from hotel to hotel. It is also an excellent way to reach the more secluded bays and islands.
   There are various options available depending on whether you wish to enjoy sailing, fishing, diving, water sports or simply get from A to B in the fastest possible time.
   Most cruises begin from the Inter-Island Quay at Victoria. Many of the charter boats are moored next to the quay. Nearby, the **Seychelles Marine Charter Association** (tel: 224679) is also a useful source of information on the availability of the smaller boats. Most vessels are licensed to operate solely within the Inner Islands, except for cruise ships and some specialist charter boats (especially dive boats). Moorings are available at Marine National Parks where a small fee is charged for entry. Some island nature reserves also charge a small fee for landing. Apart from the smaller, difficult to reach islands, secluded bays around the main islands are well worth exploring.

When to Cruise
The southeast monsoon blows from May to October bringing steady winds. Wind strength is particularly high in July and August with rough

Mahé's Marine Parks

To explore the sea at **Port Launay National Marine Park**, Jamilah Big Game and Bottom Fishing have an outlet near Port Glaud offering snorkelling at **Baie Ternay** (also a National Marine Park) and excursions to the Inner Islands, while West Rand Holdings, a diving and water sports centre a little further on, hires out jet skis and charter boats for trips. Jet skis are only allowed up to the marine park's boundary.

MAURITIUS

REUNION

SEYCHELLES

seas. Unless you have a strong stomach this is not the best time to sail far afield, though a cruise around the mainly sheltered waters of Praslin and its satellite islands can be very pleasant. The northwest monsoon from November to April brings less consistent winds, which can be squally around mid-December to the end of January. Fortunately, however, Seychelles lies outside the cyclone belt.

Activities on Board

Diving facilities are offered by larger vessels (those of over 10 berths). This may be either the main activity, with perhaps three or four dives per day on offer, or an optional choice when opportunities arise within a set itinerary. Skippers of these vessels are usually qualified divemasters. Most vessels will at least offer snorkelling equipment, comprising mask, snorkel and fins.

Some of the larger vessels will also carry a range of water sports equipment including windsurf boards and water-skis. Almost all will carry fishing tackle. Trailing a line in the water on sea passages is an excellent way to catch pelagic fish such as bonito or dorado. At anchor, bottom fishing may also be offered with opportunities to catch fresh fish for supper.

Cruising is, of course, an activity in itself and one of the most important pieces of equipment on board is the ship's tender. This will be the only way to land on most beaches as only the largest populated islands have quays.

Chartering

At the smaller end of the scale, there are a range of monohulls and catamarans available for **bareboat charter**. Professional skippers who know the islands well may also be employed. Alternatively, a **set cruise** may be taken aboard a romantic twin-masted schooner or dedicated dive boat. Small, fast **motor-cruisers** are available for those who want to get to

their destinations fast. All these options are offered by locally based operators but during the northern winter, cruise ships will also call at the islands.

You can organise yachting holidays around the islands with one week on board and another week in a hotel at home with companies such as:
Seychelles Travel: tel: 01202 877330; www.seychelles-travel.co.uk
Sunsail Ltd: telesales: 0844 463 6512; www.sunsail.com
Yacht Connections: tel: 671667; fax: 671668; www.yacht-connections.co.uk

Charter companies in Seychelles
Angel Fish Yacht Charter: Roche Caiman, Mahé; tel: 344644; fax: 344545; www.seychelles-charter.com. Offers crewed and bareboat yacht charters in the granitic islands.
Dream Yacht Seychelles: Baie Ste Anne, Praslin; tel: 232681; fax: 232812; www.dream-yacht-seychelles.com. Offers overnight charters which may also be bareboat, skippered or fully-crewed on catamarans of up to 25 metres (82 ft). Standard itineraries are 6 or 10 nights around the granitics, extending to the Amirantes in calm seas. Also based at Angel Fish marina on Mahé.
Indian Ocean Explorer Cruises Ltd: Victoria, Mahé; tel: 713626; fax: 225844; www.ioexpl.com. A dedicated dive vessel with regular cruises to the outer islands, including the Aldabra group, October to April. Also available for fly-fishing, birdwatching and island hopping charters.
Moorings: Wharf Hotel & Marina, Mahé; tel: 601060; fax: 601061; www.moorings.com. Offers crewed and bareboat yacht charters in the granitic islands.
Silhouette Cruises Ltd: tel: 324026 or 514051; fax: 380538; www.seychelles.net/cruises. Operates four twin-masted schooners and one motor yacht, each with accommodation for 15–18 passengers. The schooners are the most beautiful ships in Seychelles. Cruises are for five to six days

around the granitic islands and one week or more in the outer islands including Aldabra and Cosmoledo. Guests may participate in sailing, though vessels carry a full crew. Other activities include diving, fishing and water sports.
Sunsail (Seychelles) Ltd: tel: 601063; fax: 601064; www.sunsail.com. A company with over 1,000 vessels worldwide in many holiday centres that you can book from home. The Seychelles fleet comprises monohulls, with up to nine berths, eight catamarans and one "super-luxury" Platinum-class catamaran with full crew. Other boats are available for bareboat charter, clients providing their own food and drink, or with qualified skippers. Period or day charters may be arranged. The company offers a provisioning service if required. Advice on anchorages and other essential information is available.
VPM Yacht Charter: tel: 344719; fax: 345698; www.vpm-boats.com. Another multinational company with a Seychelles base, VPM operates a fleet of vessels, mainly catamarans. Some are available for bareboat charter and some for crewed charter. Crewed charters are skippered by professional sailors who know Seychelles waters well. A provisioning service is offered for bareboat charters.
Water World (Pty) Ltd: tel: 514735/ 247453; fax: 247607; www.seychelles.net/wworld. The ultra-modern high speed option. The motor-cruiser Shamal cruises at 24 knots with a top speed of 31 knots. It has just two standard cabins and one VIP cabin, all with en-suite facilities. Smaller vessels are also available for day charters.

Horse Riding

To enjoy the Seychelles scenery at a leisurely pace, horses can be hired from **Utegangar Riding Center** (tel: 712355; email: utegangar@gmail.com) at Barbarons on the west coast of Mahé. Bookings should be made at least 24 hours in advance. Take sun-cream and a hat as you will be in direct sunlight for much of the time.

Horses are pure bred Arabian. Riding style is English using all-purpose, synthetic saddles. Riding hats are provided. Equipment recommended should you not have riding gear is long trousers and closed sports shoes. Riding is usually done during periods of low tide because underfoot conditions are much better and the scenery is far more spectacular (all clients are

Underwater Photography Festival

There are few events in Seychelles that you would want to plan your holiday dates around. One exception, if you are a diver, might be **SUBIOS**, a three-week festival of underwater images held each March or October/November (the date varies each year), which are also the best months for diving due to the calm seas prevailing between the two monsoon winds.

Entertainment, centred around the main hotels of Mahé and Praslin, includes slide shows hosted by professional underwater photographers and photography contests. Further details can be obtained from:
SUBIOS Organising Committee, Seychelles Tourism Board, tel: 671300; fax: 620620; email: info@subios.com; www.subios.com

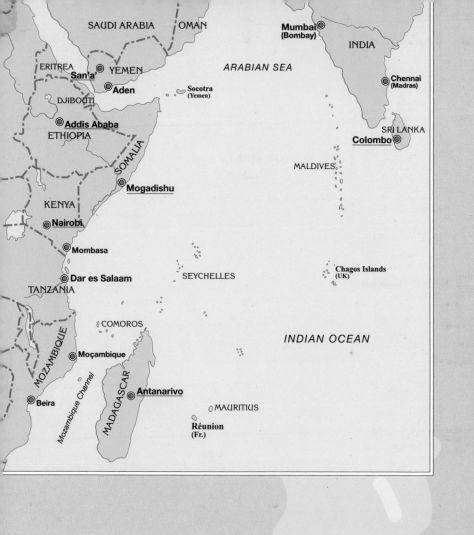

SAUDI ARABIA   OMAN

Mumbai
(Bombay)

INDIA

ARABIAN SEA

ERITREA

San'a'   YEMEN

Aden

Socotra
(Yemen)

Chennai
(Madras)

DJIBOUTI

Addis Ababa

ETHIOPIA

SRI LANKA

Colombo

MALDIVES

SOMALIA

Mogadishu

KENYA

Nairobi

Mombasa

Chagos Islands
(UK)

SEYCHELLES

Dar es Salaam

TANZANIA

INDIAN OCEAN

COMOROS

MOZAMBIQUE

Moçambique

MADAGASCAR

Antanarivo

MAURITIUS

Beira

Réunion
(Fr.)

Mozambique Channel

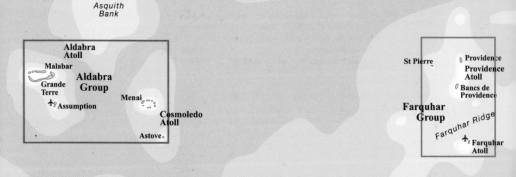

Asquith
Bank

Aldabra
Atoll

Malabar

Aldabra
Group

Grande
Terre

Menai

Assumption

Cosmoledo
Atoll

Astove

St Pierre

Providence

Providence
Atoll

Bancs de
Providence

Farquhar
Group

Farquhar Ridge

Farquhar
Atoll

Îles
Glorieuses